Mediation: An A–Z Guide

Dedication

To Alison, my wife and best friend, with all my thanks and love.

Mediation: An A–Z Guide

Stephen Walker MA (Oxon), FCIArb
Solicitor and Accredited Mediator

Bloomsbury Professional

Bloomsbury Professional Limited, Maxwelton House, 41–43 Boltro Road, Haywards Heath, West Sussex, RH16 1BJ

© Stephen Walker 2016

Bloomsbury Professional is an imprint of Bloomsbury Publishing plc

All rights reserved. No part of this publication may be reproduced in any material form (including photocopying or storing it in any medium by electronic means and whether or not transiently or incidentally to some other use of this publication) without the written permission of the copyright owner except in accordance with the provisions of the Copyright, Designs and Patents Act 1988 or under the terms of a licence issued by the Copyright Licensing Agency Ltd, Saffron House, 6–10 Kirby Street, London EC1N 8TS. Applications for the copyright owner's written permission to reproduce any part of this publication should be addressed to the publisher.

Warning: The doing of an unauthorised act in relation to a copyright work may result in both a civil claim for damages and criminal prosecution.

Crown copyright material is reproduced with the permission of the Controller of HMSO and the Queen's Printer for Scotland. Any European material in this work which has been reproduced from EUR-lex, the official European Communities legislation website, is European Communities copyright.

A CIP Catalogue record for this book is available from the British Library.

Every effort has been taken to ensure the accuracy of the contents of this book. However, neither the authors nor the publishers can accept any responsibility for any loss occasioned to any person acting or refraining from acting in reliance on any statement contained in the book.

ISBN: 978 1 78043 996 9

Typeset by Compuscript Ltd, Shannon

Printed and bound in the United Kingdom by CPI Group (UK) Ltd, Croydon, CR0 4YY

Preface

Why write this book?

Has Google killed A–Z guides? You need to know something? Just Google it.

No it hasn't. We are swamped with information on the Internet. But is it relevant? Search Engine Optimisation and Sponsored Entries order the listings on your screen.

The information in this book has been curated. You do not have to scroll through pages of headings to find one that might be relevant. That has been done for you. And the practical application of the topic to real life mediation is identified.

Who is this book for?

This is a practical and experienced-based book for anybody who is interested or involved in mediation including:

- People in disputes who know nothing about the law or mediation.
- Clients who want to understand more clearly what their lawyers are telling them.
- Lawyers who go to mediation and need a vade mecum.
- Lawyers who don't go to mediation but need to feel comfortable when the subject comes up.
- Non-lawyers who go to mediation and need a crib sheet.
- Mediators, representatives, insurers, finance directors, risk managers and those who own their own business.
- Students at all levels.

And for anyone who wants to find out more about mediation quickly and easily.

Preface

Why is it needed?

We all need to know about mediation now. Why?

In its modern form mediation has been in the UK for over 25 years. Every year it becomes more popular but also more complex. You cannot avoid it.

- There are more clients, lawyers, experts, trainers, mediators and representatives than ever before.
- More and more areas of dispute and conflict are being mediated: not just civil and commercial but also family, workplace, community, environmental, medical, peer, interfaith. The list never stops growing.
- New mediation styles and techniques develop: evaluative, facilitative, therapeutic, narrative, transformative, Med/Arb and Arb/Med. And the big development: On-Line Mediation and ODR.
- Contracts are routinely drafted to include mediation as well as or instead of traditional arbitration clauses. And the courts enforce them.
- Courts, laws and regulations increasingly require you to try mediation before issuing proceedings or attending trial. Some judges even want it to be made compulsory.

What does this book do?

This book is an up-to-date guide through the growing complexity. It defines, explains and interprets key concepts, acronyms, organisations, terms and jargon. The language is clear, simple and non-technical. As mediation grows in popularity and importance jargon proliferates. My aim, as in my previous books, is to help people get the best out of mediation. By decoding its language and demystifying the process and concepts, I hope to make mediation more accessible.

Although not a book about negotiation, psychology or economics it defines and explains key concepts from those disciplines which Mediation has imported.

Preface

The topic entries have a definition, explanation and comment. '**In practice**' bullet points also relate the topic to what actually happens in mediations in real life.

'**See also**' and '**Follow up**' headings give internal cross-references and external sources.

Not everything can be included. The book is a handy dictionary not an encyclopaedia. But suggestions for deletions or additions are very welcome.

How to use it

Look up a topic when you need to know more about it. Browse. Dip into it from time to time. Remind yourself. Refresh your memory. It is a reference book, a memory jogger, a starting point for enquiry or research and a stimulus to further thought.

The first thing to do

Look up the full entry for Mediation. You will find it on p 284. Also look at the Introduction. That introduces the **TOP TEN** elements of mediation that crop up throughout the book.

Please note

This book was written before:

- The BREXIT vote but because of the uncertainty and the inevitable transition period following the result, the EU entries and references have been retained.

- The publication of the second edition of *The Jackson ADR Handbook* which was postponed. So most of the cross-references are unfortunately to the first edition.

As in my previous books I have respectfully followed the practice of Tom Bingham in *The Rule of Law* and used 'he' rather than 'he or she' and in his own words 'hope that this will be understood in an un-chauvinistic, gender-neutral way'.

Stephen Walker
September 2016

Introduction

HOW TO USE THIS BOOK

Read the next section on "What is mediation–The Top 10".

Then come back to this page and carry on reading.

Mediation is often confused with meditation or arbitration. It is one of several forms of **ADR**-Alternative Dispute Resolution. In other words methods of resolving disputes other than through a formal legal process in a court or tribunal. Apart from direct negotiation, it is the most popular, efficient and successful method.

Originally mediation was conducted face-to-face with a live mediator meeting the parties. Increasingly mediations are conducted online either by telephone or video-conferencing such as Skype or Zoom. People in dispute therefore will in the future have more opportunity of representing themselves in a mediation. They need to be familiar with the concepts and the language.

The definition of mediation below is intended to be neutral and non-controversial. Different mediators may emphasise different elements but it covers the common ground.

When you have absorbed the definition go to the Contents Page and follow your nose. See what topics interest you. Some entries are much fuller than others. But they follow the same basic pattern.

Heading

Arranged alphabetically. Where acronyms are frequently used, such as **CMC**, the full wording is also given, eg **Civil Mediation Council**.

Introduction

The first line of the entry is the **definition.**

This is followed by an **explanation** expanding it slightly, and **comment.** This is interpretive and not every mediator will agree with what is said. Sometimes there is a heading **In reality** to highlight the difference between what the theorists say and the practitioners do.

In practice

Are bullet points to summarise the essence of the topic as applied in the real world of mediation.

See also

Are cross-references to related topics in the book.

Follow up

References to external sources such as websites, books and articles. Full listings of the titles of books appear on p 539.

What is mediation? – The Top Ten

The classic formulation is

'A voluntary confidential process where the parties to a dispute choose a neutral third party to help them find their own solution.'

These are the **Top Ten** elements:

1. Voluntary
2. Confidential
3. Process
4. Parties
5. Dispute
6. Choose

Introduction

7. Neutral
8. Third Party
9. Help
10. Own solution

1 Voluntary

In some jurisdictions, mediation is now compulsory. It is not compulsory in England and Wales. But how voluntary is it?

No one can force you to settle but the courts can pretty well force you to attend mediation.

See also
COMPULSION/HALSEY

2 Confidential

How confidential is mediation? Not absolutely confidential but still more confidential than litigation and arbitration.

Mediation, like arbitration, takes place in private. But unlike in arbitration the parties in mediation can have private and confidential conversations with the mediator.

See also
CONFIDENTIALITY

3 Process

The basic mediation model has a three stage process: Educate, Exchange, Explore.

See also
MEDIATION DAY/ THREE STAGE PROCESS

Introduction

4 Parties

Parties at mediation have much more control over the process and the outcome than they do in any other form of dispute resolution apart from direct party-to-party negotiation.

They choose who mediates, when and where they mediate, and what they mediate about. They definitely choose whether to settle or not.

See also
AUTONOMY/PARTY CONTROL

5 Dispute

Disputes in court or arbitration are framed in legal categories. Lawyers tell the parties what their legal rights and remedies are. In reality disputes are often wider than what can be included in a legal claim.

See also
DISPUTE

6 Choose

The parties can choose their own mediator. Only when they cannot agree is a mediator chosen for them.

See also
CHOOSING/MEDIATORS

7 Neutral

There is a lot of debate about what neutrality means. Is it the same as impartiality? Academically interesting but in practice of little relevance.

In this book it is assumed that

Introduction

- Neutrality means that the mediator has no personal stake in the outcome.
- Impartiality means that the mediator is not prejudiced in favour of one party or the other and acts in an evenhanded way.

See also

NEUTRALITY/IMPARTIALITY

8 Third Party

Not all negotiations are a mediation but all mediations are a negotiation. The key difference is the presence of a Third Party. In fact mediation is, essentially, assisted negotiation.

See also

MEDIATOR/TPN

9 Help

The mediator is not a judge and arbitrator. He does not tell you what to do or how to do it. He helps you to find your own way to your own solution.

See also

FACILITATIVE

10 Own solution

Judges and arbitrators impose the solution. Mediators do not.

Parties can devise their own creative solutions to their disputes in ways which a judge could never help them do even if he wanted to.

See also

AUTONOMY/PMA

Introduction

WHERE ARE WE NOW?

Mediation as a technique for solving problems and managing conflict is expanding. It has spread to pretty well every jurisdiction and country. Increasingly the formal legal structures in various jurisdictions now expressly provide for it. See the CPR – Civil Procedure Rules – in England and Wales. Some countries eg Italy made it compulsory. So you have to attend mediation before you can have a trial at court.

More trained mediators emerge every year. The best estimates are around 800 in the UK. In most jurisdictions mediators complain that they do not have enough work. There is disparity between supply and demand. In most countries the take up of mediation is disappointingly low.

Two reasons recur:

- The public's lack of understanding about mediation. People have never heard of it. When they have, they think that it is either meditation or arbitration.
- Lawyers are reluctant to use mediation instead of litigation or arbitration. When cases settle fees stop. For them **ADR** stands for Alarming Drop in Revenue.

Reasons for optimism

- Governments and court administrators promote mediation as a way of cutting costs. Cases settling earlier means less need for court buildings and judges.
- Public awareness of mediation is growing. For example in the UK family mediation was the subject of an episode in the long-running popular soap opera 'Coronation Street' in July 2014. Two years on in June 2016 the BBC ran a three-part series 'Call the mediator'. This is also about family mediation but was actual footage of real life mediations.

Introduction

- Law students are taught mediation as part of their law course. For some it is more than just a theoretical subject. They actually do gain practical experience of mediation and can qualify as an accredited mediator at the end of their course.
- Training organisations mushroom. Every year more and more conferences, seminars, workshops and mediation journals appear.
- A new profession of Conflict Resolution Professionals, which includes but is not limited to mediators has been developed.
- Lawyers, particularly those specialising in courtroom advocacy, retrain as mediation advocates to supplement their income as the number of trials falls year on year.
- Non-lawyers increasingly retrain as mediators seeing mediation as an alternative to their day job or as an attractive activity in retirement. In the UK 57% of civil and commercial mediators are now non-lawyers (2016). They do this even though the mediation market still seems to prefer to appoint lawyer mediators.
- Many mediators combine mediation with other activities such as conflict coaching, business change management, negotiation consultancy and mediation training.
- More and more research is being done into how people take decisions, group dynamics, risk analysis, game theory, behavioural economics and psychology, They look upon mediation both as a quarry for research material and as a field of applied research where their findings can be put into practice.
- Court supervision mediation is growing.

This is all good news. But there are always downsides.

As mediation becomes more sophisticated and diverse it is developing its own language and Jargon. Chat rooms,

Introduction

forums, websites and blogs fill the Blogosphere debating multiple issues arising out of mediation.

- Much of the debate seems like rival sects arguing over the One True Way in an ideological battle for doctrinal purity and the Soul of Mediation. Absorbing and important to the participants: irrelevant and confusing to the observers and practitioners.

- The big divide is between those who think that mediation is about solving problems and those who think it is about changing people. In other words those who want to seek solutions and those who want to seek resolution.

- The solvers are often lawyers or other legally orientated professions such as accountants, surveyors and engineers. The resolvers are often from the helping professions such as psychotherapists, psychologists and HR professionals.

- Through the fog of increasing discourse, one thing is clear: the traditional training model of mediation based largely on what the **Harvard Negotiation Project** promulgated as **principled negotiation** is increasingly challenged by other models. **Evaluative** mediation is growing at the expense of **facilitative** mediation.

- The role of emotion and cognitive biases rather than rational self-interest is foregrounded.

- Some mediators and commentators, such as Bernard Mayer, think that mediation is in crisis. Others think that it has had its moment like communism and is now set to fade away and be replaced by the next fashion. Still others think that it is expanding with limitless potential and the ability to change mankind for the best. Even claiming that Brexit has made this more likely. The more pragmatic believe that mediation is a cost-efficient, quicker and more satisfactory way of resolving disputes which the parties cannot sort out by themselves than arbitration or litigation. But it needs to adapt to survive and flourish.

Introduction

HOW DID WE GET HERE?

Some commentators trace mediation back to ancient civilizations, including Sumerian, Confucian, Greek and Roman. This may be of some historical interest and also provide reassurance to those still sceptical about this novel idea of mediation that it has a long tradition. In practice mediation as it is understood and practised in the 21st-century started in the 1970s.

In the 1960s in the USA there was a move to empower local communities who felt unprotected by the American court system. This had become overloaded while struggling to cope with the demands of an increasingly litigious society.

1976 was Mediation's Big Bang. In April of that year Professor Frank Sander gave his seminal speech at the Pound Conference on 'The Varieties of Dispute Processing' and the concept of the multidoor courthouse. Court-annexed mediation schemes were developed. Mediation had a counter-culture flavour and still does for many of its devotees.

In the 1980s mediation was imported into the United Kingdom and Australia and in the next decade into Europe and South Africa. Now in the 21st-century it has been embraced in Asia and even by the European Union.

This philosophical dissatisfaction is reflected in a more practical way that impacts on the way in which mediation is currently carried out. As part of the development of mediation techniques in the USA in the 1970s and 1980s the dominant theory emerged that mediation helps people find their own solution to their own problem.

In the 1990s the **Harvard Negotiation Project (HNP)** was established. This has been hugely influential on the way in which mediators now go about their work. The key text is *Getting To Yes* by Ury and Fisher. They developed the

Introduction

model of **Principled Negotiation**. This focuses on people's interests and the future.

For some practitioners and commentators mediation is an ideology as much as it is a process. They refer to mediation as a calling rather than a profession or a business. For them mediation is a way of 'doing good' in the world.

Peter Adler, the distinguished and pioneering American mediator (who is not a lawyer), explained at the 2012 ADR Group Conference in Oxford that for many of his generation mediation had lost its way. They felt that its original values had been lost, ie:

- Empowering people so they did not have to seek advice from experts on what to do.
- The ability to repair broken relationships.
- Having the choice as to whether to go to mediation and who to appoint as the mediator.
- The idea of parties creating their own negotiated solutions.

Instead, for them mediation had become an institutionalised, solution-driven process mainly used as a way of reducing pressure on overcrowded courts. Worse still the lawyers have colonised it.

There has been a reaction to this problem-solving. A solution-focused approach has emerged – transformative mediation. It uses the therapeutic techniques of examining unrecognised and unresolved conflicts in people's pasts. It is more frequently applied in family, workplace or community mediations than in civil and commercial mediations.

Even within the problem-solving model, challenges to the HNP orthodoxy are growing from those who point out the limitations:

Introduction

- All mediations have an element of claiming value as well as creating it.
- Separating the problem from the people underestimates the importance of emotions in decision making.
- Formulating BATNAs (Best Alternative to Negotiated Agreement) and WATNAs (Worst Alternative to Negotiated Agreeement) has two drawbacks.
  - It assumes that people act on the basis of rational economic self-interest which they don't.
  - Calculating your work-away figure in advance, ie your BATNA makes you inflexible and can lead you to lose sight of factors outside your BATNA.

WHERE ARE WE GOING NEXT?

Taking a five-year view the emerging trends seem to be:

- A more adjudicative style of mediation will develop such as **Med/Arb** or **Arb/Med**.
- More **online mediation** will take place.
- There will be more **TAN (Technology Assisted Negotiation)**.
- As mediation is increasingly commoditised, prices and standards drop.
- There will be great a convergence of mediation and other ADR models and styles.
- The disputes about doctrinal purity will intensify and become increasingly sterile and irrelevant.
- More and more people will mediate their disputes but not in the way that they have done over the last 25 years.

AAAA

The four functions that lawyers perform for their clients. They are:

- Analyse – consider the issues and the facts and law.
- Advise – say what the options and outlook are.
- Advocate – put the best face on the client's case.
- Assess – weigh up the changing probabilities.

Do not confuse them.

In practice

- At mediations they are often confused. Lawyers advocate when they should be assessing or advising.
- Be careful about believing your own propaganda. The mediator and the other side won't.

See also

CELLAR BLINDNESS/LAWYERS' ROLES/RISK ANALYSIS

Absentees

People who are not present at the mediation can be more powerful than those who are present.

Common examples are:

Approval: Parties rarely attend mediation with unlimited authority. They need approval when a possible settlement looks like exceeding their authority limit. Can be difficult to obtain during the mediation. The person with sign-off authority is busy or does not understand what has gone on at the mediation and/or is not prepared to increase the limit on the basis of a telephone call.

Consent: Not the same as approval because the absent parties have to agree to **any** settlement before it can be binding. Classic examples are insurers, funders, mortgagees and co-owners. Problems arise when they are not at the mediation. Insurers often exercise claim control powers under the insurance policy.

Missing evidence. Parties often refer to the witnesses that they will call at trial eg their accountant will testify that the meeting did not take place or six witnesses will say that they saw the missing agreement. Absent witnesses full of potential can be more potent than actual witnesses full of hesitation.

In practice

- Make sure that you have:
    - all the people that you need at the mediation.
    - all their telephone/Skype numbers.
- You don't usually need witnesses present.
- Absentees never made a mediator's heart grow fonder.

See also
AUTHORITY/EMPTY CHAIR/WITNESSES

Academy of Experts

London-based, founded in 1987 as both a professional society and a qualifying body. Its objective is to establish and promote high objective standards and to train experts in them.

Most of its members are not lawyers although some are. Member of the Civil Mediation Council and a provider to the Ministry of Justice's Civil Mediation Directory.

In practice

Important in mediation because:

- Its members act as expert witnesses in disputes that go to mediation.
- It trains and accredits mediators.
- It appoints mediators.
- It maintains a panel of Dispute Resolvers.

See also
CMC/MoJ

Follow up
www.academyofexperts.org

ACAS

The Advisory, Conciliation and Arbitration Service dates from 1896 when the Government set up a voluntary arbitration and advice service. Became a statutory body in 1976.

ACAS:

- Promotes employment relations and HR excellence.
- Gives expert and impartial advice on good practice in employment relations.
- Provides support in finding solutions when relationships go wrong.

Important in mediation because:

ACAS now offers mediation on both an individual and collective basis.

ACAS

1 Individual mediation is provided free of charge if there's a complaint about employment rights that could go to an Employment Tribunal (ET). If it is about something else a charge is made.

Often the employers pay the charge. The mediation is usually held on the employer's premises and follows the workplace mediation model.

2 ACAS regards mediation as similar to collective arbitration that helps to resolve disputes between groups of employees (usually represented by the union) and employers. They offer collective mediation after conciliation has failed and the parties do not wish to go to arbitration and remain committed to resolving the issues without going to law.

Their mediators are employees of ACAS.

In practice

- Their influence is confined to workplace and employment mediation.
- As a publicly funded body they provide price competition to private sector mediators.

Conciliation

It provides:

- Collective conciliation services to help employees and their representatives or trade unions to come to agreements on matters affecting groups of employees for example overtime pay. They claim a success rate of over 90%.
- Individual conciliation. Since April 2014 anybody wishing to lodge a claim with an Employment Tribunal must first send an early conciliation notification form to ACAS.

ACAS has a statutory duty to offer early conciliation for an initial period of up to a calendar month. During this time they

Accreditation

try to help the parties come to a mutually acceptable solution to avoid the expense of running a claim in the tribunal. The conciliator has the discretion to extend that by two weeks if both parties agree that extra time may help resolution.

During the period of the early conciliation the time limit of three months for lodging a claim to the ET is suspended.

At the end of early conciliation ACAS issues a certificate with a number on it and that number has to be lodged at the employment tribunal.

ACAS does not advise on the likely outcome of the tribunal proceedings, it simply tries to clarify the issues so the parties can come to an agreement. This sounds like facilitative mediation although in practice ACAS officers sometimes express their views on the merits of claims and responses.

See also

EMPLOYMENT/FACILITATIVE/JUDICIAL MEDIATION/ WORKPLACE MEDIATION

Follow up

www.acas.org.uk

Accreditation

In England and Wales anybody can practise as a mediator. There is no:

- Restriction on the use of the name as there is, for example, for architects or solicitors.
- Requirement that you receive any training before offering your services as a mediator.
- Regulation or mandatory code of conduct.

Quality assurance for the benefit of mediation users is being slowly introduced. How can the courts direct people to go to

Accreditation

mediation if they cannot be satisfied that there is a sufficient pool of properly experienced mediators?

The Civil Mediation Council has recently introduced a registration procedure. This explicitly is not accreditation. Individual mediators seeking registration have to meet certain requirements which are set out on the CMC's website. They are not onerous.

Many registered members of the CMC are also members of an approved mediation service provider's panel. That is a service provider which is registered with CMC and provides certain minimum standards of training and service. A list is maintained by the CMC.

The CMC and its member organisations require individual mediators who are on their panels or registered with them to comply with the European Code of Conduct for Mediators.

Internationally the International Mediation Institute (IMI) has introduced an accreditation scheme for both mediators and mediation advocates, which includes peer review of feedback. Details are on their website.

All these schemes are voluntary. Even the EU Code of Conduct does not have to be followed by individual mediators. At the moment the market seems able to cope with unregulated suppliers. Some think that regulation will come. One mediation-aware High Court judge has even predicted that there will be an English Mediation Act by 2020.

In practice
- Mediators are split on the issue of accreditation.
- Older and longer established mediators believe that the market should regulate itself, ie good mediators will flourish and bad ones will go out of business.

- Younger and less well-established mediators tend to favour regulation because they see that it inevitably comes in any new business activity.
- It is also a way of reassuring a still sceptical public that mediators are providing a quality service.

See also

CODE OF CONDUCT/CMC/EU CODE/IMI/REGULATION/SCMA

Follow up

CMC www.civilmediation.org

IMI imimediation.org

Acknowledgment

A key concept in mediation. Parties in dispute – particularly claimants – want to feel that they have been heard.

Mediation provides a forum for this to happen in a way that litigation or arbitration cannot. There parties only have a limited opportunity to express themselves. They are confined to answering questions from the other side's lawyers or the judge/arbitrator.

Complainants are often said to be satisfied by the offer of an apology, which is an acknowledgement. More usually they want vindication – to be proved right.

In practice

- Apologies help if sincerely given but are rarely sufficient.
- For many, acknowledgement comes in the form of a money payment.
- Acknowledgment often means vindication.

See also
APOLOGIES

Active Listening

'Nature has given men one tongue but two ears, that we may hear from others twice as much as we speak.'

Epictetus

Mediators are trained in active listening. You pay attention to what **the speaker** is saying **now** and **not** to what **you** are going to say **next**. Active listening means that you do *not* do the following:

- Think about what question you're going to ask next before the speaker has finished.
- Speak while the speaker is talking.
- Finish the speaker's sentence.
- Fill silences by talking yourself.
- Make notes while the speaker is talking.
- Hold a pen/pencil or have your mobile by you.

If you find yourself doing these you are not actively listening.

In practice

- Active listening is essential for everyone negotiating or mediating, particularly for mediators.
- You also need to be able to ask the right questions. If you do not do this you will have nothing to listen to, actively or otherwise.

See also
ACKNOWLEDGMENT/KIPLING/QUESTIONS

Follow up

Walker *Mediation Advocacy: Representing Clients in Mediation* para 6.24 for a Self Audit.

Adjournment

In England and Wales:

- Commercial mediations usually take place within a day.
- Family and community mediations have a series of meetings spread over several days/weeks.
- Workplace mediations are often concluded within a day but usually there is at least one follow-up or monitoring meeting.

In practice

- There is a trend for civil and commercial mediations not to be concluded on the day. Parties seem happy to accept that they will make progress, arrive at a point but not achieve finality.
- This has given rise to problems about where that leaves everyone?
    - Has anything been legally agreed?
    - Have Heads of Agreement been signed?
    - Are offers left on the table?
    - Do the terms of the Mediation Agreement still apply to any subsequent discussions over the telephone either between the parties or through the mediator?
- Inevitably, satellite litigation has taken place over these matters.
- If a mediation is adjourned, make sure that you are absolutely clear as to the next step.

Adjudication

See also

BINDING/CONFIDENTIALITY/HEADS OF AGREEMENT/ MEDIATION AGREEMENT/MEDIATION DAY/OFFERS/ ROLLING MEDIATIONS/TERMINATING

Adjudication

Adjudication is a simplified form of arbitration. The parties choose a Third Party Neutral to come to a decision, ie adjudicate on their dispute. The decision is binding but not final.

Adjudication is common in the construction industry where disputes arise during a project but cannot be allowed to delay it. Parties want a quick resolution. An example in England and Wales is the Housing Grants Construction and Regeneration Act 1996 (HGCRA).

Pros

- Cheaper than arbitration and litigation.
- Own choice of Adjudicator.
- Can choose an expert in the area of the dispute.
- Court supervision.
- Can be set up and concluded quickly.

Cons

- Lack of finality: often the adjudication is not a final decision but a provisional one pending a final resolution of the dispute, which may be resolved at court or in arbitration as under the HGCRA.
- Less quality control over the competence and impartiality of adjudicators than over judges. Growing concern about quality of adjudicators and their decisions.

- Time pressures can be oppressive on smaller, less well-resourced parties.
- Parties can indulge in unreasonable conduct without costs sanctions.

Adjudicative

The opposite of traditional mediation which is facilitative and non-adjudicative.

Describes a process where a third party takes a decision that is binding on the parties. For example in litigation the judge gives a judgment. In arbitration the arbitrator publishes his award.

In mediation the mediator does not do this. Instead the parties decide for themselves. A third party does not decide for them. Promoted as a positive benefit of the mediation process.

In practice

- This traditional view is under attack in commercial mediations. Commercial clients increasingly require an outcome or solution. They want finality.
- The lack of a guaranteed outcome is seen as a weakness in the mediation process.

Suggested solutions are:

- Empowering the mediator to issue recommendations if the parties cannot agree. These recommendations can be non-binding or binding as the parties choose. They may be given orally at the mediation or in writing after the mediation.
- Med/Arb.
- Arb/Med.
- MEDALOA (Mediation After Last Offer Arbitration).

ADR (Alternative Dispute Resolution)

See also

ARB-MED/AUTONOMY/EVALUATIVE/FACILATIVE/ MEDALOA/MED-ARB/RECOMMENDATIONS

ADR (Alternative Dispute Resolution)

A catch-all title for methods of resolving disputes other than by litigation. Includes both adjudicative and non-adjudicative methods.

ADR also stands for

- Appropriate Dispute Resolution.
- Amicable Dispute Resolution.
- Alarming Drop in Revenue.
- A Dose of Reality.

There is in fact a spectrum of ADR techniques and methods. See the Bar Chart summary.

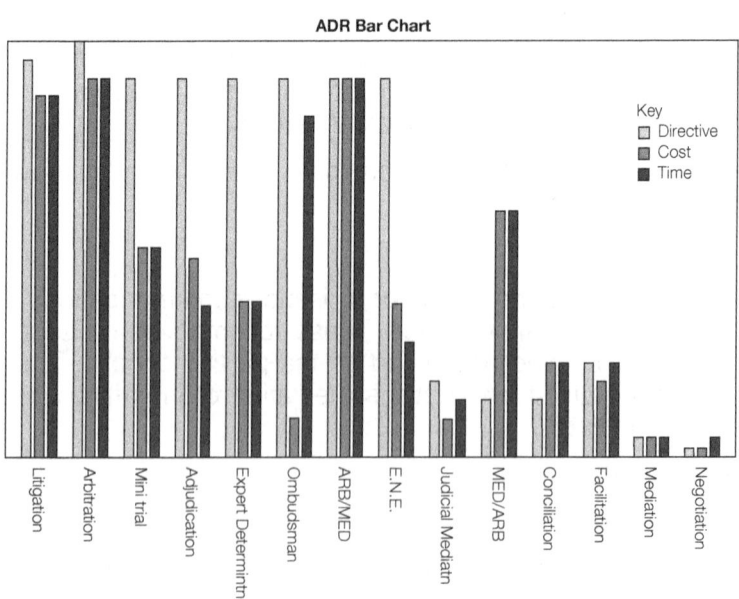

ADR Bar Chart

It compares various ADR procedures by:

- Degree of adjudication, ie litigation is the most adjudicative and negotiation the least.
- The length of time the procedure takes.
- The cost of the procedure.

In practice

- As a procedure becomes more adjudicative it becomes longer and more expensive.
- The cheapest and quickest way of solving a dispute is by direct negotiation.
- The longest and most expensive is litigation or arbitration.
- Arbitration is no longer regarded as **alternative** dispute resolution.
- Mediation stands out as the best alternative.

See also
ARBITRATION/LITIGATION

ADR Group

ADR Group or ADRg is the trading name of IDR Europe Ltd. Formed in 1989 originally based in Bristol but now in London it was the first commercial mediation organisation in the UK.

Provides training and mediation services.

Sets out to be smaller, friendlier and cheaper than CEDR but just as good.

Follow up

www.adrgroup.co.uk

Adversarial

The English (like the US) civil litigation system is based on the adversarial not the inquisitorial principle. In other words a judge sits in court and decides which of the advocates wins the argument. Although judges may ask questions they do not conduct an enquiry.

Lawyers trained in the adversarial system bring their habits into mediations.

- By instinct and training they adopt a confrontational, argumentative style of negotiation.
- They think that the objective of mediation is the same as at court – namely to destroy your opponent's case and to convince the mediator and the other side that you are right and everyone else is wrong.
- It is all about winning. They adopt a positional rather than a principled approach to negotiation.

Parties and their representatives at mediation are gradually realising that:

- They are there to make peace not war.
- The adversarial style of advocacy is not the most productive.

In practice

- In all mediations there is an adversarial element.
- Clients can be just as adversarial as their lawyers.
- Settlements are not reached by attacking each other's cases but by discussing proposals.

See also

ADVOCACY/MEDIATION ADVOCACY/PEACE/ POSITIONAL/PRINCIPLED NEGOTIATION

Advocacy

Follow up

Walker *Mediation Advocacy: Representing Clients in Mediation* Chapter 6 What is Mediation Advocacy?

Advocacy

Does advocacy have a place in mediation at all?

- Its core meaning is arguing a case and trying to persuade others including your opponent and a third party such as a judge that you are right and they are wrong.
- According to the Harvard Model mediation is not about establishing who is right and who is wrong. What the parties need to do is to attack the problem, not each other and collaboratively seek a mutually acceptable solution.
- Forensic persuasion, which is at the heart of advocacy, seems doomed to fail.

The view persists that it is an important part of mediation for each party to have the opportunity to persuade the other side and the mediator of the strength of their case. Barristers are particularly firm in this view. They hold it even when they admit that they have never been persuaded at mediation that they were wrong by the force of the other side's argument.

Is there a special brand of Mediation Advocacy?

Some draw a distinction between the Old Advocacy and the New Advocacy.

- The old advocacy was based upon destructive critical analysis of the other side's case leading to its demolition.
- The new advocacy is not about demolition. It's about assessment and explanation and the creation of solutions.

Advocacy at mediation is not about scoring points and trying to take control of the battleground. It is about nudging people towards the common ground. To promote this the UK

Agenda

the Standing Conference of Mediation Advocates (SCMA) has been set up.

In practice

- Advocates at mediation play three roles: hired gun, bodyguard and coach.
- Many advocates, especially barristers, act in exactly the same way in court and at mediation. In other words they are adversarial. They do not help the mediator or their clients.
- Advocates forget that they are there to make peace not war.

See also

ADVERSARIAL/HARVARD/LAWYERS'-ROLES/ MEDIATION ADVOCACY/OPENING STATEMENT/SCMA

Follow up

Walker *Mediation Advocacy: Representing Clients in Mediation* Chapter 6 What is Mediation Advocacy?

IMI imimediation.org

Agenda

A list of topics to be discussed at a meeting. In mediation it has a double meaning.

1. Mediators need to structure the discussions to help not hinder the settlement process. Sometimes the parties set out in advance the issues that they think will have to be worked through for a settlement. But usually they do not.

    Even when parties compile a list, it is often incomplete and self-serving. Mediators try to draw out what is important for each side and compile a shared agenda. Time, energy and goodwill are not infinite resources. Mediators need to make the best use of them. Having an agenda to work through helps.

2 The hidden agenda. All parties assume that the other party has a hidden agenda. This reflects our tendency to demonise co-disputants and attribute malign motives and intentions to them.

Skilled mediators:

- Know parties have hidden agendas and are confident in working with the ambiguity created. As rapport and trust are established hidden agendas are disclosed or uncovered.
- Are adept at drawing out unexpressed motivations and objectives through active listening and open questioning.

In practice

- Parties can be reluctant to disclose to the mediator or even to their own lawyers what their real objectives at the mediation are.
- Parties make settlements for reasons that only they fully understand.
- Without agendas, mediations flounder.
- Skilled negotiators set the agenda.

See also

ACTIVE LISTENING/COGNITIVE BIAS/QUESTIONS

Agreement

Mediation cannot exist without agreement. Its essence is that it is consensual.

The classic view is that:

1 Mediation is a voluntary process. The parties have to agree to go to mediation in the first place. No one can compel them to. There is much debate about how voluntary mediation actually is.

Aggression

2 The parties have to agree to a settlement. It is not imposed upon them. There is a distinction between:
   - being required to **attend a** mediation.
   - being compelled to **reach** a settlement.

You may be required to attend mediation but you cannot be required to settle.

Also 'agreement to mediate' is another term for mediation agreement. Most mediations take place after a formal mediation agreement has been signed.

In practice
- Attendance at mediation is less voluntary than people might think.
- Reaching agreement is the heart of the mediation process.
- Parties value the fact that they do not have to agree if they do not want to.

See also
AUTONOMY/COMPULSION/MEDIATION AGREEMENT/ VOLUNTARY/WATERFALL CLAUSES

Agreement to Mediate

See also
MEDIATION AGREEMENT

Aggression

Mediation is promoted as offering a safe place where people can express strong emotions and feelings. Some mediators

Aim High

actively encourage parties to do this. They call it venting. They claim that it dissipates anger and reduces aggression.

Aggression usually takes the form of verbal expression or passive aggressive behaviour by the parties. In civil and commercial mediations physical violence is rare but not unknown. Threats of physical violence are more common in community and family mediations.

Mediators are trained, if not in unarmed combat, then at least in non-violent communication.

Advocates sometimes take an aggressive approach when presenting their client's case. Usually they direct this at the other side whom they regard as the enemy. Sometimes they direct it at the mediator to try and intimidate them and seize control of the process.

In practice
- Aggression of any sort at mediation never works.
- Certainly it does not work in civil and commercial mediations conducted in England and Wales.
- He who swears first loses.

See also
ADVERSARIAL/EMOTIONS/GOOD MANNERS/NVC/ REFRAMING/VENTING

Aim High

Traditional advice to negotiators is to start with high figures. Doing this:
- Gives room for manoeuvre.
- Sends out a message that you are not there to compromise.

Research has shown that those who start high generally do better than those who start at a lower figure. Hence the theory of anchoring.

In practice

- Parties at mediations become discouraged when they see that the gap between them is too wide. They become disenchanted with the process even before it has started.
- Parties: be clear about your end game. Where do you want to get to? What's the best route for you?
- Think about what message you want to send when you make an offer. Listen to the mediator's health warnings.

See also
ANCHORING/ENGAGEMENT/HEALTH WARNINGS/ OFFERS/SALAMI SLICING/SIGNALS

ALF (Association of Litigation Funders)

Formed in November 2011, as the regulator of its funder members and their adherence to the Code of Conduct. The Code only applies to the resolution of disputes within England and Wales.

Check that your funder is a member.

See also
FUNDERS

Follow up
associationoflitigationfunders.com

All-In

Used a lot at mediations when presenting offers. It means that the figure offered includes all the other side's claims: their principal claim, interest, expenses and legal costs. It is all-inclusive. There is nothing else.

In practice

- Parties prefer to make "all-in, costs-inclusive," offers and to come to global settlements. Leaving costs to be assessed means that finality is not achieved.
- Make sure offers are put on the same basis to avoid misunderstanding.

See also

APPLES AND PEARS/COSTS/GLOBAL SETTLEMENT/ GROSS/NET/OFFERS

Allocation questionnaire

Form used by the court in case management. Now called Directions Questionnaire.

If a defendant files a defence the court will provisionally decide which track appears to be most suitable for the claim and send out a notice with a requirement to file a completed directions questionnaire.

When completing a questionnaire you can make a written request that the proceedings be stayed while you try to settle a case by ADR or other means. If all parties request a stay the court will automatically stay, ie put the case on hold.

In practice

- Always ask for mediation.
- Never reject it. The costs risks are too great.

See also
**COURT TRACKS/COSTS/DIRECTIONS
QUESTIONNAIRE/HALSEY**

Follow up
CPR Part 26.

AMATI

Not the family of 16th Century Italian violin makers but the Association of Mediation Assessors, Trainers and Instructors.

Established in London as a professional association for those training and assessing mediators. Its aim is to raise and standardise standards.

A worthwhile and much needed initiative.

Follow up
www.amati.org.uk

Amygdala

Currently fashionable part of the brain in mediation circles.

Identified by mediator trainers as the part of the brain which:
- Controls our fight-or-flight response. When we perceive a threat we are programmed to either stand and fight or run away.
- Governs our responses in negotiation and to risk.

This almond-shaped organ deep in the temporal lobe performs a primary role in processing memory, decision-making and emotional reactions. It has two hemispheres which are different.

Anchoring

The right is associated with:
- Negative emotions such as fear and sadness.
- Taking action in response to emotionally stressful stimuli.
- Shows increased activity in men when they watch a horror film.

The left is associated with:
- Both positive and negative emotions.
- Being linked to the brain's reward system.
- Shows increased activity in women when watching a horror film.

In practice
- No one knows the size and configuration of their amygdala. But we know how we tend to act and react.
- Women tend to retain stronger memories of emotional events than men. Men tend to respond physically to emotionally stressful stimuli.
- Ask yourself how would I respond to what I am saying to the other side. If the answer is negatively, why say it?

See also
ADVERSARIAL/ATTACK/COGNITIVE BIAS/KNOW THYSELF

Follow up
Randolph *Psychology of Conflict* p 53.

Anchoring

The theory that he who goes first wins.

Reflects the cognitive bias that we tend to rely heavily on the first piece of information that we hear. Everything else that we hear is coloured by that first piece of information. The first offer anchors all further negotiation.

Relevant in mediation where parties are usually reluctant to make the first offer. They resist by saying they don't want to:
- Bid against themselves.
- Enter a Dutch auction.
- Disclose their hand.
- Give away too much too soon.

Mediators can meet these objections by suggesting that offers be exchanged.

In practice

Experienced negotiators at mediations:
- Say that anchoring works in training but in real life…?
- Practice de-anchoring by shaking their heads, asking for basis of offer, reiterating underlying circumstances.
- End up exchanging proposals.

See also

DUTCH AUCTION/EXCHANGING OFFERS/HEALTH WARNINGS/OFFERS

Apologies

Very popular in mediation literature. Heart-warming examples of apologies leading to tears of forgiveness and shared Christmases are described. Such transformational apologies appear to be particularly common in personal injury and medical negligence cases.

Some say that apologies are all that parties really want. An apology is after all an acknowledgement that a complainant is both right and deserving.

But sorry still seems to be the hardest word. People are reluctant to make an apology. An apology is seen as:

- An admission of liability.
- A sign of weakness.
- A bargaining chip. 'I will give you an apology if you will reduce your demand for money'.

In practice

- Give apologies early. Do not sell them.
- Say sorry. Do not give an expression of regret.
- Sincerely-given apologies transform the mood for negotiation. Insincere ones wreck it.
- Apologies can backfire if insincere or used to increase your guilt burden.

See also

ACKNOWLEDGMENT/EMOTIONS/FAIR/GOOD MANNERS/VENTING

Apples and Pears

Not Cockney rhyming slang for stairs. Describes what happens when parties are not talking about the same thing. If I am offering to sell you apples and you want to buy pears the chances of us doing a deal are zero.

Common examples of this confusion at mediation are:

1. Where the parties are talking in different terms, eg net or gross.
   - Is the figure being offered net of tax?

- Plus VAT or VAT-inclusive?

    This is particularly relevant to legal costs. The rate payable in the UK is currently 20%. That can make a big difference in mediation.

- Costs inclusive or plus costs?

    Often at mediation the stumbling block is the legal costs which both sides have incurred. The payer does not want to pay them, having already incurred liability for his own costs. The receiver wants to recover as much of his costs from the other side as possible. Otherwise he has to pay them out of his principal recovery.

2 The parties talk past each other. They make their points but they do not respond to each other's points. There is no engagement or discussion.

3 The parties are on different planets. The claimant demands £10 million and the defendant offers £10,000.

In practice

Mediators try to:

- Ensure that the lawyers understand that all clients at mediation are interested in their net financial position after costs have been paid.
- Develop an agenda. Help the mediator do this.
- See what is important to each side and where there is overlap.
- Try to find a common language. This is often the language of money.

See also

AGENDA/NET/QUESTIONS/TAX/VAT

Arbitration

Part of legal systems in most jurisdictions for centuries. In reality arbitration is now a mainstream, not an alternative, method of dispute resolution.

A process where the parties select their own arbitrator who holds a hearing like a court trial except that is in private. He listens to their submissions and witness evidence and makes a decision. The arbitrator acts as a judge.

Some arbitrations are paper only, ie decided on the documents submitted with no oral hearings.

Pros

- Well established and understood in many jurisdictions.
- Parties usually able to choose their arbitrator or the appointing body.
- Experts in the subject matter of the dispute can be appointed rather than generalist judges.
- The courts retain an overarching supervisory function.
- Limited rights of appeal so that finality can be achieved.
- International treaties provide that arbitral awards can be enforced in different jurisdictions.
- Arbitration of international disputes remains a popular method of resolving cross-border disputes.

Cons

- As expensive as litigation and sometimes more expensive because the parties pay the arbitrators' fees and the appointing body's charges which are usually higher than court fees.
- Arbitrators have a more limited range of powers than judges, for example in relation to injunctive relief, orders against third parties, power to commit to prison for defying court orders.

Advisory Arbitration

- Not necessarily speedier than court proceedings and because of the more limited case management powers of arbitrators, it can be slower.
- Less quality control over the competence and impartiality of arbitrators than over that of judges.
- Absence of the deterrent of adverse publicity.
- More opportunity for parties to game the system by alleging misconduct and bias against arbitrators if they do not like the award.
- More risk of a power imbalance between a large big-spending party and a smaller poorer one affecting the process and possibly the outcome.
- In many jurisdictions domestic arbitration has become less popular because it has become so similar to litigation.

Advisory Arbitration

Can be used in a conciliation if the conciliator decides. Used in USA labour disputes but not used much in the UK. The arbitrator conducts an arbitration hearing in the normal way. He publishes his award but it is not binding on the parties. It is more like a settlement proposal or recommendation.

Pros

- An additional tool for the conciliator to help focus the parties on settlement.

Cons

- Can be a comparatively expensive way of obtaining a third party indication.
- No finality.

See also
ADR/MEDALOA/MEDIATOR'S PROPOSAL/ RECOMMENDATIONS

Arb-Med

A hybrid technique combining arbitration and mediation. Intended to deal with the biggest drawback in mediation – no guarantee of a final outcome.

Parties choose the same Third Party Neutral (TPN) to act as both arbitrator and mediator. The TPN acting as arbitrator:

- First holds an arbitration hearing in the usual way.
- Makes his award.
- Does not publish the award but places it in a sealed envelope, which he retains.

TPN then acts as a mediator. He knows what his award says but the parties do not. They can only guess what it might be depending on how they think their case went at the arbitration hearing.

The mediator conducts the mediation in the usual way:

- There is no procedural change because it takes place after the arbitration.
- There is no need to go through all the evidential and legal points in the dispute as they have been ventilated at the arbitration.
- Confidentiality still applies.

The parties know that:

- If they do not achieve a settlement at mediation the arbitration award will be published.
- There will be a definite outcome.

Arb-Med

Each party takes a decision on whether or not it thinks that the settlement offers them a more favourable outcome than they expect to receive in the award.

Pros

- It saves time and money by having the same TPN doing both jobs.
- It provides the parties with finality. They know that their dispute will be over one way or the other.
- Practitioners acting as TPNs who have been properly trained will be able to separate the different roles and also to prevent themselves during the mediation from revealing anything about their award.
- If the mediator does not hold caucuses but conducts everything in joint sessions the risk of the parties trying to wheedle information out of the mediator will be reduced.
- Much of the mediation advocacy where the parties argue their legal case and predict outcomes at trial is redundant. This makes positional negotiating less attractive and speeds up discussions about settlement.

Cons

- Parties try and read the mediator for clues as to what is in the arbitration award.
- Mediators will not be able to avoid giving clues by their body language and tone of voice or type of questions.
- The power and possibly also the temptation for mediators to manipulate the parties towards a proposal that accords with his award will be overwhelming.
- Mediators will not be able to be evaluative in any way without in fact revealing their decision in the award.
- The mindset of an arbitrator who is acting like a judge is fundamentally different from that of a mediator who is not acting like a judge.

See also
MEDALOA/MED-ARB/TPN

Arguing

What most people do most of the time at mediations. They either argue their case or they quarrel about what has happened in the past.

Lawyers love arguing their case but so do many clients. Telling the other side that they are wrong and you are right is easier than assessing the problem and exploring settlements.

Clients like to quarrel about the past rather than contemplate the future. So do lawyers as they criticise each other's conduct. None of this promotes settlement.

In practice

- Being critical is much easier than being creative. But creative is what you have to be to make peace.
- Deals are not done by arguing about evidence and law at mediations. They are done by discussing proposals.

See also
ADVERSARIAL/ADVOCACY/MEDIATION ADVOCACY/ PRINCIPLED NEGOTIATION

Art

Mediation is said to be an art not a science. This is because:
- It lacks precision.
- There is an absence of hard data.
- It is difficult to predict.

Aspirations

- It is about people.
- It deals with emotion/feelings.

Calling mediation an art emphasises the individual role and skill of the mediator.

But is this accurate? The increasing influence of research from:

- Neuroscience
- Game theory
- Behavioural economics
- Psychology
- Probability/risk analysis
- Proxemics

means that mediation is becoming more like a science than an art. The advent of Online Dispute Resolution (ODR) with algorithms and Big Data reinforces this trend.

In practice

- This debate about science versus art is sterile. Clients aren't interested.
- Mediation is a craft. You improve by doing it.

See also
CRAFT/ODR/TFN

Aspirations

Operate at three levels in mediation: the parties, the mediation community and the individual mediator.

1 Parties

Aspirations

Mediators ask parties what they want out of the process. They do not always put the question so bluntly. They may ask questions such as: Where do you want to be in three years' time? This leads on to the more interesting question: how will this dispute help you get there? Mediators encourage parties to confide in them.

- What their real needs or interests are

and

- How likely they will be able to achieve them if they do not come to a deal with the other side.

'Aspirations' in this sense is treated as a synonym for expectations, goals, desires, interests and needs. These are not all the same.

Skilful mediators:

- Disentangle them using the LIM formula.
- Encourage parties to focus on what is really important to them.
- Work out with the parties what is doable.

2 Mediation community

As explained in the Introduction the mediation community's aspirations are varied. Many want to change the world. As one of the U.K.'s leading commercial mediators, Stephen Ruttle says 'What we do changes the world.' Others are more modest in their ambitions and just want to help the parties in the room with them solve the problem of the day. The evangelists and the pragmatists jostle for market share.

3 Individual mediators

Most individual mediators want to be successful. This usually means:

- Lots of appointments as lead mediator.
- Lots of recommendations.

Assessment

- A high settlement rate.
- An agreeable sum of money by way of remuneration.

In practice

- There are those who see mediation as a calling, not a business, and want to help people have a better life.
- There are those who see mediation as a business, not a calling, and want to have satisfied clients.

See also

LIM/PRIORITIES/REALITY TESTING

Follow up

Richbell *How to Master Commercial Mediation* p 548

Walker *Setting up in Business as a Mediator* pp 5–7

Assessment

The concept of assessment is relevant in mediation in three ways:

1 Assessing costs.

 What happens when parties to litigation cannot settle or agree their costs? The court decides how much the loser should pay. This is called detailed assessment.

2 Assessing the mediator.

 Various rankings are available to help parties choose a suitable mediator.

 They are:

- In Directories such as *Legal 500* or *Chambers*.
- On mediation providers' websites who obtain feedback on their panel members from users.
- Operated by accreditation bodies, such as IMI.

Assessment

- In recommendations and testimonials highlighted on mediators' websites.

3 Assessing the situation.

What parties and their advisers should do. Instead of making a partisan presentation of your case emphasising all your best points and all the other side's weakest ones, carry out a balanced neutral assessment of the overall situation.

Look at the overall situation through both your own eyes and the other side's. Inevitably you will highlight your own good points but make sure you acknowledge your weak ones and the other side's strong points. Doing this builds credibility.

A balanced overall assessment:

- Uncovers areas of agreement, which are usually greater than they appear to be.
- Sends the message to the side that you are a credible, reasonable person who is prepared to do business. That is a much more attractive message to receive than being told during a hostile presentation that your case is doomed to fail.

In practice

- If one side had a monopoly of all the good points the other side would have settled. There would be no need for a mediation.
- Very rarely does one side have a monopoly of all the good points.
- Even if one side has a majority of the good legal and evidential points they may not have the best of the commercial advantages.

See also

ACCREDITATION/ADVERSARIAL/COSTS ASSSMENT/ DIRECTORIES/MEDIATION ADVOCACY

Assumptions

Relevant in three ways in mediation:

1 Stereotyping

Everybody does it. But it can be inappropriate and make settlement discussions more difficult than they need be. The usual ones are around gender or cultural differences.

2 Unthinking

This is where cognitive biases operate. For example:

- Reactive devaluation where we assume that if somebody suggests something it must be for their benefit and to our disadvantage.
- Confirmation bias where everything is interpreted through the prism of an existing view of the world.

This leads to each side demonising the other. They just assume the worst about each other. In fact with a skilled mediator parties realise that the similarities between them are usually greater than the differences. This helps the scoping of common ground and the discovery of mutually acceptable solutions.

3 Not checking

Good negotiators take nothing for granted. They make sure that:

- The mediator knows that something is confidential.
- The mediator understands their calculations.
- They do not assume he has read all the papers.
- They interrogate any proposal that they receive to make sure that they fully understand it and nothing is just being taken at face value.
- They make sure that everybody is talking about the same thing at the same time in the same way.

In practice
- Everyone at mediations makes assumptions.
- Keep them under review.
- Verify and modify.

See also
APPLES AND PEARS/COGNITIVE BIAS/DEMONISING

ATE Insurance

After-the-Event insurance is now a litigation staple.

It:

- Protects a party against having to pay under an adverse costs order.
- May also pay his own costs.
- Is bought as protection when both the parties and the insurer know that the risk has occurred.

Insurers assess the risk, which to a large extent is known. Often they use panels of retired judges to evaluate the merits. They are not always successful. In 2014 a leading ATE insurer revealed that after 10 years it was only correct in 60% of the cases that it funded.

ATE insurance influences mediation:

1 The party with ATE cover becomes overconfident. They think that they are fireproof from any adverse consequence. Their risk profile changes.

2 It is used as proof to the other side that their case is strong and as justifying their own confidence in their case. An independent third party has assessed the chances and backed it with their own money.

3 The decision-making becomes complicated because:
- the insured is not going to personally suffer any loss if a settlement is not reached and the case goes to court – he is not paying the legal fees.
- of the involvement of the insurer. They want to recover their outlays. Their authority to settle is often required but usually only in connection with the percentage of cost recovery that they want.

4 ATE insurers, when underwriting the risk, usually rely upon their policyholder's barrister's opinion on merits. At mediation that same barrister often has to tell the insurers whether a settlement proposal is reasonable. Under most policies cover can be withdrawn if the policyholder declines to accept a reasonable offer.

In practice

- Insurers sometimes want to accept a settlement proposal and the insured does not. And vice versa.
- This creates potential conflicts of interest for the legal advisers who are advising both their client and insurers and adds an extra layer of complexity to mediation.
- The same issues can also arise with BTE – Before-the-Event – insurance.

See also

BTE/FUNDING/INSURERS

Attack

'Attack is the best form of defence' is a maxim of generals, football coaches and unsophisticated mediation advocates. In fact at mediations defence is the best form of attack.

Attacking the other side is adversarial and aggressive. All that happens is that they become defensive. They close down, they don't open up.

Fight or flight kicks in when facing a charging tiger. It also happens when the other side's barrister tells you that your case is legally flawed and that your witnesses are liars. You concentrate on proving that he is wrong and that you are right. You do not think about the way forward and how to achieve a settlement that is mutually acceptable.

Instead:

- Provide a balanced assessment.
- Explain your position.
- Explain your understanding of the other side's position.

This is more likely to lead to early consideration of common ground and settlement proposals.

In practice

- Personal attacks never help deal making.
- Confine your attacks to the problem not to the people.

See also

AMYGDALA/ADVERSARIAL/ASSESSMENT/ MEDIATION ADVOCACY

Auction

Usually mentioned at mediation in the context of a Dutch auction. But the same behaviour displayed at auctions can be seen in mediations.

The conditions under which people make decisions overlap. For example: scarcity, time pressure, incomplete information, opportunity.

Settler's remorse is a variation of buyer's remorse. That is when the successful bidder wakes up next morning with doubts and regrets having exceeded his pre-auction budget.

Audience

Did he pay too much? Is it genuine? What will people think of him when they know how much he paid?

Scarcity error is a cognitive bias of being prepared to give a higher value to an opportunity that appears to be scarce and in danger of disappearing than to something that you already have. Applies at mediations as much as at auctions. Can lead people to pay too much or to accept a lower price than they might otherwise do.

In practice

- As mediators generate settlement momentum something like auction room fever can develop.
- Wise mediation advocates are alert to this danger. They can try and protect their client. But in the end only the client truly knows the value to him of a settlement.
- Clients may place a higher value on settlement than their advisers do. Advisers can never be certain that they know what is going through their client's mind.

See also

BODYGUARD/COGNTIVE BIAS/DUTCH AUCTION/ SETTLER'S REMORSE

Audience

All the actors in mediation have their audiences. Each actor must always be asking himself: who is my audience?

For example when preparing the Position Paper/Mediation Statement mediation advocates need to ask themselves who they want to influence:

1. The mediator?
2. The other side's lawyers?
3. Their own side?
4. The decision-makers on the other side?

During the course of the mediation when sending a message always ask – how will this be received by my audience?

Often there is an absent audience. Decision-makers have to return to their Board or spouse and explain why they decided to accept these particular terms. They may announce that they won't be able to sell this proposal when they get back. The question of authority arises.

This can be serious, especially when acting for quasi-governmental organisations. Hence mediators are sometimes asked to confirm that they think the settlement terms are acceptable or reasonable in all the circumstances. Some are prepared to do this: others are not.

In practice
- There are always multiple audiences at mediation.
- Some of them are unseen.
- Always remember your audience.

See also
ABSENTEES/AUTHORITY/MEDIATOR'S PROPOSAL/ POSITION PAPER/RECOMMENDATIONS

Authority

The issue of authority arises in four ways in mediation:

1 Authority to settle

   Mediation agreements provide that parties will send a representative to the mediation who has authority to settle. In other words finality – in the form of a legally binding contract – can be achieved on the day.

Authority

Mediators always ask the parties if they have authority to settle. When they do:

- Be punctilious about not misleading the mediator or the other side.
- Say in the Joint Opening Session that you do have authority but you may have to make a telephone call.
- Remember that doing this at the beginning of the day is much better than at the end when suddenly disclosing that you have to make that call creates enormous ill-will.

In practice

- Very few representatives have absolute authority to settle unless they are individuals without any insurance/third party funding or who own their own business.
- Limited authority is given for example by insurers, Boards of Directors, government departments etc.

2 Authority of the mediator

This arises out of:

- The mediation agreement.
- His experience and CV.
- The way in which he conducts himself with the parties on the mediation. Authority can be lost but it can also be increased.

3 Authority of the advocate

- Barristers usually assume the position of team leader. They sit at the head of the table and answer all the mediator's questions and speak on behalf of their client. All lawyers play different roles, ie bodyguard, hired gun or coach.

Mediators have to be careful:

- Not to undermine the authority of the legal advisers in front of their clients. Openly criticising the way that they have prepared the case or belittling their arguments is not helpful. Much better to have full and frank discussions in private.

- About asking to speak to clients on their own without their legal advisers present. But some very successful commercial mediators always put the principals together without their lawyers.

4 Who has authority?

It is not always clear who actually has authority to make a decision.

Within a team there is often a difference between those who created the problem and those who have been brought in to clean it up. The decision maker is usually the most senior person present and is also part of the clean up team. But not always.

See also

CLEAN UP MAN/EMPTY CHAIR/JOINT OPENING SESSION/LAWYERS'- ROLES/LYING/MEDIATION AGREEMENT/TEAMS/TRUST/WARRANTY

Autonomy

This is one of the 'Top Ten' of mediation.

The mantra is that the parties have autonomy and that this is essential to the true nature of mediation. After all:

- They decide on the process. They can decide for example whether or not they want a Joint Opening Session or they would prefer to have a caucus.
- The dispute is their dispute. They are the experts in it.
- They choose the mediator and the venue.
- They decide whether or not to settle. No one can force them to settle.

Autosettler

In practice

- Many mediators say that while the *dispute* belongs to the parties the *process* belongs to them. They see their role as process managers and are proprietorial about it. Some for example insist that there is a Joint Opening Session even if one or both parties are reluctant.
- Mediators are much less facilitative and much more evaluative than theorists and commentators admit.
- Even as process managers they intervene and direct. The more unscrupulous actually manipulate.
- Some mediators bring great pressure on parties to agree a settlement. Particularly true of novice mediators who want to get their settlement rate up.

See also

AGREEMENT/CAUCUS/EVALUATIVE/FACILATIVE/TOP TEN/VOUNTARY

Autosettler

A deadlock-breaking technique. A sophisticated version of the mediator's standby of splitting the difference.

It offers the parties the chance of doing better than splitting the difference but at the same time guarantees a settlement. It works like this. Each party makes their final offer. Whichever party moves most in absolute terms (not percentage terms) from their last stated position wins. The settlement is at that figure.

Autosettler

Here is a worked example:

PAYING PARTY	RECEIVING PARTY
£	£
100	200
Splitting the difference produces a settlement figure of £150	
Moves from £100 to £140	Moves from £200 to £170
Moves by £40	Moves by £ 30
Paying party wins. This gives a settlement figure of £140.	
The paying party is better off by £10 and the receiving party is worse off by £ 20.	

This technique introduces an element of judgement and skill. Negotiators who see themselves as poker players like it. Many negotiators secretly think that they could be world champion poker players.

One side makes an even figure offer and the other an odd figure one to avoid a tie.

In practice

- Parties need to have it explained more than once.
- When they do it they like it.
- When used it never fails.

See also

SPLITTING THE DIFFERENCE

Follow up

Walker *Mediation Advocacy: Representing Clients in Mediation* Ch 9 mediators' tricks

B

Balance of Power

Operates at mediations in two ways:

1 Power between the parties

The EU Code of Conduct for Mediators states that 'The mediator must conduct the proceedings in an appropriate manner, taking into account the circumstances of the case, including possible imbalances of power…'

People at mediation often feel vulnerable. Reasons include:

- Their first language is not English.
- They are not well educated.
- They are suffering from behavioural or medical conditions.
- They are under acute financial or personal stress.
- It is their first mediation. They find it stressful. Even seasoned business negotiators find negotiating outside their comfort zone stressful.

In practice

The parties are rarely on an equal footing. One party often has:

- More money.
- More ability to withstand the risk of losing at trial.
- Better legal representation than the other side.
- Better information than the other side.

Balance of Power

In-built inequalities such as greater wealth cannot be redressed at the mediation. Other inequalities, for example having more information can be. And the mediator can definitely ensure that the more powerful party does not abuse their power.

Some parties think that judges can even up any imbalance of power better than mediators. They forget that at court they will never have as much control over the process or the outcome as they will at mediation.

But:
- Power does not always reside with the big battalions. An individual who has nothing to lose has a great deal of power. A defendant who is being sued and has no money at all paradoxically also has power.
- What many wealthy people and organisations fear is not losing money but losing reputation. Judges can make scathing comments about them even when granting judgment in their favour. Witnesses can make embarrassing disclosures.
- Conditional Fee Agreements (CFA), Damages Based Agreements (DBA) and Third Party Funding have ameliorated economic imbalances of power.

2   Power of the mediator

Mediators can use their secret weapon. Only the mediator knows what is being said to him by each of the parties in caucus. This gives power to the mediator.

Is this secret weapon lost if the mediation is conducted in joint sessions? Is the power imbalance between the parties aggravated in a joint session where the weaker party has no buffer? Different mediators have different views.

Mediators also derive power from their authority, experience, reputation and the fact that the parties have chosen them to help sort out the dispute and have paid them to do it. This power can increase or decrease during the day depending on how the mediator interacts with the parties.

In practice

- Parties never really know what the other side might do. They can only guess. Some are better at guessing than others.
- One party may have much more power than the other eg the large financial institution pursuing a personal guarantor who is facing bankruptcy. Acknowledge this. The question for both sides remains the same: will you do better at court?
- The more options you have the more power you have.

See also

BARGAINING POWER/BATNA/CAUCUS/CFA/DBA/ EU CODE/GOODWILL/LITIGATION FUNDING/POWER/ SECRET WEAPON

Balcony

A place to take time out and look around.

In the middle of mediations leave the dance floor and go to the balcony.

As a mediator you need to:

- Get off the dance floor of the detail and see where the negotiations are going. What is happening? What are the obstacles to settlement?
- Not react if the parties are taking out their frustration and stress by attacking you. Give yourself time to think. Don't react. Go to the balcony.

Banging Heads Together

- Encourage the parties to take a broader view and see the bigger picture.

As a party you need to do the same thing:

- Step aside from the conflict and look at it from a different perspective.
- Do not get bogged down in scoring points and self-justifying arguments.
- Look at the goals and think where you will be in 12 months' time.

In practice

- Parties and occasionally mediators as well can become bogged down in the fine detail or caught up in settlement momentum.
- Time out – a walk around the block, some fresh air, a smoking break can help.

See also

BIG PICTURE/DANCE FLOOR/PERSPECTIVE

Follow up

William Ury *Getting Past No*

Ronald A Heifetz and Marty A Linsky *Leadership on the Line*

Banging Heads Together

Defined in the Oxford English Dictionary as to 'reprimand people severely, especially in an attempt to stop them arguing.'

When lawyers ask a mediator to bang heads together they don't want him to reprimand them or their clients. They want the mediator to stop the parties, especially the other side, posturing and to concentrate on what they see as the realities of life. They can be disappointed.

Mediators use different head banging techniques. For example:

- Being overtly evaluative and giving their views on the merits of the case and the likely outcome at trial.
- Trashing and bashing the parties' cases. Even telling a party that they are wrong in law.
- Asking probing questions by way of reality therapy, which go beyond simply having a challenging conversation.
- Giving very firm indications of what a settlement proposal should be.
- Concentrating on the behaviour of the parties rather than the facts and evidence of the case. Telling the lawyers for example that they are being too forensic in trying to score points rather than problem-solve.
- Pointing out the contradictions in what is being said - parties often express incompatible objectives.
- Some mediators do this in caucus sessions. Others do it in joint sessions.

In practice
- if you ask the mediator to bang heads together be prepared for some bruising and take a hard hat.
- Some mediators are natural head bangers: others are not.

See also
BASHING AND THRASHING/CAUCUS/CHOOSING THE MEDIATOR/EVALUATIVE/REALITY TESTING

Bargaining

Mediation is assisted negotiation.

Bargaining is a key element of negotiation. For some there is no difference between negotiating and bargaining. In both cases parties trade concessions in order to achieve what they want.

Bargaining is a subset of negotiation – where parties are more fully focused on the detail. This is where value is being claimed rather than created.

Many mediators think that mediation is a nobler activity. Ideally it is a mutual exploration of the issues involved and the mutual construction of a mutually beneficial settlement.

When parties are frustrated by the negotiations not going their way they describe what is happening as simply horse trading.

In practice

- At every mediation there is bargaining and horse trading.
- Be prepared for this. Do your homework. Work out your tradeables.
- Good bargainers don't offer concessions: they trade them.

See also

BATNAS//HAGGLING/HORSE TRADING/IF/ NEGOTIATON/OFFERS/TRADEABLES

Bargaining Power

Linked with the balance of power. Bargaining power lies where the parties think that it is not where it actually is.

Mediators observe during a mediation how the balance of bargaining power shifts back and forth as the parties re-evaluate what is happening and how much they are prepared to pay or give up for their desired outcome. Often they are actively assessing or reviewing their situation for the first time.

In practice

- There is often an actual imbalance of bargaining power. Be realistic. Recognise it.
- Actual and perceived bargaining power are not always the same. Exploit the difference.
- Work on your presentation skills. Maximise the positive: minimise the negative.

See also

BALANCE OF POWER/PRINCIPLED NEGOTIATION/ PREPARATION/NEGOTIATION

Barristers

The Bar Council's website defines barristers as:

> 'specialist legal advisers and court room advocates. They are independent, objective and trained to advise clients on the strengths and weaknesses of their case. They have specialist knowledge and experience in and out of court, which can make a substantial difference to the outcome of a case.'

Many mediators, solicitors and clients think that barristers at mediation are barriers to settlement. The very strengths identified by the Bar Council are weaknesses at mediation.

People go to mediation to make peace not war. This requires a different skill set and mindset. Barristers do not always find it easy to switch from the advocacy mode of the court room to the problem-solving mode of the mediation room.

Barristers

In practice

The Seven Deadly Sins of Barristers are:

1 Treating mediation as though they were making an application to court.
2 Trying to dominate their team and control their clients too much.
3 Grandstanding.
4 Boasting about their successes at trial.
5 Point scoring with the other side's lawyers.
6 Bringing along works of authority and cases.
7 Leaving the clients at the altar when it comes to settlement.

But they have distinct advantages:

1 Specialist knowledge.
2 The ability to reassure if they have given previous advice to the client.
3 A degree of detachment.
4 Being a second pair of eyes and ears.
5 Superior drafting skills.
6 Thinking on their feet.
7 Liaising with funders and insurance.

The SCMA (Standing Conference of Mediation Advocates) was established to promote mediation advocacy as a specialist skill which barristers could acquire and sell.

See also

ADVOCACY/LAWYERS' – ROLES/MEDIATION ADVOCACY/REPRESENTATIVES/SCMA

Follow up

Walker *Mediation Advocacy: Representing Clients in Mediation* pp 97–106

Barriers

The 10 most common barriers to settlement are:

1 **Stress**. This is different from pressure. Stress is a physiological reaction to excess pressure. When stressed you cannot think about settlement and the way forward. The key job of the mediator is to reduce the stress levels of everybody present at the mediation.

2 **Fear**. The commonest fears are:
   - Fear of the unknown, ie what the process of mediation is really about. This applies to clients rather than to their legal representatives.
   - The fear of being attacked or criticised. When this happens people go into defensive mode and close down rather than open up.

3 **Ignorance**. Not knowing enough about either their own case, interests or options or the other side's. Parties have not given these enough thought. Often they do not want to think about their disputes. It's unpleasant. They would rather think about something else.

4 **Lack of preparation**. Linked with ignorance and the main cause of it. Preparation is both mental and physical. Parties spend over 80% of their preparation time working up their case rather than working out what settlement might look like for both sides and how it could be structured.

5 **Greed**. When people are on a war footing they are in a state of arousal. Their demands go up and they want blood.

6 **Biases**. We are all prone to cognitive biases especially when under pressure.

Barriers

7 **Can't afford to lose and can't afford to win.** For some parties – usually the defendants but occasionally claimants – losing with the risk of both costs and damages being awarded against them means that they face insolvency/bankruptcy. They feel desperate and don't know which way to turn.

Some cannot afford to win either because:

- They cannot afford to pay the costs of going to trial.
- Going to trial and winning will still leave them with a bill for irrecoverable costs that they cannot afford.
- If they are on a CFA and have ATE a partial win will trigger payment of the mark-up and the ATE premium which could be more than they are awarded.

8 **Emotions.** Linked with cognitive biases but different from them. Some mediators actively encourage clients to express their emotions in passionate terms – aka venting. The main emotion displayed at mediations is anger.

9 **Third parties.** Decision-makers at mediation often have another audience: for example spouses, family, insurers, funders, line managers and boards of directors. They do not want to be criticised for making a bad settlement.

10 **Conflict of interest.** The most obvious one at mediations is between those providing the money and those taking the decisions, for example insurers and policyholders or lawyers and their clients. Lawyers are often accused of running cases to trial so that they earn more money. In practice this is rarely true. But funding arrangements and in particular CFAs and DBAs can give rise to potential conflicts of interest. The client wants to settle and the lawyer doesn't or just as often it's the other way round.

See also

AMYGDALA/ATE/ATTACK/CFA/COGNITIVE BIAS/DBA/ FUNDERS/VENTING

Bashing and Trashing

An evaluative form of mediation particularly practised by American (and some English) former judges.

Over 20 years ago James Alfini divided mediators into three types:

- *Trashers* love to tear apart the parties' cases. And then pressure them to be more realistic.
- *Bashers* start with the parties' opening proposals and pressure them to move.
- *Hashers* use less directive techniques to encourage the parties to reach settlement.

In practice

- Bashing and trashing still happens at mediations in England and Wales under the guise of 'challenging conversations' or 'reality therapy'.
- Don't panic. Prepare. Remember to take your body armour.

See also
EVALUATIVE /REALITY TESTING/THERAPY

BATNA (Best Alternative To a Negotiated Agreement)

A mantra of mediation. The term was given to the mediation world by the Harvard Negotiation Project and Fisher and Ury in their seminal book *Getting to YES*. It stands for Best Alternative To a Negotiated Agreement.

BATNA is a concept usable in any negotiation not just mediation. Don't just work out your bottom line. Develop

BATNA (Best Alternative To a Negotiated Agreement)

your BATNA. In other words work out what you will do if you do not achieve what you want by negotiation.

For example if you are selling your house:

- As the vendor, ask yourself what you will do if you have not sold by a certain time.
- Work out the alternatives.
- Compare them with the best price offered for the house.
- If the BATNA is better than the price reject the price.
- If the price is better than the BATNA accept the price even though it may be less than you want or think that you deserve.

The opposite of BATNA is WATNA (Worst Alternative To a Negotiated Agreement. Variations are PATNA (Probable Alternative To a Negotiated Agreement, MALATNA (Most Likely Alternative To a Negotiated Agreement), RATNA (Realistic Alternative To a Negotiated Agreement).

BATNAs, PATNAs or WATNAs can be quantified. Mediators encourage parties to do this.

BATNA (Best Alternative To a Negotiated Agreement)

	BATNA	PATNA	WATNA
Probability	70%	20%	10%
	Claimant wins on breach, causation and loss	Claimant wins on breach and causation but only partial loss	Claimant loses on causation
	£	£	£
Damages	500K	300K	NIL
Costs spent	100K	100K	100K
Costs recovered from other side	75K	65K	75K (paid to other side)
Irrecoverable costs	25K	35K	100K
Total gain	475K	265K	−175K
So 'walk-away' figure is:	475K × 0.7 + 265K × 0.2 + (175K) × 0.1	332.5K 53K (17.50K) 368K	
NB if you put a value on other non-monetary factors such as opportunity cost this figure is reduced	(50K)	(50K)	(50K)

Biases

There are dangers with BATNAs:

- People, having worked out their BATNA in a developed way will not depart from them. They become wedded to their position. Deadlock ensues.
- People are over optimistic. We are all prone to Optimism Bias. BATNAs must be doable and not in the realms of fantasy.

What does a mediator do?

Some engage in BATNA-bashing. In other words they challenge the assumptions behind the BATNA. Remember, underneath BATNA's objective, quantified logic there are assumptions.

Others ask each side to work out their own BATNA and the other side's. Comparing each side's calculations acts as a reality check and a stimulus to perspective shifting.

In practice

- The word BATNA is rarely used at mediations but the concept is.
- Variants such as MALATNA, PATNA and RATNA are more useful than BATNA which is the best as opposed to the most likely, probable or realistic alternatives.

See also

COGNITIVE BIAS/MALATNA/PATNA/RATNA/WATNA

Biases

Relevant in mediation in two separate senses: prejudices and habits of thought.

1 Bias is an 'assortment of stereotypical beliefs and attitudes about social groups'.

   One of the **Top Ten** is that the mediator is neutral and impartial. In other words he is unbiased. The current orthodoxy is that no mediator can be free of bias any more than any other human being can be. This is because our biases are what we are.

This may be theoretically interesting and even accurate but in practice is neither useful nor correct. Mediators do bring their personal influences and biases to mediation but that does not mean that they will act in a way that is prejudiced against one party. They strive to be even-handed. Usually they succeed.

2 Biases are also mental habits such as cognitive biases or heuristics. They influence our decision making and thinking without our realising and often in ways that are to our disadvantage.

In practice

- Very few mediators are accused of being biased in the sense of not being even-handed.
- Every person at a mediation is subject to cognitive biases. Be aware of them.

See also

COGNITIVE BIAS/IMPARTIALITY/KNOW YOURSELF/ NETRUALITY/TOP TEN

Big Picture – Broad/Deep

Mediators encourage parties to see the other's point of view. They try and shift perspectives.

Disputing parties start by concentrating on the micro picture. They emphasise the specific details, which explode the other side's arguments and support their own. They become bogged down. They cannot see their way through the thicket of detail to the path of settlement.

Mediators encourage them to take a macro view. They ask questions such as 'How could your life be different without this dispute?' They urge parties to place the dispute in the context of their business plans or life in general. They invite them to take a wider and longer perspective.

At the same time mediators probe below the surface of what parties tell them. Through open questioning and active listening they try to tease out the parties' real interests and needs rather than their expressed positions. Mediators go for depth as well as breadth.

Clients who are not prepared for this can find it confusing and unsettling. Some see it as hostile and think that the mediator is against them.

In practice

- Mediators will always invite you to look at the bigger picture and to take the long view.
- Visualise the macro view in advance.

See also

BALCONY/FLEXIBLITY/PERSPECTIVES/PREPARTION/ QUESTIONS

BIMA (Belief in Mediation and Arbitration)

UK registered charity based in London formed by a group of experienced mediators and arbitrators from diverse religious and occupational backgrounds. Their aim is to promote the use of ADR resolution in faith-based and/or culture-based conflict situations.

They provide training, awareness events and mediation services.

In practice

- Their processes are more like community mediation than civil or commercial.
- The Harvard Model has limited relevance.
- Most mediators who do this work are unpaid volunteers.

See also

COMMUNITY MEDIATION/CULTURAL DIFFERENCES/ FAITH MEDIATION/HARVARD/NARRATIVE/ TRANSFORMATIVE

Follow up

www.bimagroup.org

Binding

As in legally binding.

'Do I have to do this? What happens if I don't?'

Features in mediation in three ways:

Q1　Is a clause in a contract which says that before I can litigate or arbitrate I have to try mediation enforceable?

A　Yes it is. These are known as waterfall clauses. Provided that they are properly drafted the English courts will enforce them.

Q2　Is a mediation agreement a legal document? What happens if someone is in breach of it? For example they break confidentiality or do not attempt to negotiate in good faith.

A　Yes it is. Read the mediation agreement carefully before signing. They are not all the same. If a party is

Binding

in breach they can be sued in the same way as any other person who is in breach of contract.

Q3   Is a settlement agreement made at a mediation legally binding?

A   Yes it is if the parties want it to be and it is properly drafted. Most agreements made at civil and commercial mediations are intended to be, and are, legally binding. Some are turned into, or incorporated in, court orders. But even those that are not are legally binding.

But note:

- Most mediation agreements stipulate that no agreement made at mediation is legally binding until put into writing and signed by all the parties.
- Heads of Terms are not usually legally binding unless they expressly say so.
- Agreements made at community or workplace mediations are not intended to be legally binding. They are more like protocols for behaving towards each other in the future.
- Agreements made in family mediations are usually in the form of a Memorandum of Understanding which is sent to the parties' lawyers to be turned into a court order. Settlement agreements in family matters are subject to the approval of the court.

In practice

- Disputes about whether agreements to mediate, mediation agreements and settlement agreement are binding have been litigated. And the courts have handed down a series of judgments.
- Whether or not a binding settlement was reached at a mediation is a question that arises more often than you might think. Make sure that everyone has the same understanding before you leave.

See also

HEADS OF TERMS/MEDIATION AGREEMENT/NON-BINDING/SETTLEMENT AGREEMENT/WATERFALL CLAUSE

Follow up

Walker *Mediation Advocacy: Representing Clients in Mediation* pp 235–242 and Chs 13 and 14.

Bingo

Mediation Bingo was devised by a well-known and successful but frustrated commercial mediator wearied by the recurrent clichés in Position Papers and Opening Statements.

He made a list of them and marks them off as they occur:

Favourites include:

> 'We come here with an open mind to try and settle. But not at any price. If we cannot settle we will pursue/defend this case vigorously.'
>
> 'Your case is doomed on the facts.'
>
> 'We remain to be persuaded that we should change our position.'
>
> 'Any settlement must reflect the underlying realities and legal merits of our position.'

In practice

- You will hear the stock phrases at mediations.
- To increase your impact ditch the clichés.

Follow up

Walker *Mediation Advocacy: Representing Clients in Mediation* p 214 Vocabulary Blacklist

Blackmail

A word frequently used at mediations. Often as a synonym for pressure, bullying or duress.

The criminal offence of blackmail is rarely encountered at mediations. But sometimes enraged clients come close to it. In English law the definition is set out in the Theft Act 1968, s 21.

'(1) a person is guilty of blackmail if, with a view to gain for himself or another or with intent to cause loss to another, he makes any unwarranted demand with menaces; for this purpose a demand with menaces is unwarranted unless the person making it does so in the belief –

   (a) that he has reasonable grounds for making the demand; and

   (b) that the use of the menaces is a proper means of reinforcing the demand.

(2) the nature of the act or omission demand is immaterial, and it is also immaterial whether the menaces relate to an action to be taken by the person making the demand.

(3) A person guilty of blackmail shall on conviction on indictment be liable to imprisonment for a term not exceeding 14 years.'

In practice
- People do occasionally make threats and act unconscionably in ways that could undermine the confidentiality and without prejudice nature of the discussions or make any settlement agreement voidable.

- They are not aware of these risks and need to be reminded of them.

See also
DURESS/THREATS

Ferster v Ferster [2016] EWCA (Civ) 717

Blame

Anathema to mediators. Apportioning blame, ie fixing liability for what has gone wrong in the past is what judges do in court. The exact opposite of what mediators do. They look to the future and find solutions.

Nobody can resist playing the blame game at some time during the day. Not just lawyers – although barristers are particularly prone to the blame game – clients play it as well. They want to tell their side of the story and be heard and acknowledged. An understandable and reasonable requirement. Ideally they want the mediator to agree with them and become their advocate in the other room. Understandable but not reasonable.

The blame game absorbs time and energy that is better spent working out a settlement. Mediators recognise that most parties want to play the blame game at some time during the mediation day. But keep it to minimum.

In practice
- People want to feel vindicated.
- The blame game is a contact sport. If you can't take it don't play it.
- Exchanging blame will not produce a settlement. Exchanging proposals will.

See also
ACKNOWLEDGMENT/MEDIATION ADVOCACY

Blind Bidding

Usually used when liability is not in dispute and the parties want to try and negotiate a figure. Popular in on-line dispute resolution.

Parties submit bids and if they fall within a predetermined range the algorithm works out what the settlement figure is.

Variations include double-blind bidding and visual blind bidding.

In practice
- Used by insurance companies to settle thousands of small claims.
- Will be used more often.

See also
ODR

Follow up
Walker *Setting Up in Business as a Mediator* Ch 15

Bluffing

Works at poker tournaments: rarely successful at mediations.

Once your bluff is called you're finished. In poker there is very limited verbal communication. At mediation it never stops. All the more chance of being found out.

In practice:

- People bluff. Sometimes they succeed but not as often as they claim.
- Most bluffs get called.

See also
LYING/NEGOTIATION/WARRANTIES

Bodyguard

One of the three roles that mediation advocates play, along with hired gun and coach.

Bodyguards see their job as protecting their client from the other side and from himself. They want to protect their client from doing a bad deal. Bodyguards can even say: 'It would be a breach of my professional duty to allow you to sign this agreement.'

Bodyguards think that they know what is best for their client. They assume that their client has told them everything. How many clients do this? Clients often have excellent reasons for agreeing to a deal which their lawyers think is sub-optimal. It's just that they don't want to reveal these reasons to their lawyers.

In practice

- Most lawyers play the bodyguard at some part of the day.
- Most clients don't tell their lawyers everything.
- Bodyguards can become barriers to settlement.

See also
COACH/HIRED GUN/LAWYERS' ROLES

Follow up

Walker and Smith *Advising and Representing Clients at Mediation* para 10.6

Body Language

Body language is fascinating. But it is harder to read or disguise then you think.

Most people under pressure behave in a way that is not always consistent with what they are saying or doing. They can be smiling with their arm round your shoulder telling you to trust them while lying to you. Can we tell this?

Of course we can:

- Folded arms and legs means that people are defensive.
- Avoiding eye contact means that they are evasive.
- Coughing and scratching means that they are nervous or even lying.
- Leaning back means that they are bored and leaning forward means that they are interested and engaged.
- Looking to the left when answering a question means they are recalling. Looking to the right means they are inventing.

Or do they?

Sometimes they do and sometimes they don't. Someone may just have a ticklish throat, an itch or a sore back.

By all means try some tests on YouTube to see how good you are at reading body language. Observe the other team's body language. Consider whether or not it is telling you something.

Body Language

Think about your own body language. Be careful what you do with your hands and your eyes. Recent research has found that:

- face touching
- leaning back
- folding arms
- hand touching

are seen as indicating untrustworthy behaviour.

Whereas:

- leaning forward
- hands in lap
- open arm pose

are seen as indicating trustworthy behaviour

In practice

- Everybody in mediations engages in body language.
- Much less useful as a guide to behaviour than you imagine.
- Much more powerful as a signal to what you are thinking.
- Golden rule is: smile, lean forward, hands on the table and don't fiddle with your pen.
- Body language is important but it is not often the key to unlocking a good deal.

See also
NON-VERBAL/SIGNALS/SMILE

Bracketing

Follow up

David DeSteno *Association for Psychological Sciences 2012*

www.youtube.com>watch

Bottom Line

Words used at every mediation and ones that mediators don't want to hear.

The mantra is: nobody ever reveals their bottom line. Many mediations become a series of shifting bottom lines.

Most parties come to mediation with an idea of what their bottom line is. Fisher and Ury advise that this is a bad idea and that people should instead develop their BATNA.

What is striking is how many parties say that they know what their bottom line is, ie their exit point but have not worked out in advance what their first offer will be, ie. their entry point.

In practice

- Most mediations settle on terms different from the parties' expressed bottom lines.
- Most parties do not believe each other's bottom lines when they hear them.

See also

BATNA/FINAL OFFER/REDLINE/RESISTANCE FIGURE/WALK AWAY FIGURE

Bracketing

Technique used more in US than in UK mediations. Designed to overcome the sequential exchange of reactive offers that are outside the possible Deal Zone by moving them into the Deal Zone.

Usually initiated by the mediator who having spoken to both sides has an idea of where they might be prepared to go and make suggestions such as:

'If the other side offered X would you offer Y?'

'If X dropped by £50,000 would you come up by £50,000?'

In practice
- If mediators invite you to think of bracketing, do it.
- Be careful of double bracketing by splitting the split difference.

See also
RANGING OFFERS/SPLITTING THE DIFFERNCE

Brainstorming

Brainstorming, aka mind-shower, is a technique that mediators are encouraged to use at mediations. Trainers tell them that it breaks deadlocks, encourages mutualisation of problems, promotes co-operation and lowers barriers to communication.

The usual ground rules:
- Anybody can say anything.
- No idea or suggestion is ridiculed or rejected.
- Everything is written up on a whiteboard or on post-it notes, which are stuck on the wall.
- When everybody is exhausted the suggestions are sifted.

In fact researchers show that groups generate fewer original ideas than an individual sitting quietly alone. Trainers take note.

In practice

- Never used in commercial mediations.
- Occasionally used in community and workplace mediations.

See also
FLEXIBILITY/PERSPECTIVE/THOUGHT SHOWERS

Follow up

Keith Sawyer *Group Genius: The Creative Power of Collaboration*

Broken Relationship – Behind Every Dispute

The idea that behind every dispute there is a broken relationship is one developed and promulgated by David Richbell, one of the great men of commercial mediation in the UK.

In practice

- Not all mediators agree.
- For many parties at mediation the money is more important than the relationship.

See also
RELATIONSHIPS

Follow up

Richbell *How to Master Commercial Mediation* p 129.

BTE ('Before the Event') Insurance

The opposite of ATE insurance. The policy is in place before the dispute arises and the risk known.

For consumers:

BTE cover is often found in household insurance policies or as an add-on for credit cards. There is limit of indemnity usually £25,000/£50,000.

For businesses:

There are also specific types of BTE insurance such as employers' liability, public liability and professional indemnity.

In practice

- Mediations often seem to take place as the policy limit is about to be reached. This can cause much anxious discussion in the policyholder's room.
- Sometimes mediators end up mediating between the policyholder, his lawyer and the insurer.

See also
PI/PI INSURANCE/INSURERS

Bundles

A misnomer. Bundles are not loosely tied bits of fabric. In the context of mediation they are organised files of documents.

The use of bundles at mediation is a carryover from litigation. In every trial there is a trial bundle. The courts stipulate what should be included and how they are organised.

Bundles

There are no such rules in mediation. Parties can send whatever documents they want to the mediator. There is no need for parties to agree the bundle. Avoid duplication if you can but don't waste time and money arguing about what goes in the bundle.

Most parties send the mediator the bundle first and their Mediation Statement /Position Paper later. This is the wrong way round. The Position Paper should be drafted first and refer to the documents which the draftsman wants the reader to consider. Include those in the bundle.

The golden rule for compiling bundles for mediation is less is more.

In practice

- At most mediations the bundle is hardly referred to. Not surprising as mediations are not court hearings. There is no judge finding fault or establishing facts.
- Most bundles are now sent electronically which means time can easily be wasted at mediations by people scrolling to find a document. Tabbed paper bundles are much easier to navigate.

See also
POSITION PAPER

C

CAMS (Court of Appeal Mediation Scheme)

The court when considering an application for permission to appeal must consider whether or not the case should be referred to mediation. If the court decides that it is suitable the Civil Appeals Office refers it to CEDR who administer the scheme on behalf of the Court of Appeal.

The scheme has been running since May 2003. A pilot scheme ran until 31 March 2015 to test the automatic reference to mediation for appeals in certain types of cases, ie personal injury/clinical negligence/contractual claims for less than £250,000/inheritance disputes where the estate is under £500,000 and boundary disputes.

The current fees, as at June 2016, are £850 plus VAT per party. This includes four hours preparation and five hours attendance by the mediator. The Court of Appeal agrees the appointment of mediators to the panel but CEDR allocates the mediator to the case.

A party can refuse to go to mediation. But the court will consider whether or not that refusal is reasonable when awarding costs at the end of the appeal.

The success of the scheme shows that it is never too late to mediate.

See also
CEDR

Cancellations

Follow up

Details of the rules can be found on www.cedr.com

Cancellations

Most mediators charge cancellation fees.

- Some are limited to non-refundable non-recoverable items such as travel or hotel expenses.
- Other are on a graduated scale, eg cancellations more than 10 working days before the mediation date incur no fee but those within seven working days incur 50% or even 100% of the fee.

Most mediators provide that payment for mediations must be made in advance. This provides some protection if there is a late cancellation. Not all do.

Mediators take commercial decisions on whether or not to enforce their cancellation terms.

- Some take a tough line and insist. They claim that it inspires respect.
- Others hope to encourage parties to think well of them by not making a cancellation charge.

Both are often disappointed.

Some lawyers ask mediators to reserve a date knowing that they will try and settle the case before the date. Busier mediators require a deposit to secure the date. Most mediators do not and have to take the late cancellation on the chin.

In practice

- Even when the agreement stipulates payment in advance it often does not happen. Particularly when one of the parties is an insurer or government department who are traditionally slow payers.

- Cancellations are a fact of mediation life. There's no point being annoyed about them.

See also
FEES

Follow up

Walker *Mediation Advocacy* p 51

Walker *Setting up in Business As a Mediator* pp 269–283

Catharsis

Mediation can be an opportunity for catharsis. Linked with the concepts of emotion and venting that some say are important elements of the mediation experience.

The rationale is that people take decisions based upon emotion not logic. Until they have been able to unburden themselves of their emotions they are not able to think about settlement.

Originally catharsis played a part in Greek tragedy as a process of purification and cleansing of extreme emotions, which leads to renewal or restoration. Freud's colleague Josef Breuer appropriated the term when hypnotising hysterical patients.

Psychotherapists now use catharsis to describe the act of expressing or experiencing deep emotions that are associated with past events for the individual but have been repressed or denied.

This view has influenced the practice of mediation. Some mediators actively encourage parties to express their emotions and to confront any repressed thoughts. They encourage parties to be passionate and outspoken and criticise mediators who demur as being emotionally illiterate.

Not all mediators agree. Research has shown that expressing anger does not always make people feel better. In fact it can make them feel worse. Even if it does make them feel better it can act as a reward mechanism and thereby encourage a repetition of the behaviour creating a cycle of anger.

In practice
- People tell their side of the story at mediation.
- Some express their emotions more than others.
- Catharsis may be necessary for a settlement: it is never sufficient.
- Settlements happen when people stop emoting and start discussing.

See also

AMYGDALA/COGNITVE BIAS/EMOTIONS/GRIEVANCE/ VENTING

Caucus

Private meeting between the mediator and one of the parties and their representatives. Aka shuttle diplomacy/mediation.

Very common in civil and commercial mediations. The whole day can be spent with the mediator talking to one party in caucus and then seeing the other party in caucus. The parties do not usually negotiate directly. They do it through the mediator.

Some deprecate this practice. They advocate the mediation being conducted in joint sessions. Family mediation for example is usually conducted almost entirely in joint sessions.

What the parties tell the mediator in caucus is confidential until the mediator is given permission to disclose it.

A cross-caucus is where the mediator meets with some people but not all from each side. Cross-caucuses between the lawyers from both sides and the mediator are very common.

In practice

- In joint session style mediations the parties have breakout sessions either for themselves or to discuss something with the mediator or their advisers.
- Some mediations take place entirely through caucus sessions with the parties never sitting together.
- If you want a private session with the mediator or the other side, just ask.

See also
CONFIDENTIAITY/JOINT SESSIONS/SHUTTLE

CEDR (Centre for Effective Dispute Resolution)

Established in 1990 and based in London this not-for-profit organisation describes itself as 'The largest conflict management and resolution consultancy in the world'.

It provides:

- Mediation training – describes itself as the premier mediation trainer in the world having trained over 9,000 mediators in 50 countries.
- Mediations – claims it is the leading independent commercial ADR provider in Europe.

- Consultancy services to business, legal and governmental organisations to develop their conflict management capabilities.
- Research – its biannual Mediation Audit is the best source of information about the civil and commercial mediation market in the UK.

Also operates CEDR Exchange – a useful resource for mediators with up-to-date news, reviews and cases.

CEDR is a highly reputable and successful organisation. Of course it has its critics who say that:

- It is too expensive.
- The mediators that it turns out are too prescriptive in their pre-mediation requirements.
- Its training faculty are allocated too many mediations.

But there can be no doubting its deserved reputation for leadership, competence and quality.

Follow up

www.cedr.com

Cellar Blindness

The unshakeable belief that your case is fireproof. You are bound to win. There is nothing wrong with it.

Similar to the self-deception which winegrowers have about their favourite vintages. They are always perfect and better than everybody else's.

In practice

- It's dangerous to believe your own propaganda.

CFA (Conditional Fee Agreement)

- The corridors of the High Court are littered with the rusting wrecks of cast-iron cases.
- Maintain an attitude of constructive scepticism about everything to do with disputes, negotiation and litigation that you hear or believe.

See also
COGNITIVE BIAS/FLEXIBILTY/GROUPTHINK/ OPTIMISM BIAS

CFA (Conditional Fee Agreement)

Litigation funding arrangement between a lawyer and his client under which the clients pays no or reduced fees to his lawyer if the case does not succeed. Aka no win/no fee arrangements.

If the client wins, his lawyer charges both his base fees calculated in the ordinary way usually on an hourly rate and also an additional mark-up or success fee. This is a percentage increase of the base fee, up to a maximum of 100%.

Originally introduced in 1990 to provide greater access to justice for those who did not qualify for Legal Aid or did not have either legal expenses, insurance or deep pockets.

Clients who lose do not pay their lawyers anything but remain liable for their opponent's costs. ATE (After-the-Event) insurance provides clients on CFAs with protection against adverse costs orders.

CFAs were used by claimants rather than defendants. Over time the CFA regulations changed. So did the practice. Increasingly lawyers entered into hybrid CFAs. Instead of charging their clients no fees they charged a discounted base fee. The clients paid something as they went. Clients who won paid the normal rate and also the mark-up.

Choosing the Mediator

Until April 2013 clients who won at trial and received a costs order in their favour could also recover from their opponents both their mark-up/success fee and ATE insurance premium. This increased the down-side exposure for the paying party.

The regulations were fundamentally changed from 1 April 2013. Success fees and ATE premiums are no longer recoverable from the losing parties. The winners pay them out of their recoveries.

In practice
- CFAs add an extra layer of complexity to mediations.
- The interplay of ATE instalments and success fees requires detailed arithmetic at mediations to enable clients to see their net position. Best done in advance.

See also
ATE/COSTS/FUNDING/NET/RISK ANALYSIS

Choosing the Mediator

Prior to the mediation, parties have several choices to make.
- Venue
- Timing
- Scope of discussions at mediation
- Mediator

Choosing the mediator is usually the most fraught. There are two main ways:

1 Ask a mediation provider. The usual procedure is for the mediation provider to send profiles of three mediators to both parties. Through discussion they agree one. If

Choosing the Mediator

they cannot agree, the mediation provider or the court appoints somebody.

2   The parties or their lawyers exchange suggestions. Often one side suggests three names and the other picks one.

Many solicitors see the choice of a mediator as a step in the litigation and argue about it. A lot of time, money and energy is wasted on choosing mediators.

The CEDR Audit provides interesting evidence of the factors that parties take into account when selecting mediators. The 2014 rankings are in round brackets and the lawyers' rankings for 2016 are in square brackets.

Lawyers rank the following

1 Professional reputation – experience/status (3)   [1]
2 Professional reputation – in mediation style (2)   [2]
3 Sector Experience (6)   [3]
4 Fee levels (5)   [4]
5 Professional Background/qualifications (4)   [5]
6 Availability (1)   [6]

People follow different practices. Some:

- Will never use a mediator more than once. They like to experiment.
- Prefer to use mediators that they have used before. They have confidence in their abilities and approach.
- Will not use a mediator the other side has used before as they think he will be biased in their favour.
- Are happy to go along with the other side's choice because it means that they have confidence in the mediator.

In practice

- Time, money and effort spent arguing about the mediator is wasted.

Chronology

- As long as the mediator is not on your black list choose the one who can offer the earliest date.

See also
GENERALIST/SPECIALIST

Follow up

CEDR Audit 2016 www.cedr.com.foundation.research

Walker *Mediation Advocacy: Representing Clients in Mediation* Ch 3

Chronology

Mediation providers advise parties preparing for mediation to send a chronology to the mediator. Don't bother.

Chronologies are used in court applications. Judges are asked to consider what has happened in the past. This is the opposite of what mediators do. They concentrate on the future.

Remember a mediation is not a trial or a CMC (Case Management Conference).

In complicated cases chronologies and cast lists can help the mediator find his way through the documents. But not in most cases.

In practice

- The mediator reads the papers and makes his own notes of key dates.
- The sequence in which events happened is less relevant than the timetable for steps going forward to implement settlement.

See also

CMC (CASE MANAGEMENT CONFERENCE)

Follow up

Walker *Mediation Advocacy: Representing Clients in Mediation* Ch 11 Physical Preparation

Cialdini's Big Six

Professor Robert Cialdini identifies six universal principles of negotiation.

Reciprocation	People tend to return the favour.
Consistency	People like to behave in a consistent way.
Social proof	People tend to do what others do.
Liking	People like to do business with people they like.
Authority	People follow authority figures and experts.
Scarcity	People give value to something that is scarce.

In practice

- They are seen at every mediation.
- Be aware of them. Monitor them. Use them.

See also

AUTHORITY/COGNITIVE BIAS/NEGOTIATION/ RECIPROCITY/SCARCITY

Follow up

Robert Cialdini *Influence: the Psychology of Persuasion*

CIArb (Chartered Institute of Arbitrators)

Formed in 1915 the CIArb has 14,000 members worldwide in over 130 countries.

Its website says that:

- It is 'a leading professional membership organisation representing the interests of alternative dispute practitioners worldwide'.
- Its mission is to support the global promotion, facilitation and development of all forms of private dispute resolution.

It provides:

- Training for mediators.
- Rooms for mediation at 12 Bloomsbury Square in London.
- An appointment service (The Dispute Appointment Service – DAS).

Every year it organises a mediation day. DAS also puts on a 'by invitation' conference for arbitrators, adjudicators and mediators. Both usually have interesting content and are well attended.

In practice

- Although CIArb has adopted mediation to a degree its emphasis is still on arbitration and adjudication.
- Most of its members are non-lawyer arbitrators or adjudicators who seem suspicious of mediators, especially lawyer mediators.

Follow Up

See ciarb.org

Civcom Mediation

An abbreviation for civil and commercial mediation. This is one of the four traditional categories of mediation. The others are Family, Community and Workplace.

There are subcategories, for example peer mediation, environmental and public mediation.

Civcom covers a diverse range of disputes. Commercial ones are self-explanatory. Civil ones include boundary disputes, Inheritance Act disputes, professional negligence actions, for example of the purchase of a private house and employment, as opposed to workplace, disputes.

Civcom mediators are seen as the fat cats of mediation. They are often regarded as lawyer-dominated, emotionally illiterate and not doing 'real' mediation in the way of those mediating disputes between divorcing couples, warring neighbours or fractious work colleagues.

In practice

- Civcom mediators generally earn more than mediators in other areas.
- Mediating a dispute between family members over their parent's will or between founder shareholders over a company is just as real as mediating disputes about dustbins and car parking.
- Just because people do not swear or threaten violence does not mean that they are not emotionally invested in the dispute or that it is any less real for them.

See also
COMMUNITY/FAMILY/WORKPLACE MEDIATION

Clean Up Man

Not the one who created the problem. The one who has to sort it out.

The clean up man is usually:

- More senior than anyone else.
- Less knowledgeable about the events leading to the dispute than anyone else.

The mediator and the other side will want to make sure that he is fully aware of all relevant factors that will influence his decision on settlement.

Skilled mediators do this with finesse so that the authority of other team members is not publicly undermined. If that happens they become defensive and lose interest in settlement, preferring to hang on to the hope of being vindicated at trial.

In practice

- It can take time to identify who has true settlement authority. Be patient.
- Sometimes a party has to clean up its own mess.

Clerksroom

Large mediation provider based in Somerset that does not charge to be on its panel.

Some mediators swear by it. Others do not.

Follow up

www.clerksroom.com

Closing

The point of any negotiation is to make a deal. In mediation this means coming to a settlement. In the end, after all the exchange of information and exploration of issues, the parties – if they want to settle – have to close.

The crucial point is when the parties are on the edge of the Deal Zone but cannot cross into it. Mediators use various techniques to help bridge the gap:

- Splitting the difference.
- Summing up where the parties have got to.
- Review meetings.
- Emphasising progress and checking deadlines.
- Autosettler.
- Taking parties to the balcony.
- Sealed offers.

Some mediators either on their own initiative or at the request of the parties suggest solutions for example in a boundary dispute giving one party the right of first refusal in the event of sale.

In practice

- How far mediators offer proactive help in closing a deal depends on their style, philosophy, personality and experience as well as the expectations of the parties.
- Most parties welcome help in closing the deal.
- If you want the mediator to help you close the deal tell him.

See also
RECOMMENDATIONS

Follow up

Walker *Mediation Advocacy: Representing Clients in Mediation* Ch 9 Mediators' Tricks

Collaborative Law

Method of dealing with divorce outside the court structure. Not the same as family mediation.

Overlaps

- Both are voluntary, non-adversarial and non-adjudicative.
- Active participation of the spouses.
- Joint sessions.

Differences

- There is the no Third Party Neutral ('TNP') involved.
- Parties must be legally represented.

Key features

- The spouses and their lawyers commit to trying to settle without going to court. They work together to generate mutually acceptable solutions.
- The spouses' lawyers used in the collaborative law sessions cannot represent them in any litigation if there is no settlement. They sign a participation agreement to that effect.
- All sessions are four way meetings.

- There is an obligation to make full and frank financial disclosure – if your lawyer suspects that you are not doing this he must withdraw.

In practice
- Growing in popularity.
- Courts and clients are increasingly looking for ways other than the traditional hearing at court to resolve divorce disputes.

See also
TNP/THERAPEUTIC MEDIATION/TRANSFORMATIVE

Follow up

Resolution website www.resolution.org.uk for useful video, and FAQ's

CMC (Case Management Conference)

The CMC is an essential part of English litigation procedure. The court exercises case management powers through the CMC. Normally an appointment at court for a CMC is fixed between 120 and 180 days after issue of the proceedings.

If a mediation has not been arranged before the CMC takes place, there are discussions at court about why not and whether one should be arranged. Most judges, but by no means all, encourage mediation.

Some CMCs are also costs and case management conferences – CCMCs.

Judges at all levels of the judiciary have been issued with *The Jackson ADR Handbook* which should be consulted for insight into the judicial mind.

In practice
- A CMC is an inevitable step in any legal proceedings and is often a stimulus to mediation.

See also
ALLOCATION QUESTIONAIRE/ DIRECTIONSQUESTIONNAIRE/HALSEY/JACKSON/ JORDAN ORDER/UNGLEY ORDER

Follow Up
Part 26 of CPR.

The Jackson ADR Handbook (2nd edn)

CMC (The Civil Mediation Council)

Established in 2003 the CMC describes itself as the 'recognised authority in the country (England and Wales) for all matters related to civil, commercial, workplace and other non-family mediation'. It is not a regulator.

At present it includes community and workplace but not family mediation. Since January 2015 it has operated through a charitable company – CMCL.

It runs two registration schemes. One for mediation providers and one for mediators.

- Its mission is to inspire all sections of society to use mediation when managing and resolving disputes.
- Its values are Excellence, Innovation and Growth, Informed Debate, Openness and Inclusion.
- It aims to promote its values.

In the 13 years of its existence it has had mixed success. Its current chairman Sir Alan Ward, a former Court of Appeal judge has said that the aim of the CMC is to represent mediation rather than mediators. It is like the General Medical Council (GMC), not the British Medical Association (BMA).

Many mediators feel that it has not done enough to generate business for mediators or to promote their interests in its discussions with the Ministry of Justice. But:

- The CMC has broadened the representation on its board so that it is less dominated by mediation trainers.
- The CMC's registration schemes which are now operational are the first step to providing some sort of quality assurance for users of mediation.

In practice

- The CMC may not be very good but it's better than anything else.
- It's trying to improve.

See also
ACCREDITATION/MOJ/PROFESSION/QUALITY ASSURANCE/REGULATION

Follow up

www.civilmediation.org

Coach/Shepherd

Both mediators and mediation advocates can be called upon to act as a coach or shepherd at mediations. They help the parties understand the process, adjust their thinking and formulate settlement proposals to enable them to achieve what they say they want, namely, a settlement.

They do not do this by exhortation, confrontation, argument or traditional advocacy. Instead they use encouragement, guidance and nudging. Hence the terms coach or shepherd.

Coaches are not bodyguards or hired guns. They realise mediation is not about them: it's about the client. Unlike in court, the focus at mediations shifts towards the client who will have to take difficult decisions and needs all the help that he can get.

In practice

- Coaches are less intrusive but more effective than hired guns or bodyguards.
- It's harder being a coach than being a hired gun or bodyguard.

See also
ADVOCACY/BODYGUARDS/HIRED GUNS/ LAWYERS-ROLES/MEDATION ADVOCACY

Code of Conduct

There is no universal code of conduct for mediators. This is partly the result of the lack of regulation. And partly because different jurisdictions do things differently. Codes have been introduced in Europe, Australia and the USA. The basic rules are similar.

In the UK the most common code of conduct to which reputable mediators adhere is the European Code of Conduct for Mediators. Mediators who are members of the Civil Mediation Council in England and Wales will be bound by the Code because it is incorporated into the CMC Code of Practice.

In practice

- So far there has not been much evidence of ethical problems as opposed to ones of poor service.

- The mediation community is spending more and more time trying to devise standard codes. Progress is slow but is being made.

See also
CMC/EU CODE/REGULATION

Follow up

www.ec.europa.eu>adr_ec_code_coducy_en

www.civilmediation.org>governance

Richbell *How to Master Commercial Mediation* pp 325–339

Cognitive Bias

A cognitive bias is a pattern of thought and behaviour that can be replicated and leads to the drawing of irrational conclusions. Linked to but different from heuristics, which are mental shortcuts, rules of thumb or logical fallacies which are misused in arriving at a conclusion.

Behavioural economists such as Daniel Kahneman have explained their significance in decision making and negotiation. The ones that mediators see most frequently displayed are:

- *Optimism bias*. The tendency to overestimate your chances of success and underestimate how long something will take to do.
- *Reactive devaluation*. The tendency to reject something suggested by someone else because it was suggested by them and not by you.
- *Confirmation bias*. The tendency to look for, or choose, information which confirms, not challenges, what you already believe.

- *Endowment effect.* The tendency to put a higher value on something as soon as you own it or possess it.
- *Sunk cost fallacy.* The tendency to keep spending money on a course of action because you have already spent so much even though the prospects have changed.
- *Attribution bias.* The tendency to think that someone is acting as they are because of who they are, not because of the situation that they are in.

See also

DECISON TREE/DEMONISING/HEURISTICS/RISK ANALYSIS

Follow up

Daniel Kahneman *Thinking, Fast and Slow*

Walker *Mediation Advocacy: Representing Clients in Mediation* Ch 18.

Co-Mediation

Much favoured by mediators and trainers – less so by civil and commercial clients. Used extensively in community mediation.

Different from working with an assistant or observer. Co-mediation is usually carried out by two mediators of equivalent experience. Often they have different skills. For example one may be a lawyer and the other a non-lawyer sector specialist.

Perceived benefits are

- Two heads are better than one.
- In multi-party mediations tasks can be split to minimise downtime and maximise momentum.

- Meet the needs of the parties for example based on religious, ethnic and gender requirements.
- Quality control as mediators monitor each other and keep each other up to the mark.

In practice

- Mediation users see it as an unnecessary expense except in exceptional circumstances.
- Co-mediators have to work as a team without status or ego issues.
- Always a risk of diverging opinions and approaches. Usually solved by not having ad hoc pairings but by working with the same co-mediators over time.

Follow up

Richbell *How to Master Commercial Mediation* p 182

Community Mediation

This has three main types:

1. Neighbour disputes and conflicts.
2. Social housing disputes between landlords and tenants and between tenants and tenants.
3. Where the community is going to be affected by significant change, for example a new roadway, and has to be consulted. This is more to do with public engagement or environmental mediation.

Fundamentally different philosophy and process from civcom mediation.

Community mediators are more likely to:

- Co-mediate.
- Follow a narrative or transformative model.

- Unpaid volunteers
- Think that they are carrying out true or real mediation in people's homes and bleak community halls unlike the fat cat commercial mediators in their luxurious City offices and hotels.

In practice

- Community mediation is seen by novice mediators as an entry point. They do it to acquire experience on their way up the mediation ladder.
- A vital service but a difficult one it in which to make a living as a mediator.

See also

CO-MEDIATION/NARRATIVE/TRANSFORMATIVE

Follow up

Richbell *How to Master Commercial Mediation* pp 256–261 and 292–296

Complaints Procedure

Mediators who are members of the CMC or on panels operated by CMC accredited providers operate a complaints procedure. Details of the CMC procedure can be found at www.civilmediation.org/governance.

It offers a further mediation conducted by a Member of the CMC Specialist panel. To activate the process email: registrar@civilmediation.org.

Sanctions available are rebate of fees or removal from panel membership.

Anyone having complaint about a mediator who is also a member of another professional body such as a solicitor or barrister can also complain to that organisation. Normally they have a much more developed range of sanctions and greater powers of compulsion.

In practice

Most mediators will:

- Want to resolve any complaint about their service.
- Have professional indemnity insurance.

Compromise

The concept of compromise has three distinct roles in mediation.

1. The legal concept: this is about compromising a claim, ie legally settling a claim. Whether a settlement agreement made at a mediation was a legally binding compromise of a claim has been the source of much learning and jurisprudence.
2. The procedure or process of finding an agreement through communication which is mutually acceptable to all parties. How to obtain the best sort of outcome has given rise to game theory.
3. The everyday usage of agreeing to accept less than you think that you're entitled to or originally demanded in order to achieve a settlement.

Is mediation all about compromise?

Some mediators say that it is – much like marriage. Users can be put off by this thought. Compromise is still often seen as a sign of weakness. In fact mediation – being assisted negotiation – is all about trading concessions and collaborating on finding settlements that work for both parties. It is not a process of giving in.

Often compromise may sound weak and be confused with concession. Or is used interchangeably with collaboration.

Concession is unilaterally giving something up. Collaboration is mutually contributing something.

In practice
- Mediation is less about compromise and more about trading and collaborating.
- Compromise is still seen as a weakness. It's not. Giving up something in order to get something that you want is the essence of negotiation.

See also
GAME THEORY/GIVE AND TAKE

Compromise Agreements

Used in settling disputes that could go to an Employment Tribunal. Since 29 July 2013 – known as Settlement Agreements.

Despite this momentous change the same form COT 3 is used to record a settlement when it is made through an ACAS officer.

Once the claimant has signed the COT 3 form he is:
- Barred from bringing any further claims arising out of his employment including claims he doesn't know about but which do exist at the time of signature.
- Not barred from bringing claims in the future, which he does not know about and which do not exist the time of signature.

In practice
- The employer pays for the employee to receive independent legal advice on the effect of the agreement.
- If an ACAS officer is not used the independent adviser certifies that he has fully advised the employee on the

terms and effects of the agreement and that he has professional indemnity insurance.
- Useful to have an independent solicitor on standby for employment mediations to provide the certificate.

See also

EMPLOYMENT MEDIATION/EMPLOYMENT TRIBUNAL/ WORKPLACE MEDIATION

Compulsion

An essential element of the **Top Ten** of mediation is that mediation is a voluntary process. Nobody can be forced to mediate.

Compulsion to mediate arises in three ways:

1 *By contract*

Agreements have contained arbitration clauses for many years.

As arbitration fell into disrepair these contracts stipulated that a party should mediate before beginning arbitration or litigation proceedings. The courts enforce properly drawn clauses.

2 *By statute*

In England and Wales, for example, anybody wishing to initiate divorce proceedings must first obtain a certificate from an accredited mediator that they have considered with a mediator whether or not their dispute is suitable for mediation. They are not compelled to go to mediation. They are compelled to be advised about it and to consider it.

Similarly anybody wishing to apply to an Employment Tribunal must before they issue the proceedings apply to a Conciliation officer at ACAS for a certificate to say that they have tried the early settlement process.

3 *By courts*

   The courts can impose a costs sanction and deprive a winning party of their costs, if they do not have a reasonable excuse for not attending mediation. The court when considering whether or not there has been a reasonable refusal to go to mediation has in mind the six *Halsey* factors.

See also
HALSEY/TOP TEN/WATERFALL CLAUSES

Follow up
Walker *Mediation Advocacy: Representing Clients in Mediation* pp 137–148

Con-Arb

This is another hybrid process. It is the same as Med-Arb, and is sometimes used synonymously. The difference is that the Third Party Neutral acts as a conciliator instead of as a mediator.

Conflict

Conflict's place in mediation seems obvious. Without conflict there would be no need for Mediation.

But surprisingly there is not even an agreed universal definition of conflict. Is conflict a situation or a type of behaviour? Is conflict relational – about relationships or content – about process and tasks? Or is it just when people's concerns are incompatible?

Conflict, according to Ethan Katsh, is a growth area. Hence the increase in the number of conflict resolution professionals. But, according to Steven Pinker, the number of conflicts is declining. So we have the clash of the professors.

Conflict

What are mediators to do with parties in conflict? Help them resolve the conflict, manage it or even support them in it as an empowering process, which is what Bernard Mayer appears to advocate.

At times mediation seems to be like Hollywood as described by the scriptwriter William Goldman: 'Nobody knows anything'.

As a working definition people are in conflict when they are disagreeing to such an extent that it is preventing them from doing what they want to do. They can either ask a third party to tell them what to do – ie a judge – or they can ask a third party to work out with them what to do – ie a mediator.

Conflict does not have to mean:

- Aggression, hostility and anger.
- There can only be negative consequences and never positive ones.
- People are in perpetual opposition with only occasional remission.

In practice

- Theorists worry about conflict more than practitioners do. Practitioners don't spend time and energy analysing the concept. They spend time and energy solving the problem.
- At mediations, parties are in conflict because they cannot agree a course of action.
- Mediators help them overcome their obstacles to doing this. Hence settlement of their dispute.

Follow up

Ethan Katsh *The Evolution of ODR Mediation*

www.judiciary.gov.uk>2015/02

Steven Pinker *The Better Angels of Our Nature*

Bernard S Mayer *Beyond Neutrality*

Confidentiality

Conciliation

Means different things in different jurisdictions. In some, conciliation is a sort of arbitration where the arbitrator suggests settlement options to the parties. In others, it is a synonym for mediation.

In England and Wales it has many of the same features as mediation. The procedure of joint meetings, caucuses and follow-up sessions is much the same as in mediation. Conciliators and mediators use similar techniques.

The important difference is that in conciliation the conciliator takes a more proactive role in bringing his own expert knowledge to the process and in suggesting settlement solutions.

Conciliation rather than mediation is used for group disputes eg the sort of employment disputes that go to ACAS. Or where there is a desire or a need for the parties to preserve a relationship, eg where new working practices are being introduced into a series of workplaces or there is a new development with potentially adverse impact on the surrounding land.

Pros

It shares all the advantages of mediation, with the possible exception for those who prefer the facilitative mediation model of giving more power to the conciliator.

Cons

The same as for mediation namely the lack of a guarantee of finality.

Confidentiality

This is one of the **Top Ten** of mediation.

Confidentiality

Most mediation agreements stipulate that:

- The parties must keep confidential what happens at the mediation.
- The only people they can discuss this with are their legal advisers.
- What is said in a caucus between the mediator and the parties remains confidential to the mediator until the parties authorise him to disclose the information to the other side.

Most of the mediation community believe that confidentiality is a sacred value. If it is lost and confidentiality is breached the whole essence of the mediation process is damaged. They believe that you cannot have a mediation which is not on a confidential basis.

But confidentiality in the mediation context is:

- Over and above the privilege of without prejudice discussions. It's a creature of contract.
- Tripartite. It belongs to the parties **and** to the mediator. This is partly for the mediator's protection. Most mediation agreements stipulate that the parties cannot call the mediator to give evidence in any court proceedings.
- Not absolute.

The principle of confidentiality has been challenged. In England and Wales the leading case is *Farm Assist*. The court will, whether the parties agree or not and whether the mediator consents or not, enquire into what happened at a mediation if it thinks it is the interest of justice. This is another example of mediation taking place in the shadow of the law.

In practice

- Confidentiality is observed.

Contingency Fees

- The application of the principle during the mediation day does not give rise to many problems or difficulties.
- HMRC and IPs require carve outs.

See also
HMRC/LIQUIDATORS/OFFICE HOLDERS/TOP TEN

Follow up
For a brilliant and comprehensive discussion of the problems arising with confidentiality in mediation see Tony Allen *Mediation Law and Civil Practice*.

Farm Assist Ltd (In Liquidation) v Secretary of State for Environment, Food and Rural Affairs [2008] EWHC 3079.

Contingency Fees

Aka having a slice of the action. Lawyers are not paid by the hour or by a fixed fee but by a percentage of the amount recovered by their clients if they win.

Until April 2013 they were illegal in England and Wales for most types of contentious business. Lawyers can now work for their clients in litigation matters on the basis of a Damages Based Agreement.

The maximum percentage that they can be paid is capped at 25% for personal injury cases, 35% for employment and 50% for all over cases.

In practice
- Still not much used in England and Wales.

See also
DBAs/FUNDING

Control

Control

This is another of the **Top Ten** of mediation.

Parties to the mediation have much more control over the process and the outcome than they do in litigation in court.

Mediators cannot force the parties to do anything. There is no sanction that they can apply if, for example, the parties do not want to have a Joint Opening Session or want to have a private meeting without him being present.

In the end it is for the parties to decide what settlement they want to agree and sign.

Parties are often told that the dispute and the solution belongs to them but the process belongs to the mediator. He is the process manager. In fact some mediators tell the parties that the mediation day is their day and they will do what the parties want.

In practice

- Parties want some direction and framework from the mediator. Within this framework there is scope for flexibility.

- An experienced mediator anticipates what is likely to happen once he has spoken to the parties and plans the day accordingly.

- Sometimes a party or their lawyer tries to take control of the process. For example a barrister insists on going by himself to talk to his opposite number without the mediator being present. Or one side objects to someone from the other side's group being present in the Joint Opening Session.

- Tactical manoeuvring like this just slows down generating any settlement momentum. Rarely, if ever, does it actually do anybody any good at all.

See also
AUTONOMY/MEDATION STYLES/TOP TEN

Coogler Structured Model

A process used in family mediation, which emphasises having a structure so that the parties and everybody else knows where they are.

Designed to provide procedural fairness. Developed in the 1970s by an American lawyer and psychotherapist.

Follow up

O J Coogler *Structured Mediation in Divorce* 1978

Divorce Mediation for Low Income Families: A Proposed Model and related articles

www.onlinelibrary.wiley.com

Cooperation

The purpose of attending mediation is to make Peace not War. Making war is a competitive activity: making peace is a co-operative one.

Some parties, and more often their representatives, resist this, especially hired guns and bodyguards. You spend time, money and effort at mediations. You might as well get the best out of it by co-operating with the mediator.

In practice
- Whether people like it or not mediation is a team effort. Everybody has to play their part in order to achieve a settlement which is acceptable to all parties.
- Perhaps this is not the same as mutualising gains as advocated by the Harvard Negotiation Project but it

emphasises that settlements are achieved not by arguing but by discussing proposals.

See also
ARGUING/HARVARD/LAWYERS' ROLES/PEACE/ PROPOSALS

Costs

At mediation 'costs' means legal costs. What the parties pay to the court by way of fixed fees or to their lawyers for their charges.

Under the English system, with some limited exceptions, in litigation the loser pays the winner's costs. This does not mean that he has to pay 100%. He has to pay a proportion.

Despite cost shifting the general rule is still that it costs you money to go to court and win. That amount has to be deducted from your settlement or judgment to give your net recovery.

The main exception is personal injury litigation where thanks to Qualified One Way Costs Shifting a claimant can avoid paying the defendant's costs if he loses at trial.

At mediations:

1 Mediators:
- Emphasise that one of the benefits of settlement is that no more legal costs will be incurred.
- Encourage the parties to consider up-to-date schedules of legal costs that will be incurred to go to trial. Quite often this has not been done beforehand and parties are shocked to realise how much it will cost.

2 Costs become an issue in themselves and an obstacle to settlement. Parties argue about what is reasonable

to have been incurred by way of legal costs. The paying party always thinks the receiving party's costs are excessive. Some of these disputes have been obviated by the recent changes in the Civil Procedure Rules (CPR), which provides for costs budgeting and agreed budgets.

3 Clients are always concerned to know how much:
- They will receive in their hand by way of a settlement if they are the receiving party after payment of all the costs.
- How much they are going to actually have to pay out of their pocket once all the legal costs have been paid if they are the paying party.

Often a settlement sum for the principal claim can be agreed but not the amount for legal costs. As part of the settlement these can be assessed, ie calculated by the court, if not agreed. This can cause friction between lawyers and clients.

4 Funding arrangements such as CFAs aggravate this. The client wants to settle on the basis that he receives a certain net amount in his hand. His solicitor is also insisting on receiving a certain amount for his costs either from his own client or from the other side. This gives rise to a subsidiary mediation between clients and their lawyers.

5 Significant legal costs can be incurred before mediation takes place. Clients and their advisers can fall into the sunk-cost fallacy.

This is the tendency to say that because we have invested so much in this decision already we might as well continue with it even though new information suggests that this is not a sensible thing to do. As we have come this far we might as go all the way.

In litigation this is often throwing good money after bad.

6 The costs of mediation can be recovered if the case does not settle, as part of the costs which the winner

is awarded. Most mediation agreements preserve this position. But some parties, usually insurers, try to amend the agreement so that mediation costs are not recoverable if the case goes to trial.

In practice

In CivCom mediations costs are:

- A barrier to settlement if they are too large.
- An incentive to settlement if they are still modest in comparison with what they could become.
- Always negotiable.

See also

CFA/COGNITIVE BIAS/COSTS ASSESSMENT/ IRRECOVERABLE COSTS/PRECEDENT H/ RISK ANALYSIS

Follow up

Walker *Mediation Advocacy: Representing Clients in Mediation* Ch 18 Mind Traps

Brooker *Mediation Law* pp 157–161

Laura Slater ed *Costs Law: A Practitioner's Guide*

Costs – Assessment

If a party to litigation is ordered to pay the other side's costs and they cannot be agreed the court will assess how much has to be paid.

An industry of costs draughtsmen/costs lawyers advise and attend at hearings before costs judges. Despite the courts' attempts to reduce the amount of time, money and effort spent on agreeing legal costs, the industry mushrooms.

Costs – Irrecoverable

The process of trying to agree or assess costs is long, tedious and expensive. Parties treat it as a continuation of the litigation process. They exchange Statements of Case and have a hearing. Sometimes witness statements and expert reports are needed.

In practice

- Parties try and agree costs and avoid the time and expense of a disputed assessment.
- There are now costs mediations. What is mediated is how much one party should pay to the other under an adverse costs order. Even though detailed and technical, they generally produce a settlement.

Follow up

The procedure is set out in CPR Rule 44.6

Laura Slater ed *Costs Law: A Practitioners' Guide* Ch 11

Costs – Irrecoverable

Where the losing party pays a contribution, which is always less than 100%, towards the winner's costs. The shortfall between the amount actually incurred by the receiving party and amount that the paying party is ordered to pay is known as irrecoverable costs.

In practice

- At mediations lawyers assume that they will recover between 65 and 80% of the cost that their clients have to pay to them.
- The amount of irrecoverable costs is often the starting point for discussions about settlement.
- If it is going to cost you a certain amount to go to court and win why not contribute it to the settlement pot?

Follow up

CPR Parts 44 and 47

Simon Middleton and Jason Rowley *Cook on Costs 2016*

Laura Slater ed *Costs Law: A Practitioner's Guide*

Costs Management Order

This is part of the Jackson reforms designed to give the courts power to control costs so that they are proportionate.

In practice

- There is much disagreement about whether they are working.
- A good idea which has become bogged down in satellite jurisprudence.

Follow up

CPR 3D

Laura Slater ed *Costs Law: A Practitioner's Guide* Ch 1 Costs Management

COT3

A form used by ACAS officers to record terms of settlement made by parties to a dispute before an employment tribunal and negotiated through ACAS.

See also
ACAS/COMPOMISE AGREEMENTS

Court Tracks

Procedures for allocating civil cases in the courts in England and Wales.

There are three:
1. Small claims — Where the amount in dispute is under £10,000
2. Fast track — Where the amount in dispute is between £10,000–£25,000 and the trial will not take more than one day
3. Multi-track — For all claims in excess of £25,000.

There are different costs regimes for each track.

Follow up

CPR Part 26 – Case management

Counselling

Not the same as mediation, but overlaps.

A working definition is: a type of talking therapy that allows people to talk about their problems and feelings in a safe and confidential environment.

Many definitions of counselling overlap with psychotherapy. In the end both are concerned with allowing people to talk about themselves and through this to change their behaviour so that they will be able to cope better in the future. Practitioners see this as empowering.

Some descriptions of mediation sound like counselling or therapy. Many trainee commercial mediators are suspicious when told that they will learn to ask open questions, engage in active listening, show empathy but not sympathy, encourage venting and not be interventionist.

Some mediators offer counselling as one of a palette of services to their clients along with mediation, coaching, team building and change management. It is easy to see how confusion arises.

In practice

- The transformative and narrative techniques used in family, community and workplace mediations are rarely used in commercial mediation. Nor is counselling.
- Commercial mediation clients do not want to be transformed into better people for the future. They want a problem off their desk now.

Court-linked Mediation

Some courts operate mediation services. They set up a panel of mediators and allocate cases to it for mediation. Sometimes these are in-house. Some are outsourced eg CAMS or the telephone mediation services operated by various county courts.

Not universally welcomed by mediation theorists who see them as too coercive and thereby eroding the golden principle of mediation as a voluntary process.

In practice
- Mainly used for low value disputes.
- Likely to expand.

See also
AUTONOMY/CAMS/CHOOSING/VOLUNTARY

Court Settlement Process or CSP

Form of mediation provided by judges in the Technology and Construction Court (TCC) in England. More like a Settlement Hearing as practised in the USA than a conventional commercial mediation.

Known as the Court Settlement Process (CSP). With the consent of the parties the case is assigned to another TCC judge who acts as mediator. The settlement judge does not take any further part in the case if a settlement is not reached.

The procedure is regulated by the Court Settlement Order which is set out in Appendix G of the TCC Guide.

Key features:
- It is without prejudice, voluntary, confidential and non-binding.
- The judge who conducts the CSP can conduct it in any way he likes taking into account the parties' own views, the circumstances of the case and the overriding objective in the Civil Procedure Rules.
- The judge holds a preliminary court settlement conference to decide the procedure, the duration and what disclosure shall be given.
- Unless the parties otherwise agree the judge can have separate or joint meetings or communications in which he can give opinions about the dispute. A party can ask for a private meeting with the judge.
- Confidential information given to the judge by one party is not disclosed to the other without consent.
- If there is no settlement parties can ask the judge to give a written assessment on some or all of the issues,

the probable outcome at trial and his suggestions for a settlement.
- The parties' rights are fully preserved and nothing they say during the CSP prejudices any position they may wish to take in any subsequent litigation.
- Each side pays their own costs and splits the court costs unless otherwise agreed.
- The judge who has conducted the CSP takes no further part in the litigation.

Anecdotal evidence suggests that some people are happy with the procedure. Others are less so. One of the reasons parties chose mediation is to avoid a judge giving his opinion on their case when he delivers his judgment at trial. Why ask for his opinion at a CSP hearing?

Judicial time and resources are limited. They are better spent on judging.

In practice
- The number of judicial mediations is much lower than the number of mediations of the same sort of disputes using non-judicial mediators.

Follow up
TCC www.justice.gov.uk>high-court

See also
JUDICIAL MEDIATION

CPR (Civil Procedure Rules)

Rules of civil procedure used by the Court of Appeal, High Court and county courts since 26 April 1999. Constantly being amended and updated.

Their overriding objective is:

- To improve access to justice.
- For legal proceedings to be cheaper, quicker and easier to understand for non-lawyers.

Limited success in achieving these. Largely due to government funding cuts, diffident use of the new case management powers by judges and inconsistent support from the appellate courts.

Hence mediation is increasingly welcomed as an alternative to litigation conducted under the CPR.

Anybody litigating in England and Wales who disregards or fails to comply with the CPR does so at their peril.

Particularly relevant for mediation because they set out timetables for litigation and more importantly for what is said in the CPR and the Pre-Action Protocols.

The courts expect disputing parties to try and settle their dispute by mediation before trial and if possible before commencing legal proceedings. They enforce compliance with this expectation through costs sanctions.

See also
HALSEY/JACKSON/LITIGATION

Follow up
CPR rr 1.1, 1.3, 1.4

Craft

Mediation is neither a science nor an art. It is a craft.

- It is a practical not a theoretical activity.

- You get better at it by doing it. And thinking about what you're doing.
- Mediators can practise their techniques but there is no rehearsal for mediation. It is a one-off live performance. You cannot go back and repaint the picture if you do not like it. You cannot rerun the experiment.
- You have to do it in order to be any good at it at all. Hence the requirement for CPD, including a minimum number of live mediations.

In practice

- Most mediators still think that mediation is an art not a science.
- Most mediators adopt a practical not a theoretical approach.

See also

ART/CPD/TRAINING

Creating Value

The holy grail of the Harvard Mediation Model.

Achieved by 'growing the pie' and finding material gains. In other words all sides see they are better off if they work together to create something they do not presently have and could never achieve through litigation.

The opposite of claiming value.

In practice

- Mediators always explore the possibilities with the parties. So be prepared for this.
- The possibility is not always present.
- Even where there is an opportunity to create value, parties reject it. They do not always go for the optimal outcome.

See also
CLAIMING VALUE/VALUE/FAIR/GROWING THE PIE/ HARVARD

Cross-Border Mediation

A cheaper alternative to dealing with international disputes, ie where the parties are not all in the same jurisdiction than arbitration or litigation.

Often organised by international providers such as the ICC, WIPO and the Chartered Institute of Arbitrators. Domestic providers such as JAMS, CEDR and ADRg can arrange Cross-border mediations.

The IMI has developed an accreditation scheme for mediators who are qualified to participate in international mediations.

For consumer disputes the EU has introduced a Directive.

ODR and online Mediation have a particular role to play in cross-border disputes.

See also
EU DIRECTIVE/MSEO/ODR

Follow up

www.wipo.int/amc/en/

www.worldmediationforum.org

www.imimediation.org

www.iccbo.org

www.ciarb.org

Cross-Examination

Has two meanings:

1 In court, where one side's witness is questioned by the other side's advocate to discredit them or undermine their previous testimony.

2 In non-legal use, it means asking someone detailed questions.

At mediation cross-examination in both senses is an ever-present danger, particularly if barristers are there.

Most mediators explain to the parties that being at mediation is not the same as being in court:

- No one is on trial.
- The mediator is not a judge who is going to decide who is right and who is wrong.
- No one is under oath. But beware of misleading people at mediations.
- No one has the right to cross-examine anyone.

In practice

- Some advocates try and cross-examine in the Joint Opening Session.
- Some mediators allow a sort of cross-examination to take place during the Joint Opening Session.
- It is for the parties and their advisers to decide how much attempted cross-examination they are prepared to endure. They are not under any duty to endure any at all.
- Attempted cross-examination is counter-productive. It is hostile and makes the receiving party defensive. This delays the problem-solving phase of mediation.

Cultural Differences

See also
ADVERSARIAL/LYING/MEDIATION ADVOCACY/ MEDIATION PHASES/WARRANTIES

Cultural Differences

Always highlighted as an important factor at mediations. Examples of well-known ones are, for example, in Asia taking a business card in both hands and carefully looking at it.

But they are always followed by warnings about inappropriate cultural stereotyping and that it is dangerous to generalise.

There are three main areas of cultural difference:

Basic Assumptions:	Ingrained and often not spoken about
Values and norms:	What people consider as right and wrong
Symbols:	Explicit – dress, manners, gestures

These can be as important in mediations between people from the same ethnic background, but from different gender, social, educational, occupational backgrounds. Which is often the case in civil and commercial mediations.

Different languages add a layer of complexity.

In practice

- The similarities between people of different backgrounds, whether ethnic, religious, political, social or gender, are greater than the differences.
- The golden rule is if you treat people as you would like to be treated you will not go far wrong.
- Being courteous, respectful and smiling will generally see you right.

- The more there are differences the longer it will take to establish rapport, perspective shifting and enough common ground on which to construct a platform for settlement.
- You need patience at mediation.

See also
FACE/HIGH CONTEXT/TRANSLATORS

Follow up
CEDR *How to Master Negotiation* Ch 13

Cutting to the Chase

A phrase used at every mediation.

Originally used in silent films, which often ended with a climax of a car chase. Writers and directors were told to not waste time with all the boring sub-titled dialogue and cut to the chase.

Outside mediation it means get to the point quickly.

Within mediation it means to start talking about either the issues in the case or about settlement terms. Some mediators are wary about cutting to the chase too soon. Others want to do it as soon as the parties have taken their coats off.

In practice
- If said at the start of the mediation it means that the parties do not want a Joint Opening Session. They tell the mediator that everybody knows what the dispute is about, so let's get down to business.

Cutting to the Chase

- If said later, after there has been exchange of information, it means that the parties want to really see whether they can bring themselves into the Deal Zone or not.
- Occasionally it is used as a synonym for grasping the nettle or identifying the elephant in the room. In other words confronting the real barriers to settlement.

See also
BARRIERS/OFFERS/THREE STAGE PROCESS/TIME

D

DBAs (Damages-Based Agreements)

DBAs are contingency fees. They became lawful in England and Wales in April 2013.

Like CFAs the lawyers are not paid anything if their client does not win. If the client wins:

- The lawyers collect an agreed percentage of what the client recovers.
- He can recover costs calculated on the normal hourly rate basis from his opponent.

As with CFAs the client remains liable for his opponent's costs if he loses. Most clients are advised to protect themselves with After The Event Insurance.

The Civil Justice Council published a report in September 2015 on the operation of DBAs. They noted with apparent surprise the disappointing take-up.

It was originally thought that DBAs would encourage lawyers to settle at mediation. They would receive their money sooner and for doing less work than if they went to trial. So far this has not happened. In fact the take-up of DBAs has been much lower than the government expected. Changes are likely to be introduced to make them more attractive to lawyers.

In practice

- Not much used but when they are they complicate mediations.

Dance Floor

The competing mass of detail in any dispute. Mediators, parties and advisers have to get off the dance floor and go to the balcony to view the bigger picture.

In practice

- Parties' appetite for detail comes and goes during a mediation.
- Detail can be comforting. As parties become more confident they are able to take a macro instead of a micro view.

See also
BALCONY/BIG PICTURE

Deadlines

Well-known negotiating tools used in most mediations. Frequently deadlines are phantom ones not real ones.

At mediation three types of deadlines come into play:

1 Operational

The venue closes at 6 pm. One of the parties has to leave to catch a plane. These are often non-negotiable. They are the brute facts of the mediation day that have to be accommodated.

Deadlines

2 Negotiating

These are tactical. Parties impose deadlines on each other and issue ultimatums. Usually they are ineffective.

Most people receiving a deadline or ultimatum see it as a hostile act. They become defensive. They usually slow down settlement consideration rather than accelerate it.

But sometimes, if used at the right time and in the right way, a deadline can be very effective. Use sparingly. If you use them, mean them.

3 External

These deadlines are ones that nobody can do anything to change. Usually they are court dates. Trial takes place at a fixed date. An appeal has to be filed by a stated time. Or a payment has to be made by a certain date or statutory demand will be issued etc.

You just have to work with them.

In practice

- The usual deadlines are the start and finish times shown in the mediation agreement. Many mediations run past the finish time.

- Mediators ask at the outset whether or not there any time constraints such as trains, child care or theatre dates. If you have any, say so at the start of the day not near the end.

- Mediators also impose deadlines as part of their active time management of the mediation process.

- Parties try to impose deadlines by stipulating that their offer must be accepted within 10 minutes or that they must receive an offer now or they will leave.

- If you issue an ultimatum be clear what you will do if that ultimatum is not met and how this will progress settlement.

Deadlock

- Issue ultimatums sparingly. Do it too often and you create a hostile environment. The other side feels bullied. Your credibility is damaged.

See also
MEDIATION DAY/ULTIMATUMS

Deadlock

Deadlocks arise in mediation in two circumstances:

1 The mediator cannot extract a proposal from any of the parties. No one wants to go first. Or they simply repeat offers that have been made in the past and have been rejected. There is no development.
2 Both sides have made proposals. None have been accepted. There is no settlement and neither side is going to move.

Mediators use a variety of techniques to break deadlock:

To generate proposals they may:

- Use 'ranging offers', confidential proposals – for the mediator's eyes only.
- Discuss the theory of anchoring.

To bridge gaps they may:

- Suggest various closing techniques.
- Conduct a review meeting with the parties either individually or jointly and identify the progress that has been made to date and say what they think the obstacles to settlement are.

In practice

- Most deadlocks are unlocked.
- Most non-negotiables are negotiated.
- Final offers are rarely final.

See also

ANCHORING//BRACKETING/CLOSING/RANGING OFFERS

Follow up

Walker *Mediation Advocacy* Ch 9 Mediation Process: Mediators' Tricks

Deal Zone

Where you want to be at mediation with three hours to spare. Offers have been exchanged. Proposals discussed. Positions reviewed and alternative outcomes assessed.

In other words you know where you are. Both sides have shown a commitment to settlement which, although not concluded, is now a realistic possibility.

Not quite the same as ZOPA (Zone Of Potential Agreement). You have moved into the ZOPA and are now actually trying to negotiate the final figures and wording ie the deal.

Parties get nervous in the Deal Zone. The movements become smaller and more tentative. They start having second thoughts and developing 'deal twitch'.

Trust the process. Have faith in your own analysis and be prepared to take responsibility for your decisions. That is what decision-makers and dealmakers are paid to do.

In practice

- Listen to the mediator when he gives guidance on where the Deal Zone might be.
- Take note when he tells you that you are now in it.
- Saying No is easier than saying Yes.
- You want a deal? Do it.

Decision Trees

See also
CLOSING/MEDIATION DAY/SALAMI SLICING/ SETTLEMENT AGREEMENT/SPLITTING THE DIFFERENCE/SUBJECT TO CONTRACT/WALKAWAY FIGURE/ZOPA

Decision Trees

Tool to help in making decisions. Uses a treelike model of decisions and outcomes. They are a way of displaying a set of steps or algorithm.

Not confined to mediations. In the mediation context they are used as a method of risk analysis.

Decision Tree

Simple version for professional negligence action with
3 tests   : was the advice negligent?
                 : did client rely on it?
                  : did client suffer loss (causation) as a result?

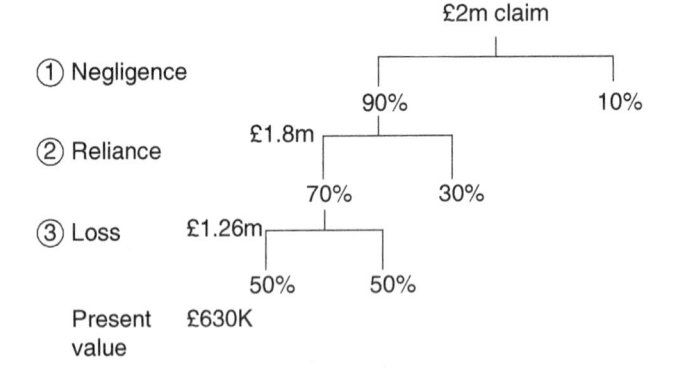

```
                              £2m claim
                         ┌────────┴────────┐
① Negligence
                        90%                10%
                £1.8m   ┌────┴────┐
② Reliance
                       70%       30%
③ Loss        £1.26m ┌──┴──┐
                    50%    50%
   Present   £630K
   value
```

Well-advised parties use them as a tool in their preparation. Mediators use them as a way of freeing up the parties' thinking when they are struggling to frame proposals to put to the other side or to assess proposals that they have received.

In practice
- Not used as much as you might expect.
- Using decision trees frees up thinking.
- Be aware that some of the conclusions can be disconcerting to those who have not carried out a Pre-Mediation Analysis (PMA).

See also
ALGORITHM/PMA/RISK ANALYSIS

Deal Mediation

Used where there is no dispute or legal proceedings to resolve but difficulties are developing. Is used in two circumstances:

1 To help ordinary non-contentious business negotiations conclude a deal that all the parties can agree to.

2 As an early warning system during a project. Often linked with Dispute Resolution Boards. A problem has occurred or looks like occurring. Instead of letting it turn into a full-blown dispute let alone legal case a mediator is brought in. An example in the UK of this is the RADAR system used by ResoLex, which interrogates data provided by feedback from those involved in the project.

Deal mediators use the same techniques as mediators use when mediating disputes.

In practice
- Becoming more popular.
- A growth area of practice for mediators.

See also
DRB

Follow up

www.resolex.com

Demonising

Tendency of parties in mediation to think the worst of each other.

They:

- Judge each other by their intentions not their actions.
- Attribute their actions to malign motives rather than to the situation that they are in.
- Succumb to reactive devaluation.

In practice

- Some demonisation is inevitable.
- Can be neutralised by exchange of information and joint meetings.

See also

COGNITIVE BIAS

Follow up

Walker *Mediation Advocacy: Representing Clients at Mediation* Ch 18 Mind Traps

Devil's Advocate

A phrase heard at most mediations. Despite the original title of the office 'Promoter of the Faith' having being abolished in 1987 the phrase lingers on. Devil's Advocates in mediation do not seek reasons why someone should not be made a saint. Instead they test what they are being told by way of debate.

Linked with the technique of reality testing. Use sparingly for the reasons given.

In practice

- The term should be pensioned off.
- It is hackneyed.
- It can alarm devout people not of the Catholic faith.

See also
QUESTIONS/REALITY TESTING

Dignified Exit

Sometimes all that a party wants is to get out of the dispute and particularly the litigation.

They know that:

- The business case for continuing with the litigation has vanished.
- Their situation will not get better.
- Their chances of winning at trial are low.
- Their chances of making a recovery are negligible.
- In essence it is a surrender with honour.
- Total capitulation is probably too much to expect. Better to allow the other side to exit with dignity than to humiliate them.

In practice

Skilled negotiators identify the exit routes. They:

- Waive some interest and costs.
- Are polite.
- Are statesmanlike.

DIPs (Disputants in Person)

- Shake hands at the end before leaving.

See also
DROP HANDS/GOOD MANNNERS

DIPs (Disputants in Person)

Increasingly clients attend mediation without any legal representative. If they are also LIPs (litigants in person) this complicates civil and commercial mediations.

Although the mantra is that settlements are not reached on the basis of legal rights or principles DIPS and LIPS often refer to their legal rights and have a touching faith that the judge will do justice and decide the case in their favour.

Even when they are justified in this belief, DIPs often have an exaggerated sense of what they will recover by way of damages and costs.

In practice

DIPs can make:

- Settlement easier – they are present and can make a decision. There are no lawyers to get in the way.
- Settlement harder – no objective advice available and they need external reassurance.

See also
REPRESENTATION

Follow up

Walker *Mediation Advocacy: Representing Clients at Mediation* Ch 19 Self-Advocacy: Representing Yourself

Directions Questionnaire

Questionnaire sent out by the Court to be completed by the parties to assist the Court in deciding on allocation of a case to a court track.

The first question is whether or not the parties want the case to be stayed for a month to see if the case can be settled by mediation or other means.

In practice

- Has to be completed and returned once the defence has been filed at court.
- Make sure that you ask for a stay for mediation.

See also
ALLOCATION QUESTIONNARIRE/COMPULSION/ HALSEY

Follow up
CPR Part 26 and Practice Direction 26
www.justice.gov.uk>pd_part26

Directive

The replacement term for evaluative mediation.

Both coined by Leonard Riskin, an American professor of Dispute Resolution.

He also coined the terms 'facilitative' and 'elicitive'.

Riskin said that when he wrote his original articles in 1994/96 he 'hoped to clarify discussions of mediation, which until that time had often been suffused with ambiguity...'

Disclosure

Sadly, despite his distinguished efforts, ambiguity, confusion and dissent flourish.

See also
ELICITIVE/EVALUATIVE/FACILITATIVE/RISKIN'S GRID

Disclosure

Has three separate meanings in the context of mediation.

1. The legal process set out in the CPR which obliges parties in litigation to exchange information and in particular documents – widely defined – which are relevant to the issues in dispute even if they support the other side's case.
2. The informal provision of information at mediation. Information gaps are common at mediations and are one of the main reasons why parties have not settled. The managed disclosure of information is often the focus of the Exchange (second) stage of the Three Stage Process.
3. Self-disclosure. This can be to either to the mediator, the other side or the party's own advisers. People have different appetites for self-disclosure. This is not necessarily because they are ashamed or worried about disclosing information. They simply do not like to do it. They are private.

In practice

Mediators:

- Try to find out from parties what their real agenda is and what their true needs and interests are. They use a combination of open questioning and reality testing.
- Know that some people find this process intrusive and close down rather than open up.
- Realise that parties will only open up whether to them or to the other side when a degree of rapport and trust has been established.

- Find that parties are often reluctant to exchange information because they think that they may be disclosing something that can be used against them.

In practice

- Non-disclosure incites suspicion and mistrust.
- Be prepared to disclose as much as you can and feel comfortable doing.

See also

AGENDA/EXCHANGE/QUESTIONS/REALITY TESTING/ THREE STAGE PROCESS/TRUST

Follow up
CPR Part 31

Disney Question

Aka 'hero question'.

Way of breaking an impasse. The parties are deadlocked. They won't move. Ask them an off-the-wall question.

> 'Suppose Super Mario or Wonder Woman are trying to sort out this problem. What would they say to you? What would they advise you to do?'

In other words it's taking parties off the dance floor and up to the balcony.

In practice

- Asking an unconventional question often unfreezes people's thinking.
- Don't assume that the mediator has lost the plot if he asks one. Answer it.

Dispute

See also
BALCONY/BIG PICTURE/DANCE FLOOR/QUESTIONS

Dispute

Being clear what dispute is to be mediated is significant in three ways.

1 Some disputes are by their nature not suitable for mediation. Suitability is one of the Halsey factors. Examples commonly cited are where:
   - A precedent is required, eg a court ruling on the meaning of a document or the interpretation on the law or custom which will have implications for a particular market or indeed the public as a whole.
   - There are allegations of fraud.
2 The definition of dispute in the Mediation Agreement can be crucial if there is no settlement. If there is a settlement the settlement agreement will define what is settled. Problems can arise when there is no settlement and someone later refers to something that others consider was covered by mediation confidentiality. The significance of the definition of dispute is that it makes clear the scope of the protection of confidentiality. That is why wider rather than narrower definitions of dispute tend to be used.
3 Disputes are not the same as 'cases' or 'claims'. These are usually legal or quasi-legal formulations of someone's rights. Disputes are wider. The issues in dispute cannot always be included within the legal formulation of rights in a 'case' or 'claim'. Mediators spend time trying to find out what the dispute is really about.

The mediation mantra is a dispute is never about what it is about. When people say 'it's not the money', it's the money, and when they say 'it's just about money', it's about something else.

In practice

In most civil and commercial mediations:

- It is all about the money and only about the money.
- People may be annoyed with each other but money usually cheers them up.
- Not many problems are immune to a money solution.
- Fraud cases can be successfully mediated and very few cases require a court ruling to establish a precedent.

See also

CONFIDENTIALITY/HALSEY

Dispute Boards/Resolution Panel Disputes Review Panel (DRP)

Also known as Dispute Boards, Dispute Review Boards (DRB) or Dispute Adjudication Boards (DAB)

The key features are:

- Usually made up of three people who are appointed by the contracting parties at the start of the project before any disputes have arisen. They visit the site at agreed intervals and have an ongoing involvement in the project, even sometimes after it has finished.
- All its powers and authority arise out of the contract. It is involved at the early stages of a dispute or potential dispute. It issues recommendations.

Pros

- It saves time, money and friction and allows projects to keep moving forward.
- It provides real time value by becoming part of the process of contract administration and can acquire a preventative role.

Dispute resolution commitment (DRC)

- The board is seen by the parties as being part of the team and their findings are more likely to be accepted than those issued by a third party outsider.
- Wider application than in the construction industry where it originated. Now used in shipping, long term projects and financial services.
- Used internationally in different jurisdictions.

Cons

- Most contracts provide that the decision of the board, as with adjudication, can be reviewed in arbitration or the courts. So no absolute finality.
- The board members have to be paid even if they are never called upon to carry out any dispute resolution.

Dispute resolution commitment (DRC)

Aka Attorney General's Pledge.

Government Departments are bound by the Dispute Resolution Commitment issued by the Attorney General's office. In 2001 the British Government made the Alternative Dispute Resolution Pledge. This was renewed in 2011 by the DRC (Dispute Resolution Commitment).

This states that government departments and their agencies commit to:

- being proactive in the management of potential disputes and in working to prevent disputes arising or escalating, in order to avoid the need to resort to the use of formal dispute mechanisms wherever possible;
- including dispute resolution mechanisms within their complaints and disputes handling procedures;
- engaging the process of appropriate dispute resolution in respect of any dispute which has not been resolved with

Dispute resolution commitment (DRC)

the organisation's normal complaints procedure, as an alternative to litigation;

- adopting appropriate dispute resolution clauses in their contracts with other parties;
- using prompt, cost-effective, and efficient processes of completing negotiations in resolving disputes;
- choosing processes appropriate in style and proportionate to the cost issues that need to be resolved;
- making informed choices by considering the benefits to the organisation, and to whoever they are in dispute with, of all available processes in achieving a resolution;
- recognising that the use of appropriate dispute resolution processes can often avoid the high cost in time and resources of going to court;
- educating their employees and officials in appropriate dispute resolution techniques in order to enable the best possible chance of success when using them

It provides guidance for government department and agencies. This can be viewed on the Webarchive. nationalarchives.co.uk/201301281112038

Paragraph 7 of the Guidance provides realistic and helpful guidance:

> '7.6 **Participants** – the team attending the mediation should be kept as small as possible but must include somebody ('the lead negotiator'), preferably a senior executive or official within the organisation with policy authority to settle on the day without reverting to others not involved in the mediation. The lead negotiator should ideally not have been closely involved in the events relating to the dispute.
>
> 7.7 Where it really is not possible for the lead negotiator to have full authority to settle, the person attending must be of sufficient authority that their recommendation of settlement is likely followed by whatever person or

body makes the final decision. The fact that the binding settlement agreement cannot be reached on the day of the negotiation and the reason for this should be made clear to the other parties in good time before the mediation.

7.8 Most mediation teams include a lawyer but a large legal representation on the team is rarely useful or necessary.

7.10 Approach – most mediations go through a stage where it seems unlikely that there will be any useful outcome yet the majority settle, so optimism and determination to solve the problem is essential.'

In practice

- Government departments are increasingly using mediation in a wide variety of disputes.
- Mediations involving government departments, particularly HMRC, have their own characteristics.

See also

GOVERNMENT DEPARTMENTS/LSS

Follow up

moj.build.squiz.co.uk

Distributive Negotiating

Aka claiming value, zero sum, win/lose or competitive negotiation. The opposite of integrative or principled negotiation.

Mediators use the example of a pie. Distributive negotiators argue about how big a slice they will receive. Integrative ones try to grow the size of the pie before slicing it up.

Distributive negotiators try and claim the biggest slice for themselves. The more that they receive the less someone else receives. Hence it is called win/lose or zero sum.

In practice

- Even the most principled/integrative negotiators recognise that some element of distributive negotiation takes place.
- Even when the negotiations are creating value there will be a time when value has to be claimed as well.

See also

GROWING THE PIE/HAGGLING/HARVARD/ PRINCIPLED/VALUE/ZERO SUM

Downtime

Important in two ways in mediation.

1 Disputes and in particular litigation are downtime for clients. This applies to both commercial and personal disputes. Clients want to be getting on with making money in their businesses or with the real stuff of their lives, which is not litigating.

 For lawyers litigation is uptime. It is how they make money. For the clients it is how they lose money.

2 During the mediation day there are lulls. Especially with the caucus model. Parties and their advisers, when left alone in a room, can switch off and become disengaged. This is dangerous.

 Mediators are not encouraged when they return to the room and find people watching the Test Match on their laptops or playing bridge on their iPads.

In practice
- Downtime during the mediation is inevitable. Warn clients in advance.
- It is dangerous to switch off.
- Avoid working on other matters. You will be distracted and take longer to re-engage when the mediator comes back into your room. Focus and momentum are lost.

See also
CAUCUS/ENGAGEMENT/MEDIATION DAY

Door of the Court

The traditional time and place for settling disputes. Preparation for trial is completed. Everyone is ready to go.

Either the night before or on the morning of the trial one of the parties' lawyers, usually their barrister asks his opposite number if 'we could have a word'. Or everyone is in court. The judge sits down and after the preliminary introductions floats the idea that the parties might like a little time for a word with each other. Sometimes the suggestion sounds more like an instruction. Off everyone goes.

The disadvantages of this approach are:
- Everyone is on a war footing – not the best frame of mind for thinking about settlement.
- Briefs have been delivered – all the expense of litigation including the first day of trial have been incurred. Parties can easily fall into the sunk-cost fallacy. Or costs are so large that they become an issue in themselves and become an obstacle to settlement.
- Clients are sidelined. The usual format of these discussions is that the two sides huddle at opposite ends of the corridor outside court and their barristers stride between them, breaking off in the middle for private chats, which they report back to their clients.

In practice

- A settlement is often reached with the clients feeling short-changed by the whole process in which they have not really participated.
- Other clients however just delighted to not have to give evidence and cannot wait to celebrate in the wine bars which cluster around court buildings.
- The peace premium has been spent. Lawyers are in pocket. Clients are out of pocket.

See also

COGNITIVE BIAS/COSTS/DIGNIFIED EXIT/SUNK COST FALLACY.

Drop Hands

The parties decide to call it a day. No one pays anybody anything. Each side pays their own costs. Aka eating your losses.

Common where the mediation day starts with each side expecting to be a net receiver because there is a claim and counterclaim.

Even where parties know that this is an unrealistic outcome one party will often insist on receiving a token payment. Its symbolic value far outweighs the monetary value.

In practice

- Absolute drop hands are rare.
- If you want a deal sometimes you just have to swallow hard and pay something.
- Quasi-drop hands with a token payment or adjustment offer a dignified exit. Not to be sniffed at.

Duress

See also
DIGNIFIED EXIT/REALISM/VALUE

Duress

Duress as a legal concept is sometimes a factor in mediations. It is much more than feelings of stress or pressure. In the context of mediation, illegitimate pressure or threats or coercive conduct can render a settlement agreement voidable (liable to be set aside).

There are two types of duress:

1 Threats – not all threats amount to duress. Only illegitimate ones do. And as Dyson J said in *DSND Subsea* 'illegitimate pressure must be distinguished from the rough and tumble of normal commercial bargaining. Legitimate threats include threats not to enter into a contract, to institute proceedings or call the police.'

2 Circumstances – where a person has no real choice and the pressure is unfair. For example a supplier demanding a substantial premium in order to continue to supply goods where there was no other supplier who could supply equivalent goods on roughly equivalent in terms.

In practice

- Parties often complain about duress when they mean pressure.
- Duress is sometimes applied at mediations but much less frequently than you might think.

See also

BLACKMAIL/THREATS

Follow up

DSND Subsea Ltd v Petroleum Geo-Services ASA (2000) BLR 530
Farm Assist Ltd v Secretary State for Environment Food and Rural Affairs [2008] EWHC 3079 (TCC)

Dutch Auction

A phrase much (mis)-used at mediations. Usually by parties wanting to avoid making their first offer.

They say 'We do not want to bid against ourselves' or 'We will not enter into a Dutch auction.' What they mean is that they want the other side to tell them what they want.

In fact a Dutch auction is where an auctioneer begins with a high asking price which he lowers until someone accepts it.

In practice

- Dutch auctions do not take place at mediations.

See also
ANCHORING/AUCTION/OFFERS

E

eADR

ADR conducted online. Has multiple meanings.

Many predict that this will be a high-growth area for mediators. Others are sceptical.

In practice

- There is a lot of gazing into crystal balls and navels.
- eADR will grow. It's just a question how much and how fast.

See also

ODR/ONLINE MEDIATION

Follow up

Walker *Setting up in Business as a Mediator* Ch 15

ED (Expert Determination)

Similar to arbitration. The parties select a TNP (Third Party Neutral) to decide who is right and who is wrong. But there are significant differences:

- The courts do not exercise as much regulatory influence over an expert as they do over an arbitrator. There is no equivalent of the Arbitration Act.
- The rights and obligations of the expert are almost entirely a matter of the contract between the parties and the terms of the expert's appointment. There are very few

ED (Expert Determination)

implied terms. Great care has to be taken in drafting the contract and in making sure that the clients understand it. Many contracts include provision for expert determination but decisions to go to ED are often taken ad hoc.

Pros

- A contract usually provides that the decision is final, ie no appeal and binding.
- The parties can choose their expert.
- Anecdotally there is evidence of concern about the level of expertise of some experts.
- It is quick and cheap compared with the other adjudicative options.

Cons

- There is no implied obligation to apply the principles of natural justice.
- There is no equivalent to the New York Convention so that a decision in one jurisdiction will not be enforceable in another.
- There is no implied obligation for the expert to give reasons for his decision.
- The expert cannot ask the court for help in carrying out a function, eg compelling witnesses to attend or that property should be inspected.
- There is no immunity for experts. Unlike arbitrators who have statutory immunity, the expert can be sued for negligence or breach of contract.
- It is a less good choice than other procedures for general contract disputes.
- Care must be taken if the expert is going to be asked to determine questions of law with no appeal to the court if he makes an error.

In practice

- ED is best suited for disputes where there are limited and clearly defined issues where only an expert will be authoritative. Most disputes are not like this.

Follow up

The Arbitration Act 1996, s 29

ZVI Construction Co LLC v University of Notre Dame (USA) in England [2016] EWMC 1924 (TCC)

Educate

Stage one of the classic mediation three-part process of educate, exchange, explore.

Mediators ask open questions to educate the parties about the case by asking them what is important to them, why it is and how they want to achieve it.

In practice

- This is something that trainers tell mediators to do but which mediators in practice seldom do, at least overtly.

See also

EXPECTATIONS/EXPLORE/THREE STAGE PROCESS

EE (Expert Evaluation)

A variation of Early Neutral Evaluation ('ENE').

The parties are in deadlock. They want someone to help them see the way through by giving an assessment of the matters in dispute. As an evaluation rather than a determination or adjudication it is not in any way binding on the parties.

Parties can agree to be bound by the evaluation, It then becomes a determination.

Elder Mediation

In practice
- Rarely used in civil and commercial mediations unless they are multi-party complex technical disputes.
- Parties should be able to make their own realistic assessments. That's what experts and QCs are for.

See also
ENE (Early Neutral Evaluation)

Elder Mediation

A relatively new, more specialised area of mediation practice. Concerns issues involving the elderly. Increasingly important as populations age.

Common areas of dispute are:
- Around care home provision. The parties are families of elderly residents, residents and care home providers.
- The conduct of an elderly person's affairs under a Power of Attorney.
- Abuse of elderly people.
- Family disputes.
- Organising estates – drafting wills, Inheritance Tax planning.
- Healthcare and disputes with healthcare providers including hospitals.

Particular issues can arise because one of the parties is elderly.

There can be problems with:
- Comprehension as cognitive capacities deteriorate.
- Simple communication as sight and hearing deteriorate.
- Concentration and memory.

- Mobility – mediations will have to often take place in an elderly person's home.
- Rigidity of thought and habit.

Many community mediators already mediate disputes involving elderly neighbours. Their co-mediation narrative model of mediation can be particularly well-suited to Elder Mediation.

Specialist training is now available in Elder Mediation particularly in Canada and the US.

In practice

- A developing and growing area for mediators.
- Hybrid use of techniques and approaches from family, community and civil and commercial mediations is needed.

Follow up

elderdecisions.com

Elicitive

The replacement term for facilitative mediation.

Both coined by Leonard Riskin, an American professor of Dispute Resolution.

He said that when he wrote his original articles in 1994/96 he 'hoped to clarify discussions of mediation, which until that time had often been suffused with ambiguity...'

Sadly despite his distinguished efforts, ambiguity, confusion and dissent reigns.

Emotions

See also
DIRECTIVE, EVALUATIVE/FACILITATIVE/RISKIN'S GRID

Emotions

The current orthodoxy is that we are creatures of our emotions. They decide for us what we do. Rational, logical, exercise of free will is impossible.

Therefore mediators and mediation need to concentrate on the parties' emotions.

But there is no universal definition of what emotions are. Emotions are often confused with emotional experiences, mood, traits, feelings or desires, perceptions and beliefs.

Some say there are six basic emotions. Others say eight. Most experts accept that there are at least six fundamental and distinct emotions:

- anger
- disgust
- fear
- happiness
- sadness
- surprise

Three questions arise:

1. Should parties should be encouraged to express their emotions – whatever they are – or to control them? Is venting a displacement activity? It is much easier than working out a settlement structure.

2. How far we can free ourselves from cognitive biases? These are often based upon emotional rather than logical reactions. Much support is drawn from research that

Emotions

suggests that our unconscious mind takes a decision on what to do before our conscious mind does.

3 How far are negotiators influenced by Cialdini's Big Six? He identified for example the tendency of people to respond to kindness, to want to be liked, to do business with people they like and to be influenced by people who they feel are in authority.

As a mediator you have to:

- Control your own emotions.
- Separate the expression of the emotion from the emotion itself.
- Decide whether expressions of emotion are tactical or genuine displays.
- Work out whether or not the emotion displayed is a message or a mask.

In practice

- The most common emotions observed at mediations are anger and fear.
- You will be not able to escape them. But you don't have to be a slave to them.
- Remember Ambrose Bierce's (author of *The Devil's Dictionary*) advice

  'Speak when you are angry and you will make the best speech that you'll ever regret.'

See also

ANGER/CATHARSIS/CIALDINI's BIG 6/COGNITIVE BIAS/FEAR/VENTING

Follow up

- Randolph *The Psychology of Conflict* Ch 3 Emotions
- Walker *Mediation Advocacy* paras 5.07–12 and 9.09

Empathy

Often confused with sympathy. Mediators are encouraged to show empathy but not sympathy.

- Empathy is the ability to understand and share the feelings of others.
- Sympathy is a feeling of pity or sorrow for someone else's misfortune.

Sometimes the difference is summed up as:

- Sympathy is 'feeling with' and empathy is 'feeling into'.

or

- A person *expresses* sympathy but *shares* empathy.

Empathy is said to be a deeper feeling than sympathy and more useful in building mutual understanding or rapport.

Be careful about:

- Expressing empathy in the standard way of saying: 'I know how you feel...' Many mediators have had their heads bitten off by an outraged client saying 'You cannot possibly know how I feel!'
- Expressing sympathy – are you, in fact, displaying partiality?

In practice

- The words are used interchangeably at mediations. Mediators often express sympathy in the sense of 'I am sorry to hear ....'
- Empathy and sympathy are not mutually exclusive.
- Both are useful in making someone feel that they have been acknowledged and heard. This is after all at the heart of the mediation process.
- If people think that you have not heard them they are not going to hear you.

See also
ACKNOWLEDGMENT/IMPARTIALITY/NEUTRALITY/ SYMPATHY

Employment Mediation

Deals with employment disputes where the relationship has broken down or is on the point of breaking down.

Different from workplace mediation which deals with disputes where the relationship is still intact and the intention is to maintain it.

In practice

- Often uses the same techniques and format as civil and commercial mediation.
- Legal representatives are usually involved and discussions are about agreeing severance arrangements including termination payments, employment references and restrictive covenants.

See also
WORKPLACE

Follow up
Lewis *How to Master Workplace and Employment Mediation*

Employment Tribunal (ET)

The ET has a judicial mediation scheme. The judge at the Case Management Discussion chooses suitable cases for judicial mediation. If all parties agree, the Regional Employment Judge will decide whether or not the case should be referred to judicial mediation.

An ET mediation operates in much the same way as other mediations.

Employment Tribunal (ET)

The key features are:
- The parties have to be committed to the idea.
- There is no continuing ACAS involvement.
- The length of the final hearing is at least three days.
- It is listed for a private hearing and all case management orders are suspended but the final hearing date is kept.
- It is now available to all types of cases – originally limited to discrimination cases.
- The mediation style is now indicative not facilitative as it was originally.
- The fee of £600 is paid by the Respondent.
- They take place at the ET premises.

Pros
- It saves time money and stress.
- Non-judicial solutions can be devised.
- The parties potentially have a greater involvement in the process and influence on the outcome.
- It is successful but not much used. Less than 1% of claims are mediated with a 50% settlement rate.

Cons
- It has some of the features of a Financial Dispute Resolution Meeting in the Family Courts with much the same advantages and disadvantages.
- It tends to take place in a 'court' setting with a real judge so that the parties can be both confused about what is really going on and also intimidated.
- Not all ET judges have been trained in mediation and there is limited court time to devote to it.
- Anecdotal evidence from mediation trainers reveals that judges, whether sitting or recently retired, find it difficult

to move from *telling* people what is important to *asking* people what is important.

- The shift from the facilitative model to the indicative model reflects the judicial mediators' proclivities. The distinction between being evaluative and being indicative is not clear. The President of Employment Tribunals has explained it as the mediator identifying the barriers to success at the final hearing that each side will face, rather than predicting the outcome or telling the parties how he would decide the case if he was going to hear it, which of course he cannot.

In practice

- A very small percentage of claims are dealt with by ET mediation. Why bother?
- From 1 October 2016 the ET will offer Early Neutral Evaluation as well. Why bother?
- Judicial time is a limited resource. It is better spent on judging.

See also
ENE/FDR – FINANCIAL DISPUTE RESOLUTION MEETING/INDICATIVE

Empty Chair

A tedious and unproductive negotiation ploy. Sometimes used at mediations. Most mediation agreements stipulate that those attending the mediation will have authority to settle.

The empty chair is usually unoccupied by someone whose authority to sign off on the settlement is required. This can be a party's spouse, the Board of Directors, line manager, Minister or even a barrister whose advice is needed.

The empty chair is often seen by the other side as either evidence of bad faith or poor preparation. They are often correct. If you are serious about trying to secure a deal turn up with everybody that you need.

In practice
- The empty chair is present at mediations more often than you might think.
- Find out who should be sitting in it early on.

See also
ABSENTEES/AUTHORITY

ENE (Early Neutral Evaluation)

The parties appoint an expert who is often a retired judge to review the evidence and the submissions and give a non-binding opinion.

Key features:
- Not much used in the UK, but has been used in complex technical disputes in the financial sector.
- Most useful where the outcome of the case in court or arbitration would not depend on contested factual evidence which would have to be tested in cross-examination but on evaluating legal arguments, established market practice or technical expert evidence.
- There is no fixed procedure. The parties agree to this process and choose the evaluator, which can be a source of disagreement. The evaluator usually decides what procedure to follow.
- Usually the parties submit written submissions and evidence. Sometimes there are oral hearings.
- The evaluator considers the material and produces a recommendation giving his assessment of the evidence, the legal arguments and the probable outcome at trial.
- The evaluator's recommendations are not binding on the parties.

ENE (Early Neutral Evaluation)

ENE can be arranged through the court in the Commercial, Mercantile and Technology and Construction Court. Details can be found in the court guides for these courts.

Also from 1 October 2016 the Employment Tribunals will offer ENE.

Pros

- At an early stage in a dispute potentially authoritative views can be obtained which can have a persuasive influence on the disputants.
- Although the recommendations are non-binding the parties can decide to adopt the recommendations to settle the dispute.
- It is cheaper than going to trial or arbitration.
- Only one party asks for an ENE of their case.

Cons

- Many think that this is an unsatisfactory procedure.
- Why would a party seek an ENE of its own case? That is what you go to lawyers for.
- Why have an ENE, which is a sort of miniaturised trial without the good bits such as cross-examination?
- There is an element of transferring responsibility for one's own decisions. The parties ask someone to tell them what the answer is but do not agree to accept it if they do not like it.
- You might as well go to court if you want a definitive answer.
- A mediation with an evaluative mediator will deliver more value:
    i The parties will be more involved in the process.
    ii The parties can make sure that issues or considerations which are not included in the

pleading or submissions which will tend to be legal are taken into account in any settlement.

 iii It is much cheaper and quicker.

Follow up

www.gov.uk/government/uploads/system/uploads/attachment_data/file/448256/technology-and-construction-court-guide.pdf

www.gov.uk/government/uploads/system/uploads/attachment_data/file/508023/admiralty-and-commercial-courts-guide.pdf

www.gov.uk/government/uploads/system/uploads/attachment_data/file/454182/mercantile-court-guide.pdf

Engagement

As Woody Allen said: 'Half of life is turning up.' But the other half is joining in.

The two main reasons for mediations not producing a settlement on the day are:

- Lack of preparation.
- Lack of engagement.

If you do not join in the process you are not going to get value out of the day or the mediator.

Lack of engagement can be interpreted as lack of commitment to mediation. Suspicion arises that you are only there for tactical reasons.

Remember that either the parties or the mediator can terminate the mediation at any time for any reason.

So listen to what the mediator says and in particular the questions he asks. If he suggests that you think about something, calculate a figure, or produce some information, do it.

In practice

- Staying engaged throughout a full day's mediation is not easy. Attention can wander. Boredom, frustration and irritation set in.
- Take breaks.
- Resist the temptation to do other work.
- Keep your eyes on the prize.

See also

ABSENTEES/AUTHORITY/DOWNTIME/EMPTY CHAIR/ PREPARATION/TACTICAL

Environmental Mediation

This has two separate meanings.

1. Where there is a *dispute* or even litigation over an environmental matter. For example someone is challenging the right to block a river.
2. Where there is a process of *consultation* prior to or during some sort of project, which has an environmental impact. This has less to do with conventional mediation and more to do with public consultation and engagement.

Although many of the qualities and techniques used – for example open questioning, active listening, allowing people to be heard, not being judgemental – are the same, there are significant differences. This is why the consultation type is often referred to as facilitation not mediation.

The main differences in consultation mediations:

- The sheer number of parties and people involved. Highly unlikely to be concluded in a day or even in a single extended session. There is usually a series of consultations. Mediators who practise in this area find

Ethics

more of their time is spent on process design than conducting the process, ie process management.
- Cultural differences, ethnic, religious, social and economic are often highlighted and have to be accommodated within the process.
- There are always empty chairs. Everybody present at the meetings has some sort of audience which is not present but is influential.
- Nothing is ever confidential.

Follow up

Richbell *How to Master Commercial Mediation* p 292–296

Ethics

You might think that the absence of effective regulation might give rise to all sorts of ethical problems. In practice there have been very few practical – as opposed to theoretical – problems.

The problems that arise about the ethics of mediators are ones concerning:
- Bias, in the sense of not disclosing a previous connection with one of the parties.
- Breaching confidentiality.
- Deliberately misrepresenting one party's position to another for example not passing on an offer that they have been instructed to make or describing the reaction to an offer incorrectly.

Mediators can be liable to the parties for breach of contract.

There have been attempts to introduce codes of conduct for mediators.

In practice

- Mediation in England and Wales has been blissfully free of ethical difficulties.
- With the huge expansion in numbers, the competitive financial pressures and the increasing diversity of mediation models this happy state may not last.

See also

CODES OF CONDUCT/COMPLAINTS PROCEDURE/ EXCLUSION CLAUSES/MEDIATORS' LIABLITY/ REGULATION

EU CODE

Sets out several principles which individual mediators may voluntarily adhere to and mediation organisations can require their members to commit to.

They are specifically without prejudice to national legislation or rules regulating individual professions.

The principles are sensible and unobjectionable.

The question is how to enforce them. Especially in the absence of regulation in the UK.

In practice

- Most UK mediation organisations have adopted a code of practice incorporating the code.
- The only sanction is to remove a mediator from a panel if he breaches the Code.

See also

CODE OF CONDUCT/REGULATION

Follow up

ec.europe.eu>adr>adr_code_conduct_en

EU Directive

The use of mediation has increased throughout the EU. Inevitably there are a myriad of differences in the way in which mediation is carried out, mediators are trained, the courts supervise mediation etc. There have been some attempts at harmonisation and the most important directives are:

- EU Directive on Mediation in Civil and Commercial cases (Directive 2008/52/EC.
  - This was implemented in the UK by the Cross-Border Mediation (EU Directive) Regulations 2011, SI 2011/1133. They only apply to cross-border disputes.
- The EU Code of Conduct for Mediators.
  - This has been incorporated into the Civil Mediation Councils own code and is adopted by many mediation providers.
- EU Directive on Alternative Dispute Resolution for Consumer Disputes (Directive 2013/11 EU).
- Regulation (EU) and 0524/20013 on consumer ODR.
  - This has been incorporated into the UK by the Alternative Dispute Resolution for Consumer Dispute (Competent Authorities and Information) Regulations 2015, SI 2015/542.
- The Alternative Dispute Resolution for Consumer Dispute (Amendment) Regulations 2015, SI 2015/1392.

In practice

Who knows what Brexit will bring? For the present these all still apply.

Evaluative

Traditionally the polar opposite to facilitative mediation. Evaluative mediators act more like judges. They follow the same process as facilitative mediators but the crucial difference is that the evaluative mediator:

- Gives his opinion on the merits of the legal case.
- Gives his view about settlement proposals.
- Lets the parties know early on that he has his views and opinions and gives them.

The civil and commercial mediation market in the UK increasingly wants evaluative mediators. Facilitative mediators are seen as purists, idealists or wimps. Evaluative mediators are tough-minded realists.

Trainers still teach the facilitative mode and refer to evaluative mediation as an oxymoron. But some now teach the evaluative model. They recognise that in many civil and commercial mediations, during the course of the mediation day the mediator will be evaluative to some extent.

What does evaluative mean? For example:

- Is it evaluative to give an opinion on the likelihood of a potential settlement being accepted by the other?
- Is it evaluative to identify the legal obstacles, which a party will have to overcome at trial?
- Is it evaluative to give an opinion on what is likely to happen at trial?
- Is it evaluative to give an opinion on whether a settlement proposal should be accepted?

Many mediators would say that:

- It is not evaluative to give an opinion about whether a settlement proposal is likely to be accepted.

Exchanging Offers

- It probably is evaluative to identify legal obstacles to be overcome at the trial although some now would say that it was 'indicative' rather than evaluative.
- It is definitely evaluative to give an opinion on how the judge will decide the case or whether a party should accept an offer.

For many commentators the distinction between facilitative and evaluative is now redundant. In fact there is a spectrum of intervention by the mediator. Some no longer use the words evaluative and facilitative. They prefer directive and elicitive.

In practice

- Changes of name make no difference.
- Experienced mediators decides what they should do based on their own experience and the dispute in front of them.
- It is for the parties and their representatives to decide what sort of intervention they want from the mediator. If they don't like what he is doing they can tell him.

See also
DIRECTIVE/ELICITIVE/FACILITATIVE/HARVARD/ RISKIN'S GRID

Exchange

This is the second stage of the Three Stage Process. During this stage the mediator encourages the parties to exchange comments, views and, in particular, information.

See also
THREE STAGE PROCESS

Exchanging Offers

There are two ways of exchanging offers: sequentially or simultaneously.

The traditional way is sequentially – one party makes an offer, the other considers it and makes a counter proposal. Increasingly mediators are encouraging parties to exchange offers simultaneously. This has advantages:

- It overcomes many of the objections people in mediations raise about making an offer, namely that they do not want to go first, bid against themselves or engage in Dutch auctions.
- The mediator can see how far apart for the parties are. This enables him to start addressing the really important questions of the day which are:
  - Why are the parties apart?
  - What are the obstacles to settlement?

Once these have been identified they can be worked on.

Mediators usually give the parties health warnings before they make offers.

In practice

- Be ready to exchange offers.
- Don't insist on sequential offers. If you do the signal that you send out will be received as you lack confidence, preparation and commitment.

See also

ANCHORING/DUTCH AUCTIONS/HEALTH WARNINGS/ OFFERS

Exclusion Clauses

Most mediation agreements limit the mediator's liability for breach of contract and/or negligence. This is because it's standard practice and also some professional indemnity insurers require them to.

Expectations

Not all mediators include exclusion clauses. They take the view that they will be unenforceable in the UK because of the Unfair Contracts Terms Act 1977. In any event the chance of a mediator being liable for the loss caused by something he did or failed to do at mediation are negligible. So why bother?

In practice

- This is not an issue.
- Likely to become more important as the courts examine mediators' conduct more frequently and closely.

See also

MEDIATION AGREEMENT/MEDIATORS'S LIABLITY/PI INSURANCE

Expectations

Mediators are trained that an important part of their job is to manage the parties' expectations both about the process and the outcome.

Expectations about process are managed by explaining the process to the parties and involving them in it.

Expectations about outcome are usually managed by:

- Asking open questions in the education phase of the Three-Phase Process, eg asking the parties what is important to them, why it is and how they want to achieve it.
- Reality testing. A technique much beloved of mediators where they challenge what you have told them and the other side about your position. Some regard it simply as a challenging conversation and others see it as destructive testing.

- Asking hypothetical questions to try and shift perspective. For example:
  - If you were advising the other side what would you say?
  - If you were the other side what would you say?
  - What if you do not settle today? What position will you be in?
  - What will life be like if you do settle? In other words what could you be spending your time, money and energy on instead of litigation?
  - What will your net cash position calculation look like?

In practice

- Parties demonise each other. They expect the worst from each other.
- Mediators try to ameliorate these negative views by explaining to each side what is influencing the other. When they do this people are often surprised.
- The only reliable rule of thumb at mediations is: expect the unexpected.

See also

BASHING AND TRASHING/DEMONSING/EDUCATE/ REALITY TESTING

Experts

The use of experts at mediation is a contentious issue.

Experts can be present at mediation:

1 In person

   In some sectors experts are nearly always present in person at the mediation. In particular construction and IT disputes.

2   By proxy

Expert reports are used in all sorts of mediations, eg:

- Surveyors' reports showing where the boundaries and rights of way are.
- Valuation evidence of properties and businesses.
- Calculation of loss in pension mis-selling cases.

Reports are usually exchanged as part of the preparation for mediation. But a surprising number are produced at the mediation. This is rarely a good idea. The receiving party never simply surrenders as soon as they see the report but says that they need time to process the new information.

3   By telephone/Skype

Experts are frequently consulted during the mediation. This can be about the merits of the case or on the viability of a settlement. For example engineers are asked whether or not the proposed retaining wall will do the job. Accountants are asked about the tax treatment of a payment structure.

The disadvantage of experts

1   They act as advocates.

Despite the requirements of CPR Part 35 and adverse judicial comments many experts still see themselves as advocates for whoever has instructed them.

2   They are opinionated.

You cannot expect experts not to have opinions. That is what they are hired to provide. Once they have expressed their opinion many experts find it difficult to modify it in any way. We all want to be consistent with what we have previously said. This love of consistency is a recognised cognitive bias.

3 They are too entrenched.

   Mediations that take place after formal exchange of signed expert reports are more difficult than those where provisional or draft reports have been exchanged on a without prejudice basis.

In practice

- Experts are more often than not barriers to settlement at mediation.
- Avoid taking them if you can.
- Hot tubbing is often very effective.

See also

COGNITIVE BIAS/HOT TUBBING/SURPRISES

Follow up

CPR Pt 35

Greg Bond ed. *Mediation Practice* p 44 for a scintillating analysis by Rosemary Jackson of the role of experts.

Explorative Mediation

A recent reformulation of mediation by Roger Seaman.

Describes itself as a respectful critique of Transformative and Narrative mediation.

The parties control the process.

The mediator:

- Follows the parties in their conversation.
- Strives for 'dialogue' by listening intently to the parties' stories to understand their feelings and perspectives.

Explorative Mediation

- Supports an exploration of the conflict by reflecting back and possibly exploring:
  - Expressions of disempowerment or reconciliation.
  - Differences in parties' views and world views.
  - Metaphors used by the parties.
  - Significant context and background impacting the conflict.

The mediator should

- Support the parties in dialogue.
- Keep his influence to a minimum or at least make influence transparent.
- Actively recognise that the mediation meeting takes place in a social and political context.
- Make it his primary task to help the parties to explain the conflict.

In practice

- Not obviously different from what narrative and transformative mediators do when they seek resolution.
- At the other end of the spectrum from the evaluative model which is gaining in popularity in civil and commercial mediations.
- Of more relevance in workplace mediation and public engagement processes than in civil and commercial mediation.

See also

EVALUATIVE/FACILITATIVE/MEDIATAING THE MOMENT/NARRATIVE/TOXIC MEDIATION/ TRANSFORMATIVE

Follow up

www.rogerseamanmediation.co.uk/docs/Presentation

Roger Seaman *Explorative Mediation at Work* 2016

Exploring

The third stage of the Three Stage Process. The mediator explores with the parties how they see their aim is being achieved by way of a settlement proposal.

See also
THREE STAGE PROCESS

F

Face

Frequently referred to in mediations. Usually as 'losing face' or 'loss of face'.

But what is it? Is it universal? How important is it?

What is face?

Face can mean different things but the core elements are:

- prestige;
- reputation;
- honour;
- self-esteem; and
- social standing.

In communications theory three types of face have been identified:

1 *Autonomy* face – where people want to appear independent, in control and responsible.
2 *Fellowship* face – where people want to appear cooperative, accepted and even loved.
3 *Competence* face – where people want to be seen as intelligent, accomplished and capable.

Is face universal?

Cross-cultural negotiation trainers tell us that loss of face is especially important to people from China and Japan. In fact researchers such as Wolfram Eberhard show that

Face

concern about loss of face is pretty well universal. Although face appears to be more important in what are described as high-context as opposed to low-context cultures. High-context cultures are those which emphasise in-groups and low-context ones are those which emphasise individuals.

How important is face?

Research into cross-cultural communication especially involving conflict resolution has shown the importance of face. As Bert Brown says 'In some instances, protecting against loss of face becomes so central an issue that it swamps the importance of the tangible issues at stake and generates intense conflicts that can impede progress towards agreement and increase substantially the cost of conflict resolution.'

Given this, why do parties at mediation insist on attacking each other in personal and abusive terms which seem to be designed to undermine all three faces – autonomy, fellowship and competence? But they do.

In practice

- To give yourself the best chance of achieving a favourable outcome at mediation avoid loss of face: yours and others.
- Treat others as you expect to be treated.

See also
CROSS CULTURAL/HIGH CONTEXT

Follow up

CEDR *How to Master Negotiation* Ch 13

Bert Brown in D Druckman (Ed) *Negotiations: Social-Psychological Perspectives* pp 275–300

Facilitative

Facilitation

This is a process where a facilitator helps all parties to work out a procedure or process for discussing settlement of the dispute. The facilitator usually then guides the agreed process.

These appointments are often ad hoc. There has to be a degree of common ground between the parties about the need for a facilitator and the choice and powers of the facilitator to launch the process.

As an ancillary exercise to a settlement procedure it can be useful. But the cost and time expended needs to be justified in the overall scheme of things.

In practice
- Not much used in the UK.

Facilitative

This is the classic model of mediation. It is still widely taught by mediation trainers in the USA and Europe. The key elements are:

- The mediator helps the parties to find their own solution by taking them through a process. He does not in any way evaluate their dispute, their case or even the proposed settlements.

- The mediator is in charge of the process but the dispute and the solution remain the property of the parties.

- In order to achieve this the mediator follows a three-stage process: Educate, Exchange and Explore.

- Mediators use a combination of techniques: open questions, active listing, reframing and summarising to help people see their way to settlement.

This model emphasises:

- The primacy of people's interests over their legal rights.
- The need for parties to collaborate to achieve an outcome that is beneficial to both sides rather than trying to win something at the other's expense.
- Every dispute can be a win-win not a zero sum game.
- Achieving a solution which is workable for the future: not trying to change people or their behaviour.

Facilitative mediators do not:

- Give opinions on the merits of the case.
- Give views on settlement proposals.
- Suggest solutions for settlements.

In practice

- Doctrinal purists, theoreticians, and novice mediators adhere to facilitative mediation.
- Most civil and commercial mediators blend it with evaluative techniques.

See also

EVALUATIVE/HARVARD/THREE STAGE PROCESS

Follow up

Walker: *Mediation Advocacy: Representing Clients in Mediation* Ch 4 Mediation Styles: What Mediators Do and Why

Fact Finding

The parties appoint a Third Party Neutral to investigate and possibly establish facts. He may be asked to reach a decision on those facts. He does not deal with questions of

FDR (Financial Dispute Resolution) meetings

law or compensation or other remedies. His findings are not usually binding.

In practice
- Not much used outside complex technical disputes.

FDR (Financial Dispute Resolution) meetings

FDRs take place before a Family Judge, but not the one who will hear the case if it does not settle. They are held at court.

The key features are:

- Before the FDR the parties will have exchanged financial information. They will both have filed a detailed questionnaire (Form E). Issues arising out of further disclosure of financial information will have been dealt with.
- It is expected the parties will attend the FDR in possession of most if not all of the financial information that they need.
- The parties attend court several hours before the appointed time for the FDR and engage in negotiations. The intention is to try and come to an agreed settlement to put before the judge at the FDR.
- If that is not possible the FDR hearing takes place before the judge. Each side briefly sets out their case and identifies the issues on which there has not been agreement.
- The judge asks questions and gives an 'indication'. This is not a judgment or a decision.
- All discussions both inside and outside the court are without prejudice.

Failure

Pros

- When it produces a settlement it is justified.
- Even when it does not produce a settlement it makes the parties and their advisers think about the issues, both legal and evidential.
- It is a reality check.

Cons

- The indications are not binding, so there is no finality.
- The FDR judge can give an 'indication' but the judge who hears the case is not bound by it. There is plenty of evidence that trial judges come to different decisions sometimes diametrically opposite ones.
- Parties can feel exhausted and stressed and do not always appreciate that when a judge gives an indication that this is not necessarily the same as a judgment.
- A lot of explanation and expectation management is required.

In practice

- Parties engaged in matrimonial proceeding have no choice. They have to attend a FDR.

Follow up

FORM E Financial Statement 104.12

Failure

Is it a failure not to achieve a settlement at mediation on the day?

Most mediation trainers and commentators say that it is not. Most clients and their lawyers say that it is.

Mediators will talk publicly about the benefits of partial settlements and clarifying issues. In private they think that they have failed if they don't produce a settlement because that is what clients want.

They console themselves with the words of a leading international mediator:

> 'You have to remember that when mediations succeed it is because of the mediator's skill. When they fail it is because of the parties.'

In practice

- Parties in civil and commercial mediations sometimes think that even if there is no settlement progress has been made. Some issues can be agreed. They have a greater understanding of their own case and the other side's.
- Partial settlements are much rarer than mediation commentators and members of the judiciary would like. There is rarely any significant narrowing of the issues in a way that reduces the time and expense of the trial.
- In multi-party mediations partial settlements can sometimes be reached with some if not all parties.
- Remember the two main reasons for not producing a settlement on the day are lack of preparation and lack of engagement.

See also
ENGAGEMENT/PREPARATION

Faith Mediation

Tries to settle by mediation disputes between peoples of different faiths or within one faith.

Fairness

Little overlap with civil and commercial mediation. Its distinguishing features are:

- A sincere belief in their faith encourages people to think that they must be right.
- By its very nature faith is not always susceptible to rational, logical or objective analysis.
- Because of the sensitivity and the diversity of beliefs and values, solving faith disputes takes more time and usually follow a programme of rolling mediation sessions.
- As with community mediation it is often carried out by unpaid volunteers.

See also

BIMA

Follow up

Richbell *Mastering Commercial Mediation* Ch 7

BIMA www.bimagroup.org

Fairness

Humans are motivated by a sense of fairness. Research shows this to be universal and applying across different cultures, social and economic groupings, age ranges and times. It may have evolutionary origins as a component of the impulse towards co-operation which humans have needed to survive.

What is it?

Fairness has different meanings for different people. People's interpretations can be self-serving. It can be considered as a social construct, which reflects power groupings rather than any absolute principle. But the concept is powerful.

Fairness

Researchers find that people will reject an optimal outcome if they think it is unfair in favour of a sub-optimal outcome, which they consider fairer. Examples can be found in the Ultimatum Game.

At mediation, parties:

- Use fairness as a pretext for not engaging in settlement discussions leading to an agreement.
- Will resist if their protestations are completely ignored.
- Often define fairness as obtaining what they think that they are entitled to in law. Hence consideration of parties' legal rights and entitlements cannot safely be relegated and exclusive prominence given to psychological and commercial considerations. People have regard to what they believe a court will award, ie their rights, as their default position.

Mediators encourage the parties to compare their:

- Definitions of fairness with the other side's.
- Default position with whatever proposals are on the table at the mediation and to quantify their chances of doing better.

In practice

- The word 'fair' is used at every mediation.
- Everybody wants to feel fairly treated.
- Most people want to be thought to be acting fairly.
- It's an encouragingly elastic concept.

See also
COGNITIVE BIAS/EMOTION/ULTIMATUM GAME.

Family Mediation

A process where a mediator helps couples resolve issues arising out of divorce or separation. They can be limited to financial issues but can also deal with non-financial issues such as arrangements for children.

There are similarities between family and civil and commercial mediations and mediators. But there are important procedural and philosophical differences. The main ones are:

- Family mediation takes place over a period of time in a number of sessions not all in one go during a single day.
- The process starts with an intake or assessment meeting. This can be held by the mediator with both parties present or just one.
- Most sessions take place in a joint meeting rather than in caucus.
- The same duty of confidentiality does not apply.
- The couple is usually not legally represented although they can seek legal advice at any time.
- Any agreement that is reached is always subject to the approval of the court.
- The range of possible outcomes if the parties do not settle and go to court is usually narrower than in a civil and commercial dispute.
- Family mediators have a different system of accreditation from civil and commercial mediators. In many ways it is more rigorous. Usually they are not members of the CMC.

See also
CAUCUS/CONFIDENTIALITY/MIAM

Family Mediation Council – FMC

The Family Mediation Council is made up of national family mediation organisations in England and Wales. It is analogous to the Civil Mediation Council.

Its members include ADR group, the College of Mediators, the Family Mediators Association, The Law Society, National Family Mediation and Resolution.

Follow up

www.familymediationcouncil.org.uk

Fear

Five fears figure in mediations:

1 Fear of regret

   Aka settler's/buyer's remorse. Parties are worried about selling themselves short and regretting what they have done.

2 Fear of not being needed

   Lawyers and in particular barristers fear this. Is there really anything for them to do at mediation? It is their clients' day. They are the ones in the spotlight. They have to take the decisions. What is there for lawyers to do?

3 Fear of the unknown

   Most clients who attend mediation have never been before and will never go again. It is different for lawyers who attend mediations regularly. The process has to be explained. Real progress at mediation only can take place once the decision-makers, ie the clients, feel at ease with the environment.

Fear

4 Fear of being humiliated

Many clients do not want to attend a Joint Opening Session. They do not want to expose themselves to attack or criticism from the other side's lawyers.

In caucuses, particularly the early ones, they can be reluctant to say much. They do not want to be criticised by either their lawyers for speaking out of turn or by the mediator for saying something inappropriate.

Some clients are afraid of what might be said when they report back. They need to feel they can justify their decision.

5 Fear of responsibility

The classic mediation model emphasises party autonomy. The clients are in control of their dispute and their solution. No one tells them what to do. This is sold as empowering. It is. But with power comes responsibility.

Many decision-makers worry about that responsibility. They:

- Look to their lawyers to be told what to do.
- Ask the mediator what he thinks about the settlement proposal.
- Will say they would prefer to go to trial and let the judge make the decision. Even if the judgment is a worse outcome for them than the settlement that they are being asked to accept they did not make the decision. They can always blame the judge.

In practice

- Everybody at mediation is afraid of something.
- Most of us are reluctant to share a fear.

- As a party at mediation who had been in conflict resolution in Afghanistan said:

  'You make a wrong decision in Helmand someone loses their life. You make a wrong decision at mediation someone loses their money.'
- Keep a sense of proportion.

See also

ADVOCACY/AUTONOMY/BARRISTERS/SETTLER'S REMORSE/SOLICITORS

Fees

Some civil and commercial mediations are done for free – on a pro-bono basis. Most are not. Mediators charge fees for their services.

The basis of charges varies. Originally mediators charged in much the same way that barristers and solicitors did.

- They charged for their time either on an hourly or daily rate.
- Disbursements, eg hotel and travel expenses, were extra.
- Preparation and travel time was often in addition to contact time at the mediation.

All-inclusive fixed fees are now more popular.

Bear in mind the following factors when agreeing fees:

- Is the fee stated per party or for the mediation?
- Does the fee include preparation time? Most quotes include reasonable or expected preparation. This is usually unspecified but some stipulate 2/3 hours. A few include all preparation no matter how much or little time it takes.
- Does the fee include travel time and expenses?

Fees

- How many mediation hours are included? The standard full day mediation is eight hours. But some charge on a seven or ten-hour basis.
- Is overtime chargeable? If so at what rate?
- Does the mediator charge VAT on his fees? A surprising number of civil and commercial mediators are not registered for VAT because their turnover is below the compulsory registration limit.
- Many mediators set their rate on a sliding scale according to the value of the claim/dispute. But more and more charge a day rate for a mediation no matter how complex, valuable or document-heavy.
- Room hire. If the mediation is not being held in a venue supplied by the parties or their lawyers some mediators can provide venues. Sometimes they will be free. More often than not a charge is made. The usual range is £100 to £250 per room per day (2016).
- Do you have to pay the fees in advance of the mediation? Most mediators require this. But by no means all.

Rates vary from as little as £500, including travel and preparation for a day's mediation to £25,000 where there is a great deal of documentation and lots of money at stake. According to the 2016 CEDR Audit the average fee for an experienced mediator for a full-day's mediation was £4,500 and for a less experienced mediator £1,545.

In practice
- Fees are negotiable.
- Fees actually charged are often below the averages given in the CEDR Audit.

Follow up

Walker *Setting Up in Business as a Mediator* Ch 16 Money

CEDR The 2016 Mediation Audit www.cedr.com

Final Offers

Always put forward at mediations. But does anyone at mediation ever really make a final offer?

People do sometimes stop making offers and bring the mediation to an end. But that is often through lack of energy or time.

Every mediator knows about firmly expressed, last, best and final offers being improved to secure a deal. The trouble is that although the decision-maker may know what his final position is he rarely shares it with the mediator or even with his own legal advisers.

Mediators often see advisers calculating a final offer, which is clearly not the same as the one that their clients have in mind.

The Harvard advice is to work out your final walk-away offer or BATNA in advance and to stick to it. This is harder to do than you think. There are often unknowns and variables. The best that most people can do is to have a range, albeit a narrow range, of final offers.

In practice
- A final offer is only final if you make it final and walk away if it is not accepted.
- Final offers often look better with time. Always leave your final offer on the table for 24 hours.

See also
BATNA/HARVARD/TERMINATION/WATNA

First Offers

'We would rather hear from them first'. Mediators often hear these words. But if you want to settle and do a deal why not make a move? Common reasons are:

1. Going first is still seen as a sign of weakness. You are giving away information which could be used against you.
2. You do not believe in the theory of anchoring.
3. You are worried about sending the wrong message to the other side, for example by making an offer that is too low/high so that it will upset them.
4. You are not ready. Amazingly many people turn up to mediations without having worked out what their first offer is. They try and do this on the day. Often they have worked out what their final offer is but not their first one.

England's most successful mediator said that the worst thing for him about mediation was 'the balls-aching first offer'. Another highly successful construction industry mediator has described 'the doom-laden experience of receiving the first offer.'

Hence more mediators are encouraging parties to exchange offers simultaneously rather than sequentially.

In practice:

- Work out your first offer in advance.
- Be clear about what message you want to send to the other side.

See also

ANCHORING/EXCHANGING OFFERS/HEALTH WARNINGS/OFFERS

Flexibility

Fishing Expedition

What your opponents engage on when they repeatedly ask for documents and information.

The opposite of what you engage in when asking for clarification so that you can understand their position better.

You suspect that the persistent questioners do not have the evidence they need to prove their case against you and are hoping to find it by asking you wide-ranging questions. You become chary about disclosing too much or indeed very much at all.

The phrase is often coupled with expressions of suspicion that the other side is only at the mediation for tactical reasons.

In practice

- Everyone takes their fishing rod with them to mediation.
- Most people are there to land a deal not a cache of information.

See also

CROSS-EXAMINATION/DEMONSING/EXPECTATIONS/ DISCLOSURE/QUESTIONS/TACTICAL MEDIATION

Flexibility

Has two separate meanings at mediation:

1 Being able to move from your opening/initial position.
2 Being open minded and able to devise new solutions in the light of new information or thinking.

To do this with confidence you need to know what your core values/principles/objectives are. You cannot make these up on the day. You have to work them out in advance.

Flip Chart

Mediators through opening question will try and find out what your 'needs' are as opposed to your 'positions 'or 'interests'.

Be alert to the danger of the consistency bias. Remember what JM Keynes said: 'When the information changes, I change my mind. What do you do?'

In practice

- No one settles by not moving an inch and sticking to what they have already said.
- Deals are done by discussing proposals.

See also

COGNITIVE BIAS/FLEXIBILITY/MOVEMENT/PIN/ POSITIONS/TRADEABLES

Flip Chart

Where would mediation be without the flipchart? First appearing in 1912 the flipchart as we know it was invented by NOBO in the 1970s.

Flipchart supporters claim that using one helps to:

- Keep people together rather than splitting into separate groups- so use joint sessions rather than caucuses.
- Pinpoint focus by listing issues and to structure discussions by working through the list.
- Generate ideas by encouraging people to say things and then acknowledge they have been said by writing them down.
- Improve comprehension by visual displays of diagrams or calculations.

In practice

- Most civil and commercial mediators do not use flipcharts in joint sessions. Family and community mediators love them.
- Some mediators use them in private sessions – for example to capture an organigram or to summarise a calculation.
- Their use is much less among sophisticated users of mediation who can find the approach too pedagogic and resist being lectured.
- As a rule of thumb the more experienced the mediator the less they use flip charts. But there are some highly successful mediators who swear by them.
- The flip chart is under threat from the whiteboard. Same considerations apply.

See also
JOINT SESSIONS/VISUAL AIDS

Funding

Parties are in receipt of litigation funding when they receive some sort of credit. Traditionally this was a loan from a bank to fund litigation – common for big money divorce cases.

New types of funding are now available:

- *Conditional fee agreements*: The lawyers agree not to receive payment of their fees until the case is concluded. They may not charge anything at all if they lose.
- *Damages-based agreements*: These are contingency fee arrangements. Again the lawyers are not paid until the case is concluded when they receive 'a slice of the action' by way of a percentage of what the client recovers.

Funding

- *Third party funding*: This brings in a new element to the lawyer-client relationship by providing funding from a third party to both the lawyers and the client.
- *Insurance*: there are two types: After-the-Event (ATE) and Before-the-Event (BTE).

Any of these types of litigation funding can complicate mediation. They can:

- Make the party who is in receipt of it feel that they have no risk. They may even think that they have a free ride to trial. Often they are disappointed in this belief. Funders whether lawyers, lenders, investors or insurers are in business to make a profit.
- Cause conflicts between the policyholder under an insurance policy and his insurers. Insurers often have conduct of the claim. They can withdraw cover if they think that the merits of the claim have changed or that a reasonable offer to settle has been received which the policyholder does not want to accept.
- Create conflicts of interest between the lawyers on a CFA or DBA and the client. There's an incentive for lawyers to settle earlier rather than later and avoid the risks of doing a lot of work, losing at trial and therefore not being paid at all.
- Give rise to interesting discussions between clients and lawyers about the terms of their funding arrangements. In particular whether or not the lawyers will waive their success to enable the client to receive the minimum amount in his pocket that he will accept in order to settle.

In practice

- Funding is increasingly important at mediations.
- It never makes a mediation easier.

See also

ALF/ATE/BTE/CFAs/DBAs/LITIGATION FUNDING/ THIRD PARTY FUNDING

G

Game Theory

The science of logical decision-making. Myerson defines it more precisely as 'the study of mathematical models of conflict and cooperation between intelligent rational decision-makers'.

Game theory is taught on negotiation courses. Mediators do not see much evidence of its application at mediations. Occasionally there is reference to the Prisoner's Dilemma to show the benefits of cooperative behaviour and that not all negotiations are zero-sum games.

The fashionable orthodoxy amongst mediation commentators and trainers is that rational decision-making is an impossibility. We are all in the grip of our amygdala and cognitive biases.

In practice

Whether this is true or not:

- Most decision-makers in civil and commercial mediations like to think that they are acting rationally and to be acknowledged as rational decision-makers.
- Mediators encourage decision-makers to engage in decision tree/risk analysis, which in part derives from game theory.

See also

AMYGDALA/COGNITIVE BIAS/DECISON TREE/NASH EQUILIBRIUM/PRISONER'S DILEMMA/RISK ANALYSIS

Follow-up

Roger Myerson *Game Theory: Analysis of conflict*. Harvard University Press (1991)

Richbell *How to Master Commercial Mediation* pp 313–323

Walker *Mediation Advocacy* Ch 7 Risk/Benefit Assessment

Generalists

Who make the best mediators: generalists or specialists?

A topic regularly debated on the mediation circuit. There is a lot of confusion.

- *Specialist mediators*: are expert in the sector or the subject matter in dispute. They have usually worked in the sector or practised in it as lawyers or advisers.
- *Generalist mediators*: do not have that sector expert knowledge. They know about mediating and how to bring parties to a settlement. They may have experience, but not specialist knowledge, of the subject.

Being a mediator who has experience of a particular type of dispute at mediation is not the same as being a specialist mediator. A mediator may mediate several franchise or rights of ways disputes. This does not make him a franchise specialist or expert. It makes him someone who knows how to settle franchise disputes.

Advantages of generalists

- Not having sector expertise they will be readier to concentrate on the settlement process and the personalities present rather than on the technical substance of the dispute.
- Mediators are not there to act as judges or to get to the bottom of all the issues of fact and law. They are there to help parties identify goals, needs and solutions.

Generalists

- Not being a specialist the mediator can ask the simple questions. These can often open up perspectives.
- Not being an expert the mediator will not feel the need to display his expertise in the subject matter and get bogged down on the dance floor. Generalists find it easier to go to the balcony and to take the participants with them.
- Generalists are less prone to cognitive biases such as:
  - The curse of information, ie where so much knowledge is known about the subject that it prevents people thinking about it.
  - Authority bias – the tendency to automatically accept what an authority figure or expert says.
  - The hammer tendency – if the only tool you have is a hammer then every problem looks like a nail.

Why object to a generalist?

Parties say that they prefer a specialist mediator because they think that they will understand the case better and more quickly. This greater understanding will mean that the mediator will both agree with that party and be better equipped to go and explain to the other party the error of their ways.

Disadvantages of generalists

- It can take them longer to bring themselves up to speed on technical issues.
- They will not be as able to meet technical experts on their own technical ground.
- Where the parties have totally misunderstood a technical issue he will not be able to identify the misunderstanding.

In practice

- Such total misunderstandings are more work of forensic imagination than negotiating reality.
- Appointing solicitors admit that they prefer non-specialist mediators when they know that their client's case is weak. The last thing they want is for it to be stress-tested in public.

Give and Take

- With experienced mediators, whether specialist or generalist, this is a forlorn hope. With inexperienced specialist mediators this can happen.
- Generalists ask those who are demanding specialist mediators: would you turn down Henry Kissinger or Kofi Anan?

See also
BALCONY/DANCE FLOOR/SPECIALISTS

Follow up
Walker *Mediation Advocacy* Ch 3 pp 51–58

Give and Take

Is mediation all about compromise?

The clichéd definition of a good settlement is one where everybody goes away feeling unhappy. This can happen. But it does not have to.

In fact people often leave mediations feeling happy that they made a settlement. They do not feel brutalised by the process in the way that litigation or arbitration can make them feel.

As one of the UK's leading commercial mediators has said: compromise is at the heart of mediation as it is at the heart of marriage.

The difficulty is that the word compromise suggests weakness and giving up something. In fact what happens in any good negotiation and mediation is that parties trade concessions.

If a party expects to achieve 100% of their demands and to achieve that by the other side capitulating under attritional arguments they will be disappointed. Hence the application of principled rather than positional negotiation.

In practice
- Never offer a unilateral compromise.
- Always trade concessions.
- Collaborate – don't compromise or concede.

See also
BARGAINING/COMPROMISE/FLEXIBILITY/HARVARD/IF

Global Settlements

Frequently used phrase in mediations to describe a deal which settles all matters between the parties. Settlement is not just limited to the issues contained in the court documents or even correspondence and position papers.

Parties often say that they want a clean break with no future disputes, conflicts or even contact with the other side.

Mediators are keen to find out whether parties want a global settlement. Asking this early on flushes out whether the parties are holding something in reserve or have hidden agendas.

In practice

Problems can arise with global settlements:
- Other potential associated claims. For example a party may have a professional negligence action against its adviser, which gave rise to the dispute. They will not want to give that up without compensation.
- A global settlement may include other entities such as group companies who are not present at the mediation. Who can sign on their behalf?

Goodwill

- A party may be prepared to give up future rights or claims which they do not know about at that moment on the basis of information provided at the time. But they need reassurance. Hence they ask for a warranty that there has been full disclosure or that the global settlement is on the basis of information currently available.

See also
AGENDA/ALL-IN/WARRANTIES

Goodwill

Goodwill between the parties is often absent at mediations. Mediators try to generate some during the day. They usually succeed.

Mediators do this by investing their own stock of goodwill. All mediators start the day with some. With any luck they retain and even increase it. But they can lose it. They therefore try and invest it wisely.

Lack of goodwill can be due to a credibility gap between the parties or simple antipathy and a taste for revenge. Confident mediators expressly identify the causes and invite the parties to suspend their critical disbelief and dislike of each other.

In practice

- A certain operational level of trust and goodwill is needed for any negotiations to succeed.
- If the parties can remember that they are mediating to make peace not war this becomes much easier.

See also
GOOD MANNERS/PEACE

Good Manners

Good manners cost nothing. Bad manners cost deals.

There is simply no point being rude or discourteous towards people who you want to agree with you. Expressing frustration in a bad tempered way does not promote goodwill.

In practice

- Bad manners lead to bad settlements. Good manners lead to better ones.
- Displays of rudeness damage credibility.

See also
EMOTIONS/GOODWILL/VENTING

Government Departments

They are bound by the Dispute Resolution Commitment issued by the Attorney General's office.

Government Departments claim that there are issues which are peculiar to them.

1 *Political factors*. They are often present. Sometimes Ministers are involved in the actual mediation, if not in person then by telephone. These political considerations are similar to the reputational considerations which commercial organisations have to take into account.

2 *Non-commercial organisations*. They emphasise that they cannot take the same commercial view. They say this even when they are acting as a commercial entity for example as an employer in a building contract or purchaser in IT contracts. In reality this is no different from what insurers say about having to consider the interests of their shareholders or policyholders.

3 *Regulators or enforcers*. For example HMRC, which has its own Litigation Settlement Strategy. It is not easy to reconcile the principles of that strategy with the Dispute Resolution Commitment. Regulators have a dual role. Any regulator when trying to settle a dispute has to have regard to its function in enforcing rules or regulations. HMRC is particularly alert to this.

4 *Large teams*. They tend to field larger teams. An issue may overlap different divisions within a department or involve more than one department who all want to be represented.

5 *Confidentiality*. This can be a problem especially with HMRC who say that they cannot be bound if they learn something at mediation that would suggest that there has been tax avoidance or more particularly evasion. This is not unique to government departments. For example office holders such as Insolvency Practitioners often have to carve out of the standard confidentiality provisions to allow them to comply with their statutory duties.

See also

DRC/LSS/OFFICE HOLDERS

Greed

Mediators often see greed at mediations. This is not always from followers of Ivan Boesky's creed that: 'greed is all right... Greed is healthy. You can be greedy and still feel good about yourself'.

Greed is usually seen:

- At the start of the mediation when inflated figures are demanded.
- Towards the end when someone is holding out for a minor additional sum, which cannot make any financial difference to them. In these circumstances greed seems

to be not an insatiable desire for more but an expression of the need:

- to be a winner and score points;
- to be vindicated;
- to inflict pain and obtain revenge;
- to obtain assurance out of feeling of insecurity.

We have different greed levels. Paul Piff provides sobering insights from his research into the effects of wealth on people. It seems that the rich are indeed greedier than the poor.

In practice

- Greed is present at every mediation.
- Most parties eventually restrain any greed impulses in order to achieve settlement.
- Greed is not good at mediations.

Follow up

Paul Piff – www.ted.com/speakers/paul_piff

Ivan Boesky speech University Of California, Berkeley 18 May 1986.

Grievance

All parties at mediation have a sense of grievance. Mediators know that. What they want to find out is how that sense of grievance can be assuaged.

1 One way is by venting. Letting the aggrieved person express their grievance in all its bitterness. Not all mediators agree with this.
2 By making an impact statement.
3 By meeting the other side in private for a heart to heart.

Gross

Feeling aggrieved, and telling the other side that, is one thing. How you express your grievance is quite another.

In practice

- Mediators observe the calming effects on people of feeling that they have been listened to.
- People do not listen when you shout at them.
- Mediation rooms are a better forum than court rooms for obtaining relief for a sense of grievance.

See also
ACKNOWLEDGMENT/VENTING

Gross

Mediators routinely tell the parties at the start of the day that they need to have some working figures.

Leaving aside issues of liability, unless as a matter of arithmetic figures can be agreed settlement will be difficult. How can you agree how big a slice of the pie people are to receive until you know how big the pie is?

A recurring reason why figures can't be agreed is that they are calculated on different bases. When calculations are compared there is often a difference between the use of gross and net figures.

When exchanging offers be clear whether the figures offered are gross or net. Also be clear whether they:

- Include legal costs.
- Are after deduction of the costs of sale if property is going to be sold as part of the settlement.

- Include or exclude VAT.
- Take into account what tax will be paid either by the payee or the receiver.

In practice

- Settlements falter despite apparent good progress when the parties realise that one was talking gross and the other was talking net.
- Too much time is often spent on producing working figures on the mediation day that could have been saved with better preparation.

See also

APPLES AND PEARS/NET/PREPARATION/WORKING FIGURES

Groupthink

The tendency for people in a group to act in a more extreme way than they would if they were acting individually.

Often seen at mediations where people egg each other on and reinforce their self-belief in the strength of their case. Decision-makers worry about losing face with other group members.

In practice

- Not usually an insuperable barrier to settlement but better avoided by fielding as small a team as possible.

See also

CELLAR BLINDNESS/TEAMS/SIZE

Growing the pie

A homely synonym for creating value which all sides to the dispute can share. The recipe is identifying the parties' interests and needs cooperatively working out how they can be satisfied to mutual advantage.

Hence the phrase 'growing the pie'. Much used by mediators in training but never in mediations.

In practice

- Often the only type of pie that can be grown is humble pie. That can still be valuable.
- Everyone at a mediation wants to be acknowledged.

See also

ACKNOWLEDGEMENT/APOLOGIES/HARVARD/ PRINCIPLED NEGOTIATION

H

Haggle

Haggling as in 'We're just haggling' is a pejorative term at mediations. Haggling is not something that principled negotiators do.

At its simplest, haggling is arguing about the price. In some cultures haggling is a daily activity when buying the staples of life. Other cultures rarely do it except when buying a house or car.

Haggling can be a pleasurable tussle of strength between equals or an uncomfortable demeaning affair. Most people at mediations like to think that they are engaged in a higher activity than haggling.

Haggling is a zero sum game. The more that you pay me the less you have in your pocket. But even in well conducted Harvard style value-creating mediation the parties want to claim the value that has been created. There is a distributive element even in the most integrative negotiation.

The key to haggling is:
- Keep your temper.
- Keep smiling.
- Remember flattery gets you everywhere.
- Take baby steps.
- Don't fall in love with the object. If you can't walk away you can't haggle.

In mediations:

- Never let the process become the problem.
- Sometimes the hagglers are so caught up in the contest they lose sight of the problem that they are trying to solve as they tussle over the last £2,000.

In practice

- There is always an element of haggling at mediation.
- Keep it to a minimum.
- Join in and enjoy it for what it is.
- Don't let the activity get in the way of the outcome.

See also

DISTRIBUTATIVE BARGAINING/HORSE TRADING/ZERO-SUM

Halsey

Halsey was a 2004 medical negligence case in the English Court of Appeal that had a huge impact on mediation in the UK.

It set out guidelines for when parties to a dispute can safely ignore going to mediation without the risk of cost sanctions. If you unreasonably refuse to go to mediation you may not be awarded your costs even if you win at trial. The *Halsey* factors are always mentioned. These are:

1. The nature of the dispute.
2. The merits of the case.
3. The extent to which the other settlement methods have been attempted.
4. Whether the costs of ADR would be disproportionately high.
5. Whether delays in setting up and attending ADR would be prejudicial.

6 Whether ADR had a reasonable prospect of success.

The upshot of *Halsey* and the subsequent cases and changes to the CPR is that anybody who refuses to go to mediation risks an adverse costs order even if they win at trial.

In practice

- Despite the clear and repeated warnings from the courts, parties – and particularly their lawyers – are resistant to mediation.
- No one can afford to ignore the *Halsey* factors. To do so is to risk costs sanctions for clients and a negligence action for advisers.
- Not always followed.
- Always useful in freeing up thinking about settlement.

See also

CIVIL PROCEDURE RULES/COSTS

Follow up

Halsey v Milton Keynes NHS Trust [2004] EWCA Civ 576

The Jackson ADR Handbook paras 11.08–11.09

Walker *Mediation Advocacy: Representing Clients in Mediation* paras 8.12–8.14

Harvard – HNP

In the mediation context Harvard means the Harvard Negotiation Project (HNP). Established in December 1979 it developed the method of Harvard Principled Negotiation (HPN).

This has been a massive influence on negotiation. Its basic principles underpin the teaching, if not always the practice, of mediation in most countries.

The five key principles are:

1 Separate the people from the problem.
2 Focus on interests not positions.
3 Invent options for mutual gain.
4 Insist on using objective criteria.
5 Know your BATNA.

See also
BATNA/FACILITATIVE/INTEGRATIVE BARGAINING/ WATNA

Follow up
Fisher and Ury *Getting to Yes*

Apart from being a great book it's a good read.

Heads Of Terms

HOTs appear in all sorts of commercial activities. Aka letters of intent, memorandums of understanding, heads of agreement, term sheets, protocols.

In the negotiation context
They are used:
- At the start of negotiations to set out the issues or principles on which people need to come to agreement.
- At a later stage of discussions as a reminder of where the parties have got to.
- An agenda of items for further discussion.
- To represent an agreement in principle which is subject to either due diligence or formal legal drafting of an agreement.

Heads Of Terms

- In these circumstances they are nearly always said to be not legally binding. The only clauses which might be legally binding are ones relating to:
  - confidentiality
  - exclusivity
  - abortive costs

In a mediation context

HOTs can mean something different. They are an alternative to a settlement agreement.

- The parties have made a lot of progress but have run out of time. They can't draft the formal settlement agreement. But they want to record that they have made progress.
- There may even be an agreement but under the terms of the Mediation Agreement it is not legally binding until both sides have signed a document recording the agreement.

A real danger is confusion over whether there is a legally binding agreement. In the absence of an express statement that the HOTs are legally binding there will not be. Parties can change their mind and nobody can complain. Although they usually do when this happens.

In practice

- If clients have come to an agreement they do not mind being bound by legally binding HOTs. It is their lawyers who are nervous about the outline nature of such a document compared with the completeness of a properly drafted settlement agreement.
- Sometimes commercial daring trumps legal caution and sometimes it doesn't.
- Lawyers have to be careful in not doing what their clients want them to. Remember it's the client's deal.

Heuristics

See also

BODYGUARDS/MEDIATION AGREEMENT/ TERMINATING

Health Warnings

Mediators usually give the parties health warnings before they make offers.

- The process of trying to achieve settlement at mediation is a process of convergence.
- Parties should be careful about setting that process back by the sort of offer that they make.
- Think twice about making the sort of offers that promote reactions such as: 'This is derisory. This is insulting. We're wasting our time. We might as well leave now.'

Whenever you make an offer, whether simultaneously or sequentially, think about:

- what message you want to send with that offer; and
- what message you think that the other party will receive.

In practice

- Health warnings are usually disregarded in the first exchange of offers.
- Health warnings are heeded when both sides realise that all they are doing is irritating each other.

See also

EXCHANGING OFFERS/FIRST OFFERS/OFFERS

Heuristics

These are mental shortcuts that make decision-making easier and quicker.

The simplest and best known is trial and error. Another one we use all the time is stereotyping.

Heuristics are usually coupled with and sometimes confused with cognitive biases.

Be aware of them at mediations.

In practice
- We all use them.
- They save time but can lead to flawed decisions.

See also
COGNITIVE BIASES

Follow up
Kahneman *Thinking, Fast and Slow*

Walker *Mediation Advocacy: Representing Clients in Mediation* Ch 18 Mind Traps

High Conflict

This has a special meaning in mediation devised by family mediators. It does not just mean people are very angry or even violent. Indicators of high conflict are:
- Rigid positions with a black and white view of the world.
- Tendency to blame everybody else for problems.
- Not listening to what is being said to them even when there is communication.
- Absolute confidence they will be vindicated in court.
- Repetitious retelling of their story with no development towards resolution or solution.
- A tendency to attach themselves to the mediator.

High Context/Low Context

In practice

- At nearly every mediation at least one party will display High Conflict behaviour at some time.
- HIgh Conflict behaviour tends to be temporary. If it persists settlements are rarely achieved.

See also

Richbell *How to Master Commercial Mediation* Ch 3 pp 136–141

High Context/Low Context

Another phrase which has a special meaning in mediation. Especially in cross-cultural mediations. It refers to styles of communication.

Based on the work of Edward T Hall a distinction is drawn between those people from low context cultures who tend:

- To be English, American, Australian, German, Dutch or Scandinavian.
- Not to spend time and effort investigating surrounding circumstances but to focus on objective facts.
- To view themselves as open, truthful and direct. They say what they mean and mean what they say.

People from high context cultures tend to:

- Be from France or other Mediterranean nationalities, Asia or the Middle East.
- Place a premium on the surrounding circumstances when interpreting data. Factors such as gesture, tone of voice, posture, social status and setting are vital.
- See themselves as respectful, cautious and polite.

High context communicators see low context communicators as rude, impatient, insensitive, and too direct.

Low context communicators see high context communicators as unreliable, evasive time wasters who will not say what they mean or mean what they say.

In practice

- When communicators are from different contexts confusion is inevitable.
- Skilled negotiators/mediators are aware of this. They try to ameliorate by taking extra care to appear respectful, to listen very carefully and to check at all stages that the message that they are sending is the one that is being received.

See also

ACTIVE LISTENING/CROSS CULTURAL/FACE/ MESSAGE/REFRAMING/SIGNALS/SUMMARISING

Follow up

Richbell *How to Master Commercial Mediation* pp 136–141

CEDR *How to Master Negotiation* Ch 13

Hired Gun

Lawyers, particularly barristers, who sense that their lives lack drama like to describe themselves as hired guns.

At mediations they see their job as exactly the same as in court.

- They are there to argue their client's case not to discuss settlement proposals.
- The have been hired to destroy their clients' opponents. Their preferred weapon is cross-examination.
- They chafe at the restrictions on them to cross-examine the other side.

- They take every opportunity of being adversarial, aggressive, forceful and unyielding.
- They find it easy to criticise and hard to create.

In practice

- Hired guns are barriers to settlement.
- They waste their own time and their clients' money.

See also

ADVOCACY/BARRISTERS/LAWYERS' ROLES/ MEDIATION ADVOCACY

Follow up

Walker *Mediation Advocacy: Representing Clients in Mediation* para 6.22

Horse trading

An even lower form of mediation activity than haggling. Deprecated by all, practised by most.

See also

DISTRIBUTIVE BARGAINING/HAGGLE/ZERO SUM

Hospitality

A neglected topic at mediations. Mediation theorists stress the importance of the physical environment. Not much thought is given to hospitality.

The choice of venue is one thing. What is provided in it is another.

The golden rules are:

- The paying party should always be given the best room. You want them to be relaxed, not tense, so that their generosity is not constrained.
- Water and fresh tea, coffee and biscuits should be available all day long. Usually mediations finish around 5/6 pm. Apples, bananas and oranges are also a good idea. The impact of low blood sugar on decision-making is well documented. People are meaner when they are hungry.
- The idea that exposing people to sensory deprivation increases the chances of settlement is popularly held and regularly disproved.
- Low blood sugar levels have been found to impair cognition and rational decision making
- Keep people fed and watered and connected to the Internet.

See also

SANDWICHES/VENUE – for checklist

Follow up

www.forbes.com>sites>2012/05/22

ftp.iza.org

psycnet.apa.org>journals>bul

Hot Tubbing

Putting the experts together so that they can give evidence or discuss their differences.

Now part of the of the court procedure in England and Wales under CPR Part 35.

Hot Tubbing

Mediators often suggest that the experts meet with them to discuss why they do not agree.

In practice
- Experts are always willing to meet each other to discuss areas of difference. They can't wait to prove that they are right.
- Usually a surprising amount of common ground emerges.

See also
EXPERTS/WITNESSES

Follow up
CPR 35 and Practice Direction 35

www.justice.gov.uk>pd_part35

ICC

Headquartered in Paris, the International Chamber of Commerce was founded in 1919. It has, since 1923, through the International Court of Arbitration, promoted international commercial arbitration. It continues to administer international arbitrations and has administered more than 20,000 cases involving parties and arbitrators from over 180 countries.

More recently it has developed ICC Mediation Rules, which are administered by the ICC International Centre for Mediation.

ICC actively promotes the adoption of and training in mediation.

- For example it has since 2005 run the International Mediation Competition for law students, which in 2016 had 66 universities from over 40 different countries participating.
- Provides useful resources for mediation on its website.
- Operates as a mediation provider.

Follow up

www.iccwbo.org/products-and-services/arbitration-and-adr/mediation/rules/

IDRC

The International Dispute Resolution Centre. Not to be confused with the ICDR which is the International Centre for Dispute Resolution being the international arm of the American Arbitration Association.

IDRC was established in 2000 and is located at 70 Fleet Street near the High Court and the Inns of Court. It is the U.K.'s leading facility for arbitrations and mediations.

Superb facilities for any size or type of mediation. Its annual biscuit bill is legendary.

Follow up

www.idrc.co.uk

If

The most powerful word in negotiation.

Mediation like any other negotiation is a process of trading concessions not making unilateral compromises. Before you make a proposal make sure that you know what you want in return, eg If you can pay within 48 hours we will accept £100K.

At mediation the general rule is that nothing is agreed until everything is agreed. Most mediation agreement stipulate that nothing is legally binding until a document containing all the terms of settlement has been signed by the parties. These are ideal conditions for trading concessions.

In practice

- Using the word 'if' helps preserve the state of suspended commitment.
- 'If' is a much better word to use than 'unless'.

See also

COMPROMISE/NON-BINDING/NOTHING IS AGREED/ RECIPROCITY/YES BUT

Imbalance of Power

Present at many mediations. Something which the EU Code for mediators requires mediators to address.

In practice

- Much easier to recognise and acknowledge than to address.
- Mediators can prevent abuses of any power imbalance.

See also
BALANCE OF POWER/EU CODE OF CONDUCT

IMI (International Mediation Institute)

Based in The Hague the International Mediation Institute is a not-for-profit charity that was established in 2007. Its mission is to develop mediation as a profession in its own right through promoting transparency and high standards of competence.

IMI describes itself as a unique organisation because it:

- Does not provide any services in the market for mediation.
- Has no income-generating activities.
- Is not a membership organisation.
- Is not a referral body.
- Does not compete with anybody else.
- Is internet-based.

It has established international certification programmes for mediators and mediation advocates. These are worth applying for.

On its website there are valuable resources such as decision tree model, online dispute analysis model, model contract clauses and videos and blogs/reading lists/podcasts.

Impact

See also
REGULATION

Follow up

imimediation.org

Impact

A key element in risk assessment.

Parties often work out the likelihood and cost of losing at trial. They rarely work out the impact on their lives or business. Your chance of losing may only be 1:4 but the impact if you lose is devastating – you go out of business or lose your home. Paying a premium to buy off this risk is an attractive option.

Can you afford to pay it? Can you afford not to pay it? An eternal question at mediations.

Impacts can be positive as well as negative. For example:

- By settling, a business being able to release provisions for legal costs and damages can be an immediate benefit.
- The freeing up of time of senior management to concentrate on the business of the business not on the downtime of litigation.

In practice

- Mediators ask 'What if' questions. Often parties need time to answer. They have not thought about these before.
- Parties need to compare:
    - the negative impact of losing at trial with the positive impact of settlement; and
    - the positive impact of winning at trial with the negative impact of settlement.

There is never a positive impact of losing at trial.

See also
DECISION TREE/IMPACT STATEMENTS/RISK/ UNCERTAINTY

Impact Statements

Usually made at the Joint Opening Session. Clients often want to say something at mediation.

Their lawyers worry about what they may say in the heat of the moment. It could be damaging if the client speaks uninhibitedly at a Joint Opening Session. How to balance the client's need for expression with prudence?

In practice

It's better if the client:

- Does not present the assessment of the problem or their case.
- Confines themselves to making an impact statement.
- If the client speaks after their lawyer.
- Explains what the impact of the dispute, injury, bankruptcy etc has had on them, their business/family and their lives.
- Delivered sincerely and concisely impact statements can have a big emotional influence on the other side's decision-maker.

See also
ACKNOWLEDGEMENT/JOINT OPENING SESSION/ VENTING

Follow up

Walker *Mediation Advocacy: Representing Clients at Mediation* p 186–188

Impartiality

An essential quality in mediators but generates much debate and confusion.

- Is impartiality the same as neutrality?
- Are either of them in fact attainable?

Mediators are human just like the parties and their lawyers. They have their own prejudices, biases and influences. Try as they might they will not be able to completely exclude them from their own conduct at mediation. Good mediators are aware of them and control them.

In reality impartiality and neutrality are often used synonymously.

The key difference is that neutrality defines a mediator's position to the parties of the dispute. Impartiality defines his conduct towards the parties.

You can be neutral but not impartial. You can be impartial but not neutral. Parties expect mediators:

- Not to favour one party or the other.
- Not to take against any party.
- Not to have a personal interest in the outcome of the mediation.
- To treat all parties in an even-handed and fair way.
- To be trustworthy.
- To avoid conflicts of interest.

Therefore mediators should:

- Disclose any prior relationship or dealings with any of the parties.
- Scrupulously observe the duty of confidentiality.
- Not accept success fees.
- Not accept presents from any of the parties.

- Refrain from expressing their personal views about the merits of the parties' cases unless expressly asked to do so.
- Accurately relay messages/information/proposals from one room to the other.
- Treat everybody with the same degree of courtesy and formality.

In practice
- There is little evidence of lack of impartiality.
- If you feel that the mediator is not being impartial tell him.
- You may feel under fire if the reality testing is too robust and be tempted to think that the mediator is biased against you. Ask him if he is beating up the other room as well.

See also
BIAS/NEUTRALITY/REALITY TESTING

Follow up
Bernard Mayer *Beyond Neutrality*

Indemnity

An agreement where one person agrees to hold another person harmless. In other words pay any liability which they incur.

An indemnity is similar to but different from a guarantee because the indemnifier is the primary debtor. A guarantor is a secondary debtor.

At mediation:
- As part of a settlement one party may agree to pursue a third party (who is not a party to the mediation) for damages. Any recovery will be shared with the other party to the mediation. They usually seek an indemnity

Indicative

against any costs or expenses which they incur in doing this.

- The phrase 'limit of indemnity' is also heard. This refers to the maximum amount under an insurance policy that the insurer is liable to pay out.

In practice

- If you think that an indemnity (or guarantee) will be part of a settlement take a template with you. Drafting them from scratch wastes so much time at mediations.
- Remember an indemnity is only worth what the person giving it is worth.

See also
INSURERS

Indicative

A mediation style that is apparently a halfway house between evaluative and facilitative mediation.

The mediator:

- Does not give his own views on the merits of the case or the likely outcome at trial.
- Indicates the legal hurdles which the parties will have to overcome in order to succeed at trial. This encourages the parties to consider how easy it will be for them to jump those hurdles. It's another form of reality testing.

Said to be practised to great effect by the judges in the Employment Tribunals who do judicial mediations.

In practice

- The indicative style is used in most mediations to some degree as part of reality testing.
- Is often a synonym for evaluative.

See also
EVALUATIVE/ET/FACILITATIVE/REALITY TESTING

Informality

Mediations are not as formal as court hearings. Mediators are trained to encourage people to feel relaxed and at ease. This makes it easier for them to open up and speak frankly.

Mediators often ask the parties if they would like to be addressed by their first name. Some mediators go further and ask people – even the lawyers – not to turn up in suits.

Others insist on everybody being referred to as Mr or Mrs/Ms. They want to preserve a professional distance. Although ADR may stand for an Amicable Dispute Resolution they do not want to appear over-friendly with any particular party.

Usually during the day the atmosphere becomes more informal as people get used to each other. But it can change. The degree of informality is stress-tested if the mood turns antagonistic.

Mediators should be polite, courteous and open towards the parties and their representatives. To start with it is safer to be formal rather than informal in modes of address and conduct.

In practice
- People work out their comfort level of informality.
- People do business with people they like. So be likeable.

See also
CIALDINI'S BIG 6/GOOD MANNERS/INTERPERSONAL SKILLS/RAPPORT

In Place of Strife

A mediation provider that operates an invitation-only panel of experienced mediators.

Follow up

www.mediate.co.uk

Information Exchange

People in dispute often have different perspectives because they have different information available to them. Mediators try to achieve as much pooling of information as possible.

In practice

- Information gaps are one of the biggest obstacles to settlement in mediations.
- Know in advance what you want to know about the other side.
- Have your information ready to disclose if the mediator asks.
- Be as open as you can. Playing your cards close to your chest suggests that you have a weak hand.

See also

DISCLOSURE/EXCHANGE/PREPARATION/THREE STAGE PROCESS

Insurers

Insurers are leading actors in the mediation world. Their involvement arises in four ways:

1. They insure one of the parties in respect of the claim. For example professional indemnity or employers' liability claims. They are usually representing the defendants.

Insurers

2 They provide legal expenses insurance. They do not insure the damages part of the claim. They can be representing either defendants or claimants in providing either Before-The-Event or After-The-Event insurance.

3 They bring subrogation claims. Although usually brought in the name of their insured the insurers in fact bring the claim in order to recover their outlays.

4 They are in dispute with the policyholder about coverage or the conduct of a claim.

In (1) and (2) insurers are not a party. But they do have considerable influence over the conduct of the claim and whether or not settlement terms can be agreed.

They may not have the absolute final decision on whether or not a proposal should be accepted. Their ultimate sanction is to withdraw cover and to leave the party uninsured.

In (3) and (4) they are the party who makes the decision.

Insurers are serial users of mediation. Their claims handlers are often very experienced. Although they take external legal advice they usually have their own opinions, which they are not reluctant to express.

Insurers often do not attend the mediation. They rely upon telephone reports from their lawyers. This usually slows down settlement momentum.

In practice

Most insurers:

- While constantly saying that they want to reduce claims handling costs and to pay promptly on proper claims, have not embraced mediation.
- When they attend mediation can be formulaic. They like to wait until mid-afternoon to make an offer.

- Tend to regard mediations as mini-trials and often appear to take an un-commercial and overly legalistic approach.
- Do not realise that their chances of settlement are higher when they attend the mediation.

See also
ATE/BTE/PI INSURANCE

Intake Meeting

An initial assessment meeting held by the mediator with the parties either individually or together to discuss whether or not their dispute is suitable for mediation.

Currently in England and Wales these are compulsory in family proceedings. They are referred to as MIAMS (Mediation and Information Assessment Meetings).

The Government is considering introducing them for civil cases as well.

See also
FAMILY MEDIATION/MIAMS

Integrative Bargaining

The opposite of distributive or positional bargaining. Here the parties try and grow the pie to create greater value by combining the interests of the parties.

- It emphasises the value and benefit of cooperative rather than confrontational behaviour.
- It does not treat negotiation as a zero-sum game.
- It looks for win-win solutions.

Interest

In practice

- Always referred to at mediations but not always adopted.

See also

DISTRIBUTIVE/FACILITATIVE/GROWING THE PIE/ HARVARD/POSITIONAL

Interest

Features at every mediation in the sense of being money payable in addition to the principal claim.

The four main types are:

- *Contractual* – where the rate is stipulated in the agreement.
- *Statutory* – for example under the Late Payment of Commercial Debts (Interest) Act 1998 the rate is 8% above base rate.
- *Discretionary* – what the courts will order in addition to damages. The period and rate is discretionary.
- *Judgment* – on the judgment debt until it is paid. The rate is 8%.

In the absence of contractual or statutory interest most parties still claim 8% for pre-judgment debt even though the courts in 2016 are awarding around 50% of that.

Most settlement agreements provide that interest shall be payable on instalments but not always and sometimes only in the event of default.

In practice

- The interest element of any claim is something that the receiving party is usually willing to discount.

Interests

Referred to in every mediation book and training session. Distinguished from positions and needs.

- Positions are what you say you want, ie what you would ideally like.
- Interests are what would benefit you, ie what you would like to have if you can.
- Needs are what you have to have, ie what is necessary

Mediators encourage parties to focus on needs and interests. The more that interests can be satisfied the more likely there is to be a settlement that everybody can be happy with. If needs cannot be met the chances of a settlement are reduced.

Hence parties must be very clear in advance about what are their:

- Real needs.
- Realistic interests.

Don't confuse them. Carry out a Pre-Mediation Analysis (PMA).

In practice

- Clients do not always know what their interests are.
- Clients often do not tell the mediator or their lawyers what they are.

See also
LIM/PMA

Interpersonal Skills

Valued and vaunted by mediators. Not always possessed by them.

They are told to be patient friendly, humorous, empathetic, wise, positive and humble.

In practice

- Even some successful mediators have a restricted range of them.

See also

ACTIVE LISTENING EMPATHY/GOOD MANNERS/OPEN QUESTIONS/SYMPATHY/UNICORN MEDIATOR

Interventions

The current orthodoxy is that mediators are neither evaluative nor facilitative. They are interventionist.

In other words they make suggestions or ask questions to help the parties find their way through the undergrowth of disputed facts and law to the path of settlement.

Conventionally defined according to the Heron model. This divides interventions into authoritative and facilitative.

Authoritative ones are:

- Prescriptive – 'I think that you need to reconsider…'
- Informative – 'If you look at it from their point of view then you can…'
- Confronting – 'How have you calculated your risk?

Facilitative ones are:

- Cathartic – 'How do you feel about this?'
- Catalytic – 'What would happen if you…?'
- Supportive – 'That's a very helpful suggestion.'

See also
EVALUATIVE/FACILITATIVE/INDICATIVE/QUESTIONS

Follow up

Heron *Helping the Client* 5th edn

Walker *Mediation Advocacy: Representing Clients in Mediation* paras 4.19–20

Intimidation

Physical intimidation with violence, threats, table-banging, shouting and aggressive gestures does take place at mediations. Far more common at community and family mediations than at civil and commercial ones.

Verbal intimidation is encountered at civil and commercial mediations. Some parties, or more likely their lawyers, want to dominate the proceedings.

- They talk about giving the mediator a hard time.
- They seek to undermine his authority by taking control of the process and convincing everybody at the mediation that they know more about the dispute than anybody else and so what they say must be right.
- They try to intimidate their opposite number by personal attack on their competence as well as extravagant criticism of their factual analysis.

In practice
- If the objective is to derail settlement it works.
- If the objective is to promote settlement it does not.

See also
ADVOCACY/GOOD MANNERS/MEDIATION ADVOCACY

J

Jackson

In UK mediation circles Jackson means two things:

1 *The Jackson ADR Handbook* published in 2013 (2nd edn, 2016).

   Sir Rupert Jackson having reported on his Costs Review called for a 'a single authoritative handbook, explaining clearly and precisely what ADR is (without either 'hype' or jargon) and giving details of all reputable providers of mediation.'

   Lord Dyson, the then Master of the Rolls said: 'this book deserves to be the first and only port of call for every student of ADR irrespective of whether they are a litigant, a law student, a lawyer, or a judge. I'm sure that it will be.'

   A team of three academics from the City Law School City University in London produced the book. They were helped by an editorial advisory board of 16 and The Judicial College, The Civil Justice Council, the Civil Mediation Council jointly endorsed it.

   This collectivist provenance guaranteed a rather bland text. It has not become the first and only port of call as Lord Dyson anticipated. Instead:

   - Anybody taking an academic course in mediation will find it very useful.
   - Busy practitioners and anyone attending mediations wanting practical help, especially if they are not lawyers, will find it much less useful.

- Several High Court judgments have referred to it when the court was considering whether there has been an unreasonable refusal to participate in mediation.

2 Legal costs.

In 2009 Sir Rupert Jackson produced the Review of Civil Litigation Costs Final Report. The mantra was that litigation was becoming too expensive for everybody:

- Users, ie the parties.
- Providers, ie the Court Service.
- Funders, ie the Government and the Legal Aid system.

He made many recommendations. One was the more active promotion of mediation as an alternative to litigating through the court system.

This recommendation, which has been implemented through the CPR and various court judgments was expected to be transformational for the mediation industry. It has not been. The take-up of civil mediation in England and Wales is still disappointingly low.

The 2016 CEDR Audit estimates that there were 10,000 civil and commercial mediations in England and Wales in 2015.

One trigger for transformation was expected to be changing legal costs rules on recovering ATE insurance premiums or CFA success fees. Successful parties at trial can no longer claim them from their opponents. They have to pay them themselves.

Many mediation purists are concerned that:

- Judicial impetus towards mediation is driven by cost considerations rather than by a desire for justice, party autonomy or self-determination. Judges and their employers – the Government – want fewer people using court facilities because they are too expensive. Instead, they say, go private and mediate.

JAMS (Judicial Arbitration and mediation Services)

- Mediation is seen a denial of justice not as an access to it. Strangely this view does not seem to be shared by the clients who mediate and come away with a settlement of their dispute.

In practice

- The *Handbook* needs to be consulted regularly by lawyers so that they are aware of the official guidance given to judges.
- Judicial enthusiasm for mediation is costs orientated and patchy.

See also

ATE/CFA/COSTS/CONTIGENCY FEES/JUSTICE/ MEDIATION.

Follow up

CEDR Mediation Audit 2016 www.cedr.com

JAMS (Judicial Arbitration and Mediation Services)

JAMS claims to be the largest private alternative dispute resolution provider in the world. Founded in 1979 and headquartered in Irvine California it has some 300 full-time neutrals.

JAMS provides a range of ADR options including facilitative and evaluative mediation, binding arbitration, neutral case evaluation, settlement conference, mini-trial, summary jury trial, neutral expert fact-finding, special master, discovery referee, class action settlement adjudication, project neutral and dispute review board services.

In 2011 JAMS International, headquartered in Fleet Street London was formed.

Most JAMS mediators in the USA are former judges. Their style is evaluative rather than facilitative. They nearly always provide a mediator's proposal. They do not follow the Harvard Model of Mediation although individual mediators might use some of the HNP principles.

In the UK the panel is drawn more widely from senior London-based lawyers who have specialised in commercial litigation.

In practice

JAMS provides:

- More arbitration than mediation in UK.
- Tends to be more evaluative than facilitative in its approach.

See also

HARVARD/MEDIATOR'S PROPOSAL/PANELS

Follow Up

www.jamsadr.com

www.jamsinternational.com

Joint Opening Sessions

The death of the Joint Opening Session is a topic regularly debated by mediators. Certainly it is falling out of fashion among sophisticated users of mediation.

The original reasons for holding a Joint Opening Session were to:

- Enable the mediator to explain the ground rules to everybody at the same time.
- Check that the parties present had the necessary authority to settle.

Joint Opening Sessions

- Set the mood for settlement by emphasising the non-adversarial nature of the process.
- Give the parties and their representatives the chance of speaking directly to the mediator and to each other.

Most mediators prefer to have a Joint Opening Session. Some insist upon it. They think that it is not a good omen if the parties cannot even say "Good morning" to each other or nod when the mediator asks if they have authority to settle.

Common objections to Joint Opening Sessions are:

- Relations between the parties are so bad that there will be a row, which will set back the process of settlement.
- One party feels intimidated by the other.
- The parties and particularly their lawyers have been corresponding about the case for so long that everybody knows all the details and the points that can be made. They just want to cut to the chase.

Many parties and their advocates make the mistake of thinking that the Joint Opening Session is like an opening speech in court. They:

- Make all their best legal and evidential points.
- Try to convince the other side that they are going to lose at trial.
- Load up the other side with a sense of guilt.

This approach never works. When people are attacked their defences go up. The whole point of mediation is to get people to open up not close up

Advocates who provide a reasoned and reasonable assessment of the overall situation rather than a tendentious and partisan presentation of their own case achieve much better results. They appear credible and business-like. The other side are encouraged to think that settlement is possible.

In practice

- Increasingly mediations do not begin with a Joint Opening Session. This seems to have little impact on settlement rates.
- If you have one use it to explain your position and your understanding of the other side's position. Do not just attack the other side.
- Joint Opening Sessions do more good than harm.

See also

ADVERSARIAL/ATTACK/AMYGDALA/ADVOCACY/ ASSESSMENT/CUT TO THE CHASE/MEDIATOR'S OPENING STATEMENT

Follow up

Walker *Mediation Advocacy: Representing Clients in Mediation* Ch 10 pp 185–191

Joint Sessions

Another contentious issue in the mediation community. Should mediations be conducted in joint sessions or in private ones (caucuses)?

Most civil and commercial mediations in England and Wales are conducted on the caucus basis. Family mediations are conducted on the joint session basis. Workplace and community mediators use both models.

Supporters of the joint session says that it allows the parties to:

- Have greater autonomy.
- Have more control over the content of the discussion as well as the outcome.
- Have more opportunity to see that they are being heard and acknowledged.

Joint Sessions

- Experience more readily and openly what the other party is feeling.
- Feel more willing to engage in collaborative behaviour if they are together for longer.
- Be more involved in what is going on than if they are in separate rooms with their involvement being limited to when the mediator is present with them in their room.
- Have more control over the process. In particular it restricts the power of the mediator to manipulate parties. In the caucus model the mediator has a secret weapon, ie only the mediator knows what is happening in both rooms.

Supporters of the caucus models say:

- Joint sessions often degenerate into arguments and do not develop into discussions.
- Parties and in particular their lawyers cannot resist the temptation to score points.
- Lawyers feel the need to grandstand and show off in front of their clients.
- Not everybody has the same capacity for self-disclosure. Some people simply like to discuss things in private before doing it in public.
- It is naive to expect people in dispute who have invested time, money and energy to suddenly feel able to discuss everything openly with their sworn enemy.
- In reality the parties and their lawyers rarely are completely frank and open with the mediator or each other let alone with their opponents.
- Not many lawyers believe that their clients have told them everything that would be useful.
- A mediator who only uses joint sessions can end up being a moderator rather than a mediator. His value to the parties is reduced if he cannot have open and frank conversations in private with one party.

- Shuttle diplomacy gives the parties an opportunity to have private time in which to reflect on what has been discussed with the mediator during a caucus while the mediator is having a caucus with the other side in their room.
- The more vulnerable party, and there is usually one party that is more vulnerable than the other at mediations, can feel intimidated in joint sessions.

In practice
- Most civil and commercial mediations use the caucus model.
- It is rare for there not to be at least one joint session with some if not all of the attendees.

See also
CAUCUS/SHUTTLE

Jordan Order

One of the tools available to judges when exercising active case management.

As part of CPR P D 29 para 4.10(9) the court can direct parties to consider ADR at CMC. They make ADR orders sometimes referred to as Ungly orders or Jordan borders.

See also
CASE MANAGEMENT CONFERENCE

Follow Up
CPR PD 29, para 4.10(9)

Joint Settlement Meetings ('JSMs')

Joint Settlement Meetings ('JSMs')

Aka Round Table Meetings ('RTMs') or Three Room Meetings.

Key Features

- There is nothing new about these procedures. The parties to the dispute meet to try and settle it.
- No third-party neutral is involved.
- They have been described as mediation without a mediator. This is more confusing than helpful. Mediation has been described as assisted negotiation. If that is correct then JSMs are unassisted negotiation. They have nothing to do with mediation.
- Their use has increased given the courts' encouragement to parties to try and settle. Some judges regard them as a form of ADR. If they are at all, they are a very weak form of ADR.
- The Three Room Meeting is a variation that proved popular in personal injury cases. There is a joint session and then the parties break up into their private rooms. The barristers go into the Third Room and have private discussions in the absence of their clients. They come back and report what has being going on.

Pros

- They are cheaper. You do not have to pay the mediator's fees. But barristers are usually also instructed on both sides so there are their fees to include.
- They can be quicker to arrange because you do not have to worry about the mediator's availability.
- They are more informal and do not generally last as long as mediations although they can go on for hours.

Joint Settlement Meetings ('JSMs')

Cons

- They are not significantly cheaper. The only difference in cost between a well-prepared JSM or RTM and mediation is the cost of the mediator. The advantages of having a third-party neutral present far outweigh the cost. A significant number of mediations take place after a JSM and or RTM has failed, which means that there is an extra layer of cost.
- There is no agreed procedure which is monitored by a Third-Party Neutral. This gives more scope for people to play games instead of attending to the job in hand which is to achieve a settlement.
- There is less reality checking so that parties maintain their positions longer.
- There is no external source of encouragement to keep the parties engaged and the momentum going when they reach the Wall at 15.30.
- Most lawyers at JSMs or RTMs cannot resist the forensic urge to argue their case. They see their job as demolishing the other side's case. They cannot easily resist the temptation to grandstand in front of their clients. To be fair some of the clients demand a bravura forensic display on their behalf.
- They tend to be lawyer-dominated with the clients having less personal input into the discussion than at mediation.
- Clients do not have the same opportunity of being acknowledged by a new audience, ie the mediator.
- There is no one who actually has a duty to address any imbalance of power and to make sure that the powerful, well-resourced and represented party does not try and intimidate the other weaker and poorer party.

In practice

- They sometimes work.
- Generally they do not work as well as mediation.

- Personal injury lawyers are clinging on to them.

See also

RTMs (Round Table Meetings)/THIRD PARTY NEUTRAL (TPN)

Judicial mediation

In England and Wales this is practised in the Technology and Construction Court (TCC) and in the Employment Tribunals (ET).

The rules and procedures are different but there are some common principles:

- A judge acts as a mediator. That judge can no longer take part in the litigation process.

- The mediation usually takes place when the case has been developed. Pleadings or statement of case have been exchanged and disclosure or even exchange of witness statements have often also been concluded.

- Judicial mediators see it as their job to narrow the issues and to confront the parties with the reality of their legal positions by indicating the legal obstacles that they will have to overcome at trial in order to succeed. This is sometimes referred to as being indicative.

- Some judicial mediators practice a model that is very close to being Early Neutral Evaluation.

Many mediation users and commentators regard judicial mediations as:

- Settlement conferences. They are usually limited to sorting out the issues in the case as legally formulated. They are not able to encourage creative solution finding by the parties.

- A waste of time. Judges should be spending their time doing what they do best namely judging. If they did that

Justice

rather than mediating it would speed up the time taken to hear cases and to deliver judgments.

But lawyers particularly those who appear as advocates in the TCC and ET on a regular basis quite like judicial mediation. They are in a familiar forum before a tribunal that they normally work with. It's not like appearing in a solicitor's office with a mediator that they have never heard of let alone met before. In other words they are in their comfort zone.

In practice

- Not much used. Some judges seem to want to do more of it.
- A better use of scarce judicial resources is to let judges judge and mediators mediate.

See also

TCC/ET/INDICATIVE

Justice

What clients at most mediations say that they want.

Above the doorway of the Federal Supreme Court of Switzerland in Lausanne are carved the words: 'Lex, Justitia, Pax', ie law, justice, peace.

How many people think that all three concepts can be obtained in a courtroom no matter how federal or supreme? Remember the words of Justice Oliver Wendell Holmes: 'This is a court of law not a court of justice'.

Mediation supporters believe that all three can be obtained at mediation by negotiation and cooperation between the parties.

In reality there is no universal definition of justice. Most disputing parties interpret it in a self-serving way that fits their own interpretation of their legal rights.

Justice

Of the three concepts

- Law is the least important factor at mediation.
- Justice at mediation depends on the parties' own interpretation of justice, not as in court on a judge's interpretation.
- Peace follows if a settlement is voluntarily reached not compulsorily imposed.

Some commentators believe that mediation is inimical to justice. Prof Hazell Genn has eloquently if stridently asserted that mediation can be a denial of justice. In her words mediation is 'not about a just settlement it's just about settlement.'

She overlooks the fact that settlement is often what people actually want. Especially those who have been in dispute for any length of time. They want peace above justice or law.

Above all they want to be acknowledged and to be treated fairly. If they can feel that this has happened they are usually satisfied with the outcome. Who is to say that they are wrong to want this?

In practice

Bear in mind the following words:

- 'Injustice is relatively easy to bear: it is justice that hurts.' HL Mencken
- 'There is no such thing as justice; in or out of court.' Clarence Darrow

See also

ACKNOWLEDGMENT/FAIRNESS

Follow up

Hazel Genn *The Hamlyn Lectures 2008*

K

Killer Points/Questions

These are the ones that all cross-examiners love. They ask them and watch the witness squirm.

Opportunities are limited at mediation for clients and their lawyers to ask direct killer questions. But mediators can ask them.

Some mediators think that their job is to destabilise the parties and their advisers. They want to shake their confidence in their position and legal case.

Others simply ask questions which go to the heart of the matter. They are not trying to destabilise anybody, just clear through the undergrowth of points, positions, and detail to see the path to settlement.

In practice

When preparing for mediation think about what questions:

- You would ask yourself if you were the mediator.
- You want the mediator to ask the other side.

See also
EVALUATIVE/QUESTIONS/REALITY TESTING

Kilmann Test

A conflict style inventory.

Know Yourself

See also
PERSONALITY/THOMAS-KILMANN MODEL

Kipling

An English writer who gave rise to one of the worst jokes ever.

Q 'Do you like Kipling?'

A 'I don't know. I've never been kipled.'

But Kipling did provide a useful mnemonic for mediators.

'I keep six honest serving-men

(They taught me all I knew);

Their names are What and Why and When

And How and Where and Who'

In practice
- These are the open questions, which every mediator is trained to use and everybody attending mediation should be ready to answer.

Know Yourself

Work out what your own values, influences and biases are. If you are aware of them you can spot when they start to influence your conduct and in particular decision-making at mediations.

You can take tests such as the Thomas-Kilmann or Myers Briggs which will assign you to a predetermined category. Or you can reflect on what you tend to do or avoid doing, what pleases you or annoys you.

In practice

- At mediations monitor your own weaknesses and play to your strengths.

See also

Thomas-Kilmann Model

Follow up

www.myersbriggs.org/mymbti-personality-type/mbti-basics

Kubler Ross Grief Cycle

Aka DABDA.

Describes the five stages of coping with loss:

- denial
- anger
- bargaining
- depression
- acceptance

Originally designed to describe the grief following bereavement. Similar stages of behaviour can be observed at mediations. Some theorists have imported it into mediation saying that you have to let parties move through the stages during the mediation process.

The Kubler Ross cycle has been challenged. It is based on very little evidence. The current orthodoxy is that grief is not linear.

In practice

- Some parties at mediation are in denial, angry, and depressed.

Kubler Ross Grief Cycle

- Some also achieve acceptance through bargaining.
- Practitioners never refer to it at mediations.

See also
NARRATIVE/THERAPEUTIC/TRANSFORMITIVE

L

Law

In theory

The relationship between law and mediation is a troubled one.

Are they in opposition? Do they complement each other? Can mediation be effective without the law in the background? Can it be effective with the law in the foreground?

Some mediators say that:

- Disputes are settled not on the basis of legal rights but on the basis of commercial interests and personal needs.
- Deals are done not by arguing about evidential and legal points but by discussing proposals.
- Mediations are not mini-trials or arbitrations.
- Mediators are not judges.

Mediators who emphasise this approach tend to be non-lawyers. This is understandable as they usually know no law.

Others, including the most senior judiciary, say that:

- Mediation takes place in the shadow of the law.
- At mediations lawyers and their clients assert their legal position and the law.
- The law is the default position. If the parties cannot reach a settlement they have the option to continue to trial.
- A party's conception of fairness is related to their understanding of their legal entitlements.

Mediators who emphasise this tend to be lawyers. This is understandable as they sell legal advice or enforce the law.

In practice

Mediators may not like it but mediation in the UK takes place under the general supervision of the courts. Parties can apply to the courts to:

- Enforce a contractual obligation to undertake mediation.
- Set aside an agreement made in mediation.
- Decide whether or not a binding agreement was made at mediation.

To help them do this the English courts have decided that they can look behind the veil of confidentiality and consider the conduct of the parties.

- But law and legal principles do not predominate in securing settlements at mediation. Parties let their personal or commercial interests override the legal points made on their behalf by their lawyers.
- Paradoxically, despite law not being the most important factor at civil and commercial mediations, the market prefers lawyer mediators to non-lawyer mediators.

See also
CONFIDENTIALITY/DURESS/WATERFALL CLAUSES

Lawyers

At least one lawyer is present at most civil and commercial mediations in England and Wales – either as a mediator or as a representative. By contrast most family, workplace and community mediations do not have a lawyer representative present – but the mediator may be a lawyer.

The main reason is that community and workplace mediations are not intended to result in legally binding agreements. Civil and commercial mediations are.

Lawyers

Family mediations usually result in a Memorandum of Understanding. This is the basis of a legally binding agreement that has to be converted into a Consent Order to be approved by the court. Parties to family mediation often take legal advice at this stage.

You do not need to take a lawyer to mediation for it to be successful. The one area where most non-lawyer clients feel exposed is drafting a legally binding agreement. In reality if both parties are unrepresented the mediator does it. Otherwise non-binding heads of agreement can be signed and sent to the lawyers to be turned into a legally binding formal document.

Lawyers can be barriers to settlement at mediation. They can take an overly legalistic view.

Lawyers are the gatekeepers of mediation in England and Wales. This applies to both family and civcom mediation. It is less true of workplace and community mediation. In other words people in dispute go to their lawyers who point them in direction of mediation and help select the mediator.

Many academic commentators complain that mediation has become colonised by lawyers and has lost its original party-based freedom and empowerment. They acknowledge with sadness that this trend does not look like abating. But CEDR reported in their 2016 Mediation Audit that 57% of civil and commercial mediators are non-lawyers. This is the first time that non-lawyers have been in the majority.

In practice

- Lawyer mediators find it easier to obtain appointments.
- Most civil and commercial mediation clients prefer lawyer mediators.
- Lawyers are present, directly or indirectly, at nearly every mediation.

Lawyers – Roles

See also
BARRISTERS/LAWYERS-ROLES/SOLICITORS

Follow up

Booker *Mediation Law*

Walker *Mediation Advocacy: Representing Clients in Mediation* paras 6.94–104

Lawyers – Roles

Lawyers can be confused about their role at mediation. In practice they see themselves as:

- Hired Gun – they destroy the other side.
- Bodyguard – they protect their client from the mediator, the other side and himself.
- Coach – they nudge, show and guide the client towards achieving what he wants by way of settlement.

In practice

- The golden rule for lawyers is: Do not become part of the problem. Stay part of the solution.
- Do not become an obstacle to settlement.
- Never fall out with your opposite number so badly that you cannot be used as a communication channel.

See also
BODYGUARD/COACH/HIRED GUN/MEDIATION ADVOCACY

Follow up

Walker *Mediation Advocacy: Representing Clients in Mediation* para 6.22

LIM

Useful acronym in negotiation:

L stands for Like

I stands for Intends

M stands for Must

Helps people identify and structure their priorities.

In practice
- All parties at mediation have to prioritise.
- This is much easier if they have thought about their priorities in advance.

See also

ASPIRATIONS/GOALS/PMA/RISK PROFILE/ STRATEGY/WALK AWAY FIGURE

Listening

Clients and advocates who spend most of their time at mediations listening instead of talking end up with better outcomes. Clients and advocates should practise Active Listening. If you find yourself thinking of the next question before the speaker has finished answering your first question you need to do this. Mediators are trained in Active Listening

Take a self audit on active listening and consciously listen to yourself.

In practice
- At mediation people generally prefer to talk rather than listen.
- Seasoned negotiators prefer to listen rather than talk.

See also
ACTIVE LISTENING

Follow-up
See the audit at Walker *Mediation Advocacy: Representing Clients in Mediation* p 106

Litigants In Person (LIPs)

People who represent themselves in litigation without a lawyer.

In England and Wales the withdrawal of Legal Aid has meant that there are many more LIPs. Judges complain that this increase of LIPs appearing before them leads to delay, confusion, greater expense and more work for them.

Mediators have also seen an increase in the number of disputants in person representing themselves (DIPs). This does not make their job harder except when it comes to drawing up settlement agreements.

In practice
- Do not be afraid of going to mediation without legal representation.
- Do find out what you have to do to get the best out of the process.

See also
DIPS

Follow-up

Walker *Mediation Advocacy: Representing Clients in Mediation* Ch 19 on Self-Advocacy

The Litigation and Settlement Strategy (LSS) – HMRC

HMRC (Her Majesty's Customs and Revenue) are more prepared to mediate tax disputes including back tax cases. They are a Government department but appear to have an idiosyncratic interpretation of the Attorney-General's pledge.

In 2007 they promulgated the LSS (The Litigation and Settlement Strategy) which was refreshed in 2013.

The LSS sets out the principles within which HMRC handles all tax disputes subject to civil law procedures.

Paragraph 16 states:

> 'In certain cases Alternative Dispute Resolution can help support the resolution of disputes either by facilitating agreement between the parties or by helping the parties to prepare for litigation'.

Page 30 of the Commentary, which is described as practical guidance for HMRC staff on the application of the LSS states:

> 'Alternative Dispute Resolution (ADR), and more specifically, mediation is a flexible dispute resolution tool available to HMRC, which – in appropriate cases – can help HMRC and its customers resolve disputes (or reach key decision points) in a cost-effective and efficient manner.
>
> The LSS applies to the resolution of all disputes through civil procedures; therefore any agreement to resolve a dispute between HMRC and a customer – whether it is

The Litigation and Settlement Strategy (LSS) – HMRC

facilitated by the use of ADR or not – must accord with the terms of the LSS.'

The principles that apply include:

- Minimise the scope of disputes and seek non-confrontational solutions.
- Base case selection handling on what best closes the tax gap.
- Resolve tax abuse in accordance with HMRC's considered view of the law.
- Ensure that the revenue flows potentially involved make any dispute worthwhile.
- (In strong cases) settle for the full amount HMRC believes the Tribunal or Court will determine, or otherwise litigate.
- (In 'all or nothing' cases) do not split the difference.
- (In weak or non-worthwhile cases) concede rather than pursue.
- Don't do package deals.

In practice

- It can still be worth mediating with HMRC rather than litigating before a tribunal or court.
- Confidentiality carve out may be required.
- It will be a different type of mediation experience.

See also
CONFIDENTIALITY/DRC/GOVENMENT DEPARTMENTS

Follow up

www.gov.uk/government/publications/litigation-and-settlement-strategy-lss

Litigation

'Litigation is a process where out of the clash of lies emerges truth.' Anon.

There is truth in this. Litigation is a process where proceedings are brought in court to enforce a particular right. ADR is the alternative to this.

Claimants and defendants hire lawyers to prepare and argue their case in court. The judge listens to both sides and decides the winner.

The object is to demolish the other side's case through cross-examination of their witness and forensic dismantling of their legal arguments and factual evidence.

The lawyers who do this proudly proclaim that they are hired guns.

The Civil Procedure Rules are the procedural rules under which litigation is conducted in England and Wales. They are complicated and not designed to be readily understood by non-lawyers.

Litigation is now widely seen as being too expensive, complex and slow. Despite reforms cases often take a long time to come to trial – rarely less than six months and more likely 12–18 months. ADR, and in particular mediation, is seen as a better way.

A feature of litigation in England and Wales is that the winner can recover a substantial part of his legal costs from the loser. The cost of going to court in England and Wales is unfavourably contrasted with the legal costs in Europe and in particular in Poland, Germany and France which are substantially lower and often on a scale or fixed fee basis.

The risk of adverse costs orders deters people. Some see it as an impediment to the access of justice. Hence the opportunity for mediation.

Litigation Discount

A new hybrid of litigation/mediation called structured mediation is developing – where the procedural steps for preparation for trial are abbreviated but incorporated into the pre-mediation preparation.

The court's attempts to manage litigation more closely with costs budgets and sanctions for minor procedural lapses — usually submitting documents late — have prompted a revival in ADR services. Arbitration services for family and personal injury disputes are being set up to circumvent the cumbersome and heavy handed litigation procedure.

An Online mediation court for all claims under £25,000 with reduced involvement of lawyers has been proposed in the Briggs Report (July 2016).

In practice

- You cannot ignore litigation and it is increasingly expensive and user unfriendly.
- But mediation is not the continuation of litigation by other means. A lesson not fully understood by many who attend mediations.

See also
COSTS/CPR/HIRED GUNS/LAWYERS-ROLES/ STRUCTURED MEDATION

Follow up
Briggs Report www.judiciary.gov.uk>civilcourt

Litigation Discount

Lawyers never give clients a 100% guarantee that they will win their case. They always apply a litigation discount for the risk of losing.

Litigation Discount

The discount may be:

- A small one based upon the inherent risk of litigation – sometimes known as 'the mad judge factor' – and be as low as 5% or 10%.
- More usually it is 15–20% to reflect the fact that there is always a risk that witnesses do not do themselves justice in court or that the judge simply prefers one person's version of events to another.

Experienced lawyers rarely advise clients that they have more than a 75/80% chance of winning. Clients usually ignore the litigation discount when thinking about going to trial. Having to consider it at mediation makes them uncomfortable. But it's part of risk analysis.

Hence the need for a PMA (Pre-Mediation Analysis) which reduces the level of stress on clients during the mediation day making it easier for them to think creatively about settlement and make an informed decision.

Research shows that even experienced lawyers who are prepared to predict the outcome of cases in a systematic way frequently overestimate their chances of success. Both claimant and defendant lawyers habitually do this.

In practice

- Most lawyers know that there is always a discount for litigation risk to be factored into any settlement discussions.
- Most habitually overestimate their own chances of success and are prone to optimism bias.

See also

BARRIERS/COGNTIVE BIAS/PMA/PREPARATION/RISK ANALYSIS/STRESS

Follow up

Greene and Bernstein *Cloudy Forecasts* www.uccsedu/Documents

Goodman-Delahunty, Granhag, Hartwig, Loftus' Insightful or Wishful Thinking' Psychology. Public Policy and Law Vol 16(2) May 2010

Litigation Funding

Third-party funding for litigation is a growth area industry in the UK. It received a boost when in April 2013 the rules about champerty and maintenance were relaxed.

Funders are:

- Usually rewarded with a slice of the action between 25% and 40% or a multiple of the amount invested – a minimum of three times.
- Investing their own money. They are not lending the money to the party. If a funded party does not win the funders lose their money.
- Not the same as pure funders who:
  - have no personal interest in the litigation;
  - do not stand to benefit from it;
  - are not funding it as matter of business;
  - in no way seek to control its course.

Funders normally make money by receiving a percentage of the recovery. They hope that they win more often than they lose. They do not appear to be better than anybody else at predicting outcomes of trials. One of the leading funders reported in 2014 that over 10 years they had a 60% success rate. And this was after the selection of cases was vetted before acceptance by a panel of retired High Court judges.

There is an Association of Litigation Funders (ALF). Their code of conduct prevents its members from exercising control over the litigation. But negotiations at mediation are influenced by:

- The fact that one of the parties is in receipt of third-party funding and will therefore have to pay a percentage of their recovery to the funders.
- CFAs or DBAs which are another form of funding albeit by the parties' lawyers.

There are those who think that if the President of the Supreme Court, Lord Neuberger, is correct in describing third-party funding as 'the lifeblood of the justice system', that the life expectancy of the justice system is not a long one.

See also

ALF/CONDITIONAL FEE AGREEMENTS/DAMAGES BASED AGREEMENTS

Follow up

www.associationoflitigationfunders.com

Liquidators – Trustees

Insolvencies, both corporate and personal, give rise to disputes that go to mediation.

Insolvency practitioners (IPs) whether liquidators of companies or trustees in bankruptcy (TIBs) bring claims against the bankrupt or shareholders and directors of insolvent companies and their associates.

An IP's job is to collect in the assets for the general benefit of creditors. They are officeholders and have statutory duties under the Insolvency Act. This gives rise to some special features of mediations involving IPs.

- They often act on a speculative basis. They only get paid if they make recoveries.
- They often employ lawyers on a speculative basis, ie CFAs. They were granted an exemption in the April 2013 Jackson reforms to allow them to continue to recover success fees and ATE insurance premiums. This expired on 31 March 2016.
- They have statutory duties to investigate the conduct of directors of companies. They need less strict confidentiality provisions to allow them to carry out their statutory duties.
- They may need sanction from creditors in order to compromise proceedings.
- Assignments of causes of action, now easier since 1 October 2015, are common features at mediations. Either the claimant is an assignee or as part of a settlement a cause of action is assigned by the IP to the paying party.

In practice
- Many mediations involving IPs are about costs: the IP's costs and those of his lawyers.
- Often there is little or no chance of a dividend to creditors.

See also
CONFIDENTIALITY/OFFICE HOLDERS

Follow Up
Insolvency Act 1986, s 246ZD

Looping

Technique used by mediators to make sure that they and the parties understand each other. Similar to but not exactly the same as active or reflective listening.

The four simple stages are:

1 Understand each party.

2 Express your understanding.

3 Ask for confirmation from the parties that they have been understood by the mediator.

4 Receive confirmation from the parties.

Often overused by mediators which can cause mediation to become a drawn out and patronising process.

Effectively used when:

- The mediator senses that one of the parties needs to receive confirmation that they have been understood.
- There is a lack of understanding or there is a misunderstanding that needs to be cleared up.

In practice

- Experienced mediators naturally make sure that they are understanding the parties and vice versa without consciously deploying the technique of 'looping'.

See also
ACTIVE LISTENING/OPEN QUESTIONS/RAPPORT

Lose-Lose

The opposite of Win-Win beloved of HNP and principled negotiation.

Defeatist mediators define a satisfactory mediation settlement as one where both parties leave feeling dissatisfied. In other words that they both think that they have lost something by negotiating a settlement.

Realist mediators say that although they are routinely told by both sides that they are going to win at trial that is impossible. Only one side can win at best.

So why should the parties feel dissatisfied if they go to court?

Sometimes both sides can lose because the judge:
- Does not agree with either side's analysis and decides to express his disagreement by coming up with an idiosyncratic one of his own which satisfies neither party.
- Expresses his disapproval of what has been presented to him by making an order for costs which means that the recovery for both sides leaves them in a worse net financial position as result of having gone to trial.

In practice:
- Both sides are often better off settling at an early stage than fighting through to trial.
- Especially true if indirect costs such as the opportunity cost and loss management time are factored in.

See also
COSTS/HARVARD/PMA/RISK ANALYSIS/

Losing the Room

The mediator's nightmare.

For mediators building rapport is essential. Without it, they cannot create the degree of trust necessary for frank discussions about settlement options and disclosure of interests and needs.

Lying

Sometimes rapport is never established given the personalities and attitudes of those present. But usually some is. All mediators start with a fund of goodwill which can increase or decrease depending on how they get on with the parties.

As the day wears on tension and friction can rise. Lawyers may feel under pressure, not only from the other side or the mediator, but also from their own clients. They transfer this to the mediator telling him that he has lost the confidence of their side. Clients who feel that the reality testing is too testing may say the same thing.

If this happens the only sensible course for a mediator is to offer to terminate the mediation and stand down. This invitation is almost never taken up.

In practice
- Mediators do lose the room but not often.
- More usually advocates lose their way and clients lose their appetite for trial.

See also
GOODWILL/RAPPORT

Lying

Exaggerating, holding back, bluffing are all part of what people do in negotiations and at mediations. The boundaries between this and lying are not always clear.

Most mediation agreements includes a clause that the parties are there to negotiate in good faith. Parties assure each other they are there in good faith.

Lying

This is a considerable move from the traditional judicial view of Lord Ackner:

> 'However the concept of the duty to carry on negotiation in good faith is inherently repugnant to the adversarial position of the parties involved in negotiations.'

Is there a line between exaggerating, holding back, bluffing and misrepresenting? Even the robust Ackner LJ conceded that:

> 'Each party to the negotiations is entitled to pursue his (or her) own interest, so long as he avoids making misrepresentations.'

Philip Collins, a former speechwriter for Tony Blair, distinguished three types of lies:

- Those statements that you know not to be true when you make them.

- Those statements which you believed to be true when you made them, but which turn out to be false.

- Those statements about which you were reckless as to whether or not they were true when you made them.

Most of us think that we can detect when someone is telling us lies. Reading body language gives it away – the averted gaze, the itchy nose, reddening earlobes, etc etc. But reading body language – and especially the micro signs – is difficult and requires much training. Most people in mediations do not have this level of proficiency.

We therefore rely upon gut feeling or instinct. If you think that the other side is lying, then:

- Ask for a warranty that the statement is true. Incorporate it in the settlement agreement.

- Ask for direct proof. For example If they say they have a witness statement which proves their point but are reluctant to disclose it to you at this stage, ask them to show it to the mediator who can verify that he has seen it.

Lying

- Treat their statements as a lie and make your proposals accordingly. When challenged say that you do not believe what they are telling you and that is why you are making the proposal that you are. In other words call their bluff.

Under para 708-1 of the Bar Standards Board Code of Conduct:

> 'A barrister instructed in a mediation must not knowingly or recklessly mislead the mediator or any party or their representative.'

In practice

- Never expect to be told the truth the, whole truth, and nothing but the truth, even in the post-modern world of multiple truths.
- This does not mean that people will not tell you the truth. Just don't be disappointed when they don't.

See also

BLUFFING/BODY LANGUAGE//TRUST/WARRANTIES

Follow up

Walford v Miles [1992] 2 AC

Part VII of *Bar Standards Handbook* www.barstandardsboard.co.uk

M

Manipulation

A dangerous word in the mediation community. The Oxford English Dictionary defines 'to manipulate' as:

- 'to handle or control (a tool, mechanism, information etc) in a skilful manner; or
- to control or influence (a person or situation) cleverly or unscrupulously.'

Mediators practising the facilitative, transformative, narrative or 'mediating in the moment' models deny that they manipulate but claim that other types of mediators are prone to it.

'Manipulative' is a pejorative term. Most mediators object to being labelled manipulative. They accept that they do manipulate in the first dictionary sense – namely to control information in a skilful manner or to influence the person or situation cleverly – but deny that they are unscrupulous.

They accept that they do this by:

- the questions they ask;
- the way they ask them;
- the information they emphasise; and
- the way they look at people.

But they insist that that they do this for honourable purposes, ie to help the parties see their own way to their own settlement.

If clients or advocates think that the mediator is trying to manipulate them in any other manner they can simply stop the mediation. All mediation agreements provide that the parties can leave at any time for any reason.

In practice

- Mediators provide guidance, give a steer, coach and advise on how to close a deal. Is this manipulation?
- If it is, it is benign.

See also

CLOSING//MEDIATION AGREEMENT/PERSUASION TERMIINATING

Maslow's Hierarchy

A description of the five needs devised by Abraham Maslow in the 1940s.

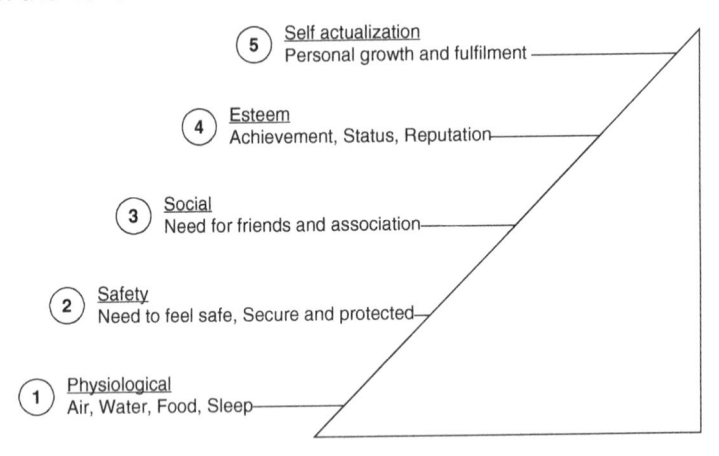

- (5) Self actualization — Personal growth and fulfilment
- (4) Esteem — Achievement, Status, Reputation
- (3) Social — Need for friends and association
- (2) Safety — Need to feel safe, Secure and protected
- (1) Physiological — Air, Water, Food, Sleep

In ascending order they are:

- Physiological.
- Safety.
- Love/belonging.
- Esteem.
- Self-actualisation.

Maslow's Hierarchy

Maslow referred to the first four as deficiency needs or D needs, being esteem, friendship/love, security and physical needs. Only when these fundamental needs have been satisfied can people think about the higher needs of self-actualisation. Some mediation theorists have imported this into mediation.

In practice this is what is observed in mediation:

- Physiological — People have to be fed and watered. They should not be too hot, cold or uncomfortable. If they are any of these things they will not be thinking about settlement.
- Safety — This is not physical safety so much as emotional or psychological safety. People do not want to feel threatened, attacked or at risk of being humiliated.
- Love/belonging — People want to feel liked. The need to be loved or to belong can be seen in the broken relationships that lie behind many disputes. The chance to repair these relationships can meet this basic need.
- Esteem — People do not want to lose face in mediations. They want to be acknowledged and feel they have been heard.
- Self-actualisation — These can be seen when the parties are asked where they want to be in three years' time. What do they need in order to be able to rebuild their lives?

See also
**ACKNOWLEDGMENT/FACE/HOSPITALTY/
INTIMIDATION/RELATIONSHIPS/SANDWICHES**

MEDALOA

This means Mediation After Last Offer Arbitration. It is a technique derived from baseball arbitration in the USA.

Key features:

- If at mediation the parties cannot achieve a settlement the mediator acts as an arbitrator.
- His sole purpose is to decide which of the proposals submitted to him by the parties he prefers as being the most reasonable.
- He picks one and that becomes the arbitral award.
- The idea is that each party will have the incentive to put forward the most reasonable proposal in the hope that the arbitrator will choose their proposal.
- The parties will have the benefit of having had discussions with the arbitrator during the mediation when he was acting as a mediator before formulating their proposal for submission to the arbitrator. This can give them the opportunity to read his mind

Pros

- It guarantees an outcome.

Cons

- There are no obvious ones, once the parties have decided that they would rather have a Third Party tell them the answer than work it out for themselves.
- You have to be confident that you choose the right person to decide which of the competing proposals is the more reasonable.

Med-Arb

In practice

- Not used very often in the UK in civil and commercial mediations.
- Commercial clients are becoming more interested in it.

See also
PENDULUM DECISION

Med-Arb

This is the opposite of ARB-MED: the mediation takes place first. If it produces a settlement that is the end of the matter. If there is no settlement the mediator then acts as an arbitrator. He conducts a hearing in the usual way and makes and publishes his award.

Pros

- The imminence of the arbitration concentrates the parties' focus on settlement.
- The Johnson effect. This can encourage parties to see the realities of their positions more clearly and to stop believing their own propaganda. The bluffing might stop earlier. 'Depend upon it, sir, when a man knows he is to be hanged in a fortnight, it concentrates his mind wonderfully.'

Cons:

- The parties will try and game the mediator so as to influence him when he acts as arbitrator.
- They will withhold confidential information from him because it might influence him even unconsciously at the arbitration.
- They tell him, confidentially, of action that they intend to take, eg bring fraud charges against the other side in the

hope that it has some influence on his view of the other side.
- An arbitrator cannot be certain that he has excluded information or impressions which he gained in private confidential discussions with one of the parties during the mediation. As arbitrator he should take his decision based upon evidence that is put before him at the hearing by both parties in presence of each other.
- It could encourage mediators to be more evaluative knowing that if no settlement is reached they will be entirely evaluative, so they might as well let the parties know how they provisionally see things.
- There are mediators who practise it but it is not widespread. The English courts have not been encouraging. In *Glencot Development* the decision of a mediator who having conducted a failed mediation then sat as an adjudicator – not arbitrator – was set aside.

Lloyd J. said:

> 'Mr T went to and fro between the parties. We do not know what he heard or learned... nor given that the content was "without prejudice" and confidential ought there to be an enquiry as to what happened. These private discussions could have conveyed material or impressions which subsequently influenced his decision.... In the adjudication Mr T was asked to decide certain points about which there was no documentary evidence. These are areas where unconscious or insidious bias may well be present.'

In practice

- Although disapproved of by many mediation theorists more interest is being shown by clients and mediators.
- Likely to be used more widely.

See also

ARB-MED

Follow up

Glencot Development and Design Co Ltd v Ben Barrett & Son (Contractors) Ltd [2001] EWHC Technology 15

Samuel Johnson, *The Life of Samuel Johnson* LL.D.

Mediating in the Moment

A relatively new approach to mediation. Its mantra is:

> 'Mediation is conducted solely in the present moment. The challenge for the mediating parties is to remain present as each moment unfolds rather than intellectually jumping ahead in time to what might be a possible solution.'

It relies upon:

- Intuition, the unconscious mind and unlearning analytical thinking and knowledge.
- Maintaining a sense of reverie, ie the capacity to make sense of what is going on in unconscious processes.
- Being able to sit with the uncomfortable tension of the moment without irritably reaching after fact or reason.

This approach asserts that:

- The mediator's task is not to understand or analyse the nature of what is happening in the particular environment but to intuit that unconscious reality of the moment by becoming at one with it.
- Unconscious thinking is an antidote to the addiction to intellectualising problems instead of developing the ability to sit with them, totally present in the moment.
- Time is the mediator's friend. It's the currency in which mediators trade. The more time the mediator can spend with the parties the more opportunities there are for relationships to rebuild and options to emerge.

Mediation

- Joint sessions and the facilitative model should be used.

Those who do not practise this approach point out that:

- Parties do not want to pay for a lot of mediator's time, especially in civil and commercial mediations. They are very cost conscious.
- Clients are just as likely as their lawyers to prefer private sessions to joint ones.
- It sounds more like therapy than mediation. Commercial clients often object to mediation on the grounds that it is too touchy-feely.

In practice

- Not much used in UK mediations.
- Limited relevance for civil and commercial mediators.

See also

FACILITATIVE/JOINT SESSIONS/NARRATIVE/ THERPEUTIC

Follow up

See the work of Greg Rooney 'Shifting the Focus from Mediating the Problem to Mediating the Moment 2012' – www.papers.ssrnc.com

Mediation

The best known of the ADR (Alternative Dispute Resolution) methods. In essence an assisted negotiation. A mediator helps the parties negotiate their own solution to their problem.

Please go to TOP TEN in the INTRODUCTION

Mediation Agreement

The document which the parties sign agreeing to go to mediation. Usually also signed by the mediator and/or the mediation provider. Sets out the rules for the appointment and terms of the mediator and may refer to the rules of procedure.

The key terms in most mediation agreements are:

- Identifying the parties fully and accurately.
- Defining the dispute comprehensively and clearly.
- Mediator's fees – how they are calculated, when they are paid, overtime and preparation.
- The duty of confidentiality on all signatories.
- Warranty that the parties have authority to settle and are attending the mediation in good faith.
- Limitation on the mediator's liability.

It:

- Sets out the rules of procedure for the mediation.
- Confers upon the mediator such authority as he may have.

In practice

- A crucial document that is often not read by the parties until the day of the mediation.
- In community mediations often not signed before the mediation starts.

Follow up

Walker *Mediation Advocacy: Representing Clients in Mediation* Ch 13 for a template and clause by clause commentary

Mediation Advocacy

A term that Andrew Goodman claims to have invented in 2004 before going on to found the Standing Conference of Mediation Advocates (SCMA).

The rationale for the SCMA is that there is a difference between what advocates do and say in court and what they do and say at mediation. Or at least there should be.

The term:

- Is not universally liked as it connotes legal qualifications and destructive argument rather than commercial, collaborative problem-solving. Alternatives have been suggested such as representative, advisers, assistant or skilled helpers. None have been widely accepted.
- Seems to be immovably entrenched. The IMI have established a certification programme for Mediation Advocates.
- Is differently interpreted. Some thought leaders believe that the aim of effective advocacy at mediation is 'to overwhelm the opposing party and to deflate his expectations.'

The current view is that mediation advocacy is much less to do with critical argument and debate and more to do with assessment, constructive problem-solving and coaching.

This has been recognised:

- In the UK by the establishment of the SCMA.
- Internationally by the IMI's qualification in Mediation Advocacy established in 2013 Its programme has two annexes with a list 'Mediation Advocacy General

Mediation Advocacy

Knowledge Requirements' – which has 24 separate headings and 'Mediation Advocacy Practical Skills Requirements' – which contains 110 items.
- By the specialist courses now offered on mediation advocacy and books written specifically about it.
- By competitions which encourage trainee lawyers to acquire competence. For example the ICC mediation competition which has been held annually in Paris since 2005.

In practice
- Advocates play three roles: hired gun, bodyguard and coach.
- Many advocates, especially barristers, act in exactly the same way in court and at mediation. In other words they are adversarial.
- Mediation advocacy = deal making.

See also
ADVERSARIAL/ADVOCACY/IMI/LAWYER ROLE/ MEDIATION ROLES/SCMA

Follow up

Walker *Mediation Advocacy: Representing Clients in Mediation*

Goodman *Mediation Advocacy*

IMI/imimediation.org>mediation-advocacy

Mediation Day

Mediation Clock

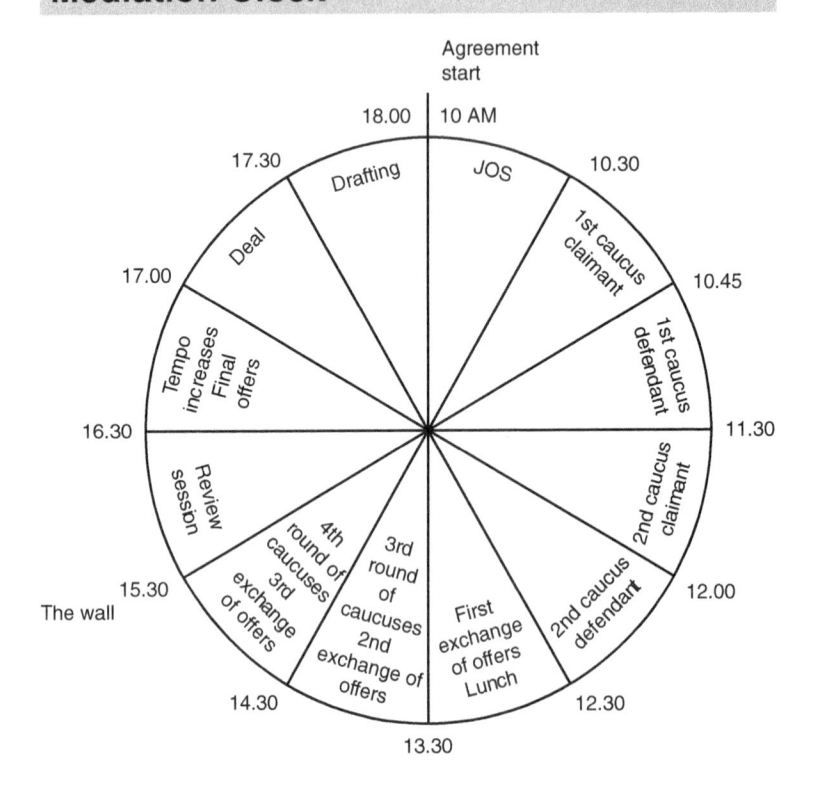

```
                    Agreement
                    start
         18.00  |  10 AM
    17.30              JOS        10.30
         Drafting
                                      1st caucus
    17.00    Deal                     claimant    10.45
          Tempo                          1st caucus
          increases                      defendant
    16.30 Final                                   11.30
          offers
           Review                      2nd caucus
           session                     claimant
                4th    3rd
                round  round
    15.30       of     of    First       2nd caucus  12.00
    The wall    caucuses caucuses exchange  defendant
                3rd    2nd    of offers
                exchange exchange Lunch
                of offers  of offers
         14.30                        12.30
                    13.30
```

This shows how time at a typical civcom mediation is spent. Sadly there are very few typical civcom mediations. The clock gives a guide on how to spend the time but it is not a prescriptive timetable.

See also
MEDIATION DAY/THREE STAGES

Mediation Day

The stages of a typical mediation day for a civil and commercial mediation with two parties.

Mediation Pledge – DRC (Dispute Resolution Commitment)

Stage I	Arrival
Stage II	Private chats between the parties and the mediator in their own room
Stage III	Joint Opening Session
Stage IV	Caucuses with the mediator
Stage V	First exchange offers
Stage VI	Lunch
Stage VII	Second exchange offers progress
Stage VIII	Caucuses continue
Stage IX	Low point aka The Wall
Stage X	Review session
Stage XI	Caucuses – review section
Stage XII	Settlement
Stage XIII	Drafting settlement agreement
Stage XIV	Signature and copy making
Stage XV	Farewells

Follow up

Walker *Mediation Advocacy: Representing Clients in Mediation* Ch 10

Mediation Pledge – DRC (Dispute Resolution Commitment)

In 2001 the British Government made the Alternative Dispute Resolution Pledge. This was renewed in 2011 by the DRC (Dispute Resolution Commitment).

See also
DRC/GOVERNMENT DEPARTMENTS/LSS

Mediation Service Provider

Aka Panels.

Organisations that appoint mediators and administer mediations. They are proliferating in England and Wales as mediators group together to promote their services.

The quality, charges and range varies enormously. The impact of ODR (Online Dispute Resolution) on mediation providers is now being felt and in some cases proving to be transformational.

Some providers are:

- Well-funded and established with professional administrators.
- DIY groupings of mediators for marketing purposes.
- More recently established by entrepreneurs who have moved into the conflict resolution business offering mediation services often at a low cost and paying their mediators for example as little as £30 a case.

Reputable providers are registered with the CMC who stipulate requirements for mediation service providers. Details are on the CMC website.

The advantages of providers are:

- They take over the administration.
- They implement their complaints procedures.
- They have professional indemnity insurance for their panel members.
- They provide referrals for mediators.
- They may be more expensive than going direct to mediators but by no means always.

In practice

- They do not guarantee to provide work for mediators but they are a shop window.
- They simplify the administration for both parties and mediators.

See also

ADR GROUP/CEDR/CLERKSROOM/IN PLACE OF STRIFE/JAMS /PANELS

Follow up

Civil Mediation Council – www.civilmediation.org

Medical Mediation

Does not just mean disputes involving medical staff. Has a more specialised meaning of resolving conflicts between health professionals and families about what is in the best of interests of a child with a serious or life-limiting illness.

Conflicts can arise because of:

- Differing religious or ethical beliefs.
- Different clinical teams having different opinions on the best course of treatment.
- The child may have a different view from its parents.

In practice

- Where these disputes cannot be resolved by health professionals they often go to court for decision.
- Courts are not always the best way forward especially as they tend to be binary with winners and losers.
- That is why specialist medical mediation organisations have been set up.

Follow up

www.medicalmediation.org.uk

Mediator

The mediator is a Third-Party Neutral ('TPN') appointed to act as a facilitator and intermediary in the dispute between the parties.

According to one of the U.K.'s most successful mediators:

> 'The mediator must be patient, tenacious, enthusiastic, positive, energetic, humorous, humble, wise, non-judgemental, accepting and encouraging. In other words, a saint, or an angel - probably both.'

In England and Wales Civil and Commercial mediators are according to the 2016 CEDR Audit:

Male	65%	Female	35%
Lawyers	43%	Non-lawyers	57%
Average Age	57 (M)		50 (F)
White	92%	Non-white	8%

Most family mediators are women. There is much greater gender equality in workplace and community mediation.

Mediators approach their job in different ways depending on their experience, personality and style. But they derive their authority from the mediation agreement.

Most adopt the conventional wisdom that the dispute belongs to the parties and the process belongs to the mediator.

In practice

- Most mediators adopt the process that the parties would like to follow. There are mediators who impose their process on the parties.

- Mediators adopt a diverse range of styles, methods and techniques.
- There is no regulation of mediators.
- There is very little sanction against them apart from a claim for breach of contract or negligence.

See also

GENERALIST/MEDIATION AGREEMENT/MEDIATORS' LIABILITY/REGULATION/SPECIALIST/TPN/TRAINING/ UNICORN MEDIATOR

Follow up

Richbell *How to Master Commercial Mediation* p 11

Walker *Mediation Advocacy* Ch 3

Mediators' Liability

Mediators in England and Wales do not have immunity from being sued, unlike arbitrators or judges.

Mediators can be liable under the ordinary tests of negligence:

- Did they perform to the standard of an ordinarily competent mediator?
- If they did not – did their act or omission cause loss?

An obvious example is drawing up a settlement agreement, which turns out to be unenforceable.

Mediators cope with this as follows:

- Most mediation agreements contain limitations or exclusions of liability. Many mediators doubt whether they are effective especially against consumers at mediation because of Unfair Contract Terms Act.
- They buy professional indemnity insurance. Mediators who are members of the CMC or other reputable panels are required to have it.

Mediator's Opening Statement

Mediators will be sued more in future. In California a client has sued both the provider and the mediator for misrepresenting the area and level of the mediator's expertise.

In practice

Most complaints about mediators are not for negligence but for breach of contract, particularly for poor service. For example:

- Turning up late.
- Not reading the papers.
- Falling asleep.
- Terminating the mediation prematurely.
- Steam-rolling the parties towards settlement.
- Breaching the confidentiality provisions.

See also
EXCLUSION CLAUSES/PROFESSIONAL INDEMNITY

Follow up
Walker *Mediation Advocacy* paras 12.17–19

PGP Mediation 12 August 2016 @bloggtrottr.com

Mediator's Opening Statement

Mediators make their opening statement at the Joint Second Session. They can use this to set the mood and explain the ground rules.

The mediator usually:

- Introduces himself.
- Asks the parties to introduce themselves.
- Checks that the mediation agreement has been signed.

- Explains the key elements: the purpose of the mediation is to settle, it is voluntary, confidential and without prejudice.
- Asks the parties to confirm they have authority to settle.
- Asks if they want to say anything.

In practice
- The style and content varies a lot.
- Some mediators emphasise their own expertise and achievements.
- Others keep this to a minimum and explain the underlying philosophy of mediation and namely that it is a process designed to achieve settlement.

Follow up
Walker *Mediation Advocacy* paras 10.08–10.09

Mediator's Proposal

Commonly used in mediations in the US. The mediator says where he thinks the settlement range is or should be. Aka mediator's number.

Less common in UK mediations.

Not to be confused with a mediator's recommendation. This is where the mediator says what he thinks a sensible and reasonable settlement proposal would be. This is increasingly common in UK commercial mediations.

In practice
- In the UK mediator's proposals are not often formally given.
- Often they are informally given or hinted at.

See also
EVALUATIVE/FACILITATIVE/RECOMMENDATIONS/ JAMS

Follow up

Walker *Setting Up in Business as a Mediator* para 5.35

Memorandum of Agreement

Aka Memorandum of Understanding or Heads of Agreement, Heads of Terms.

More usually a synonym for a document that records an agreement that is not yet final or legally binding.

In family mediations in England and Wales the parties cannot come to a legally binding agreement without the Court approving the consent order embodying it. They produce a Memorandum of Understanding, which is usually passed to the parties' lawyers to turn into a Consent Order which is put before the court for final approval.

See also
HOTs/NON-BINDING

Merits-Based Settlement

Most parties at mediations emphasise that although they are prepared to settle it will not be at any price. Their lawyers highlight how any settlement must reflect the underlying legal merits of the case. Usually included in a platitudinous peroration in the Position Paper or Opening Statement.

This is more a rights-based approach to settlement than an interest or needs-based approach promulgated by principled negotiators using the Harvard model.

Can lead to an inflexible approach to mediation. Assumes that the merits are self-evident and that one party's assessment of the merits is shared by everybody.

In practice

- Legal merits play a part in any assessment of settlement.
- Financial realities, psychological needs and commercial interests usually prevail.

See also

ACKNOWLEDGEMENT/FAIR/HARVARD/MEDIATION ADVOCACY/NEGOTIATION

Message

Mediators often ask parties what message they want to send to the other party. Frequently they are not given a clear answer.

Parties at mediations must be very clear about what message they want to send and be aware of what message they think that the recipient will receive.

As Frank Luntz said 'It's not the words that you say it's the words that they hear'.

Examples in mediations of where you must be clear about your message are:

- Drafting your Position Statement – who are you addressing it to? What do you want them to understand from what you say? What is the message to them?
- Joint Opening Session when you're speaking to the other side. What message do you want them to receive? If you want them to believe that you are there to try and do business why launch a partisan attack on them or their lawyers?

Message

- When making a proposal – what message do you want to send? If you make a very low offer will you be telling them that you are hardboiled negotiators who are here to stay a long time or that you're not really interested and are just going through the motions? Is this the message you want to send?

Remember messages can be verbal or non-verbal. The way you shake hands, look at someone, or what you do when they are talking to you all send out a message. So can unconscious body language such as leaning back instead of forward when someone is making a point to you.

Mediators often tell parties:

- Don't shoot the messenger – this is when they bring bad news from the other room when shuttling between caucuses.
- Don't just use me as a messenger – the parties are paying the mediator not just for being present but also for guidance and experience. If you just use the mediator to send messages for you what value are you getting?
- If you just want to tell the other side something you can always do it yourself.

In practice

Parties

- Ask mediators to frame a proposal as though it was the mediator's rather than the proposers. They think that this reduces the risk of reactive devaluation and invests the proposal with more authority and credibility.
- Do not consciously think about what message they want to send to the other side and how it will be received.

See also

BODY LANGUAGE/COGNITIVE BIAS//POSITION STATEMENT/SIGNALS

Follow up

Frank Luntz *Words that Work*

Walker *Mediation Advocacy* paras 10.10–10-.16, 11.09–11.20

MIAMS (Mediation Information and Assessment Meeting)

Used in family mediation. Since 22 April 2014 most divorcing or separating couples in England and Wales who want to use the court system to resolve any disputes about children or money have to show that they have attended a MIAM before they can apply for a court order.

They attend before a mediator who explains the mediation process to them. They can attend individually or separately. They do not have to agree to go to mediation.

There are exemptions eg where there are allegations of domestic violence.

See also
FAMILY MEDIATION/INTAKE MEETING

Follow up

Family Mediators Association www.thefmaco.uk/miams/

The Family Mediation Council www.familymediationcouncil.org.uk

Mini-Trial

A form of ADR. Not really a trial but more a settlement process where the parties present a summary of their respective cases to a panel.

MLATNA (Most Likely Alternative to a Negotiated Agreement)

The panel is made up of party representatives plus a neutral who acts as umpire. This is the key difference between a mini-trial and a mediation. The mediator is never the advocate for any particular party. He is neutral.

The mini-trial panel is not there to adjudicate or make a decision but to try and settle the case.

The term is also used at mediations in the sense of telling the parties that the mediation is not a quasi-trial. The mediator is not a judge. Therefore there is no point in adopting an adversarial forensic approach to negotiation.

In practice
- Why bother with a mini-trial?
- Just go to mediation. It's cheaper and quicker.

MLATNA (Most Likely Alternative to a Negotiated Agreement)

Another variant of BATNA/WATNA and demonstration of academics' love of acronyms.

In practice
- This is the alternative that most parties concentrate on during mediation.
- BATNAs and WATNAs are discarded at an early stage as being unlikely to happen. They are not useful benchmarks for any proposals put on the table during the mediation day.
- Nobody ever uses the term even when using the concept.

See also
BATNA/PATNA/RATNA/WATNA

MoJ (Ministry of Justice)

The Ministry of Justice was formed in 2007. Its priorities are to:

- Reduce reoffending and protect the public.
- Provide access to justice.
- Increase confidence in the justice system.
- Uphold people's civil liberties.

Nearly all its work takes place in England and Wales.

It operates a Civil Mediation Provider Directory Service. It only lists mediation providers that are registered with the Civil Mediation Council.

As at February 2016 the costs of mediation by the Online Directory Service were:

VALUE OF CLAIM	FEES PER PARTY	LENGTH OF SESSSION/HOURS
£5000 or less	£50	1
	£100	2
£5–15,000	£300	3
£15–50,000	425	4

All figures are plus VAT.

In practice

- Many in the mediation community think that the MoJ does not do enough to promote the use of mediation.

See also
National Helpline

Moral Support

Momentum

George W Bush refers to the 'Big Mo'. In other words the energy and direction needed to make progress.

At mediations parties often complain about being frustrated and bored:

- In the caucus model when they are on their own while the mediator is in another room.
- In the joint session model where the parties are going round and round the same point while the mediator is being in the moment for everyone.

To generate and maintain momentum mediators try to:

- Keep the sessions shorter so that people are not left for too long on their own with nothing to do.
- Leave parties with things to do or think about while they go to the other room.
- Establish a framework of settlement proposals and parameters so that people can make progress towards where they think they may end up.
- Be energetic, optimistic and encouraging.

See also

ENGAGEMENT/EXPECTATIONS/MEDIATION DAY/ MOVEMENT/PMA

Moral Support

Mediators often complain that mediating is a lonely job. It may be, but it is not as lonely as being the decision-maker.

Moral Support

This is why clients often bring spouses, partners, friends, and other family members with them.

They want to share the burden of having to:

- Process new information.
- Review their position and change their mind.
- Do something which previously they said they would not do. For example if they want to accept less than 90% of the amount claimed, they want someone to tell them that it is a good idea and to be complicit in the decision.

Some mediation agreements provide that nobody can attend mediation without the consent of the mediator and the other party.

Be careful about refusing to allow a party to bring someone along. This can be seen as a display of dominance behaviour and trying to seize control of the process. You may also undermine the decision-maker's ability to take a decision on the day if the people that he thinks that he needs to help him are not there.

Sometimes supporters help achieve settlement. They can also do the opposite:

- They egg on the client.
- They have some undisclosed stake in the outcome. For example they are owed money by the client who is relying upon receiving a certain sum by way of settlement in order to pay them off.
- They may be undisclosed business partners/associates.
- They may just like exercising the status of trusted adviser.

In practice

- Decision makers at civil and commercial mediations are rarely there on their own.

Motives

- Skilled mediators who see that the moral supporter is becoming an obstacle will say so. Be prepared for this.

See also
ABSENTEES/AUDIENCE/DIPS/FEAR/GROUPTHINK

Motives

Mediators frequently see parties attributing the worst motives to each other.

- They demonise each other.
- They display reactive devaluation – rejecting suggestions from the other side because they must be inspired by malign motives.
- They attribute the other side's actions to personal wickedness rather than situational imperatives. They are discomfited when asked what they would do in the same situation.

On the other hand the parties judge themselves by their intentions – always good – and the other side also by their actions – usually bad. Rarely do they judge themselves by what they have done but by what they intended to do. This is attribution bias.

This mismatch of perspectives often explains why people have lost the habit of communication and need a mediator to help them see the way to settlement.

In practice

- A useful test at mediation to ask 'Why am I saying/doing this' and 'Why are others saying/doing that?'
- If you ask these questions in advance before the mediator does, answering them will be less stressful.

- A party may never reveal their true motives to anyone, sometimes not even to themselves.

See also
AGENDA/COGNITIVE BIAS/PERSPECTIVES/TACTCAL

Movement

Mediators thrive on movement. They are like share dealers. If the share price does not move nobody can make any money.

So it is with mediations. If the parties do not move mediators cannot do anything. Mediators need something to work with – at least a message that they can take to the other side that movement is possible.

Work out in advance your negotiation strategy so that you can see where you are prepared to move, when and how much. Make it a framework not a rigid and immutable timetable. Doing this:

- Will enable you to take the initiative and not just be reactive.
- Make the whole process of decision-taking during the day will be less stressful.

In practice

- Both sides have to move to achieve settlement.
- Don't confuse movement with concession.
- When movement becomes momentum you are in business.

See also
COMPROMISE/FLEXIBILITY/IF/MOMENTUM/ TRADEABLES

MSEO (Mediation Settlement Enforcement Order)

A means under the EU Mediation Directive by which an agreement reached through mediation in a cross-border dispute within the EU can be recorded in a court order.

In England where proceedings have already been started an application is made under CPR Part 23 or where they have not under the CPR Part 8 procedure (as amended by CPR Part 78.24 and Practice Direction 78) for a MSEO.

The court will usually make an MSEO without a hearing. If one of the parties defaults the order can be enforced in the same way as any other judgment or order of the court.

See also
CROSS BORDER

Follow up

CPR Part 23

CPR Part 8

CPR Part 78.24

CPR Practice Direction 78

Mutualising

Mediators are trained to mutualise the problem and its solution. The Harvard-HNP model (Harvard Negotiation Project) emphasises this as one of its five key elements – working for mutual gains, ie win-win situation.

Mutualising

Mediators need to find out how much common ground there really is. They often find that there is more than is apparent from the public exchanges. It can be expanded by the parties sharing more information about the problem and themselves.

Parties always have different needs and interests. Mediators ask parties to consider if they will be better off going to trial, even if they win, than by settling. They do this by encouraging the parties to:

- Look at their net financial position after the conclusion of a trial.
- Consider what ideally they would like to achieve and to compare that with what could be achieved by litigation and the remedies that could be awarded to them by the court if they won.

When parties do this they usually see that:

- The risk-reward ratio is narrower than they had thought.
- There is a gap between what they ideally would like to achieve and what the court will give them even if they win.

When each side sees that they have something to gain by settlement rather than trial the more chance there is of achieving settlement. This is why before you go to mediation work out:

- What you want/need.
- What you think the other side wants/needs.

All mediators recognise with a warm glow the moment when the parties start collaborating to find the answer to a particular issue or problem. It may be:

- Something technical such as how to structure a settlement most tax-efficiently or how to ensure that an option to purchase land runs with the land rather than being a personal right.

Multi-Party

- Something more commercial such as how they can cooperate on winning business together from a third party or a new licence agreement.

Creative structuring of settlements is more fun, more valuable and more satisfying than the critical destruction of each other's cases.

In practice

- Some degree of mutualisation and cooperative problem-solving happens in most mediations.
- But mutualisation is rarer than the idealists would like.

See also

CREATING VALUE/DISCLOSURE/EXCHANGE/ HARVARD-HNP/LIM/PROBLEM SOLVING

Follow up

HNP Model – Fisher and Ury *Getting to Yes*

Multi-Party

Most mediations involve two parties. In some sectors multi-party mediations are the norm, for example in construction and reinsurance disputes.

They are more complicated simply by being larger with more agendas and competing interests in play. This means that:

- More time and care has to be spent before the mediation in designing the process for the day.
- They often last for more than one day.
- Co-mediation is more common.
- They are more expensive both in the amount of time as well as money spent.

- More downtime, ie the periods when one party is in a room on their own with no mediator is longer because the mediator, even if co-mediating, has more rooms to visit.
- The risks of becoming disengaged, bored and frustrated are higher.
- Mediators have to work a lot harder to earn their money.
- Settlements can be more complex to construct and record.

In practice

- Most mediations are between two sides.
- Multi-party mediations are often more complicated and time consuming than they need to be.

My Legal Advice

This has two meanings at mediation.

1 The client's meaning:

All parties say that they recognise that mediations are not courts of law. They are there to settle, not to have a mini-trial. They understand the importance of personal, psychological and commercial factors. And still at every mediation they refer repeatedly to their legal advice.

Nobody ever says that they have been advised that they are going to lose at trial. Everybody has been advised that they will win. At worst they have been advised that the case is a 50/50 one.

Clients always think that their legal advice is stronger or more bullish than the lawyers who gave it think that it is. We all hear what we want to hear. Clients filter out the lawyers' caveats.

My Legal Advice

2   The lawyer's meaning:

Lawyers sometimes tell the mediator in private what their actual legal advice to their clients is. This is usually different from what they have said it was in the Joint Opening Session or what their clients have described to the mediator.

Occasionally they ask the mediator to help them make their client understand and accept their legal advice.

Some lawyers advise their clients against accepting a settlement. They say that: 'My advice is that we can do better than this at trial.' Mediators see the indecision in the client's eyes. For commercial and personal reasons he wants to accept the settlement. But he has paid his lawyers for their legal advice. He does not want to be seen to be wasting his money or being disloyal to his lawyers.

Hence lawyers and clients must in advance of the mediation frankly consider the implications of any legal advice and their confidence in it.

In practice

- Mediators remind lawyers and their clients that everybody, including mediators, is prone to optimism bias.
- It is the client's decision but sometimes it seems that the lawyers are taking it for them. This is dangerous.
- When cases do not settle more often than not the parties regret not having settled at mediation. But not always.

See also

BODYGUARD/COGNITIVE BIAS/CONFIRMATION BIAS/ OPTIMISM BIAS

N

Narrative

Narrative mediation draws on the therapeutic tradition. Michael White and David Epston in Australia in the 1990s pioneered Narrative Family Therapy. They have applied those techniques to mediation.

- It has a post-modernist flavour with its insistence that there is no such thing as objective truth. All points of view are necessarily subjective not objective and derived from a person's socio-cultural context.
- It assumes that people see the world in terms of stories or narratives: their own and other peoples. The role of the mediator is to encourage the parties to tell their own narratives and to understand the other side's narrative. The mediator tries to unsettle each party's belief in their own narrative and to persuade them to adopt a new collaborative one for the future.
- It prioritises relational over substantive issues.
- It adheres to the post-modernist view that language creates reality and that language is a socio-economic construct, which reflects the power structure of the society in which it is used.
- Hence its popularity with mediators working with marginalised groups.

Narrative mediation has three stages. Instead of Education, Exchange and Explore there are:

1 Engagement.

2 Deconstructing the conflict-saturated story.

3 Constructing an alternative story.

Narrative

In fact the Engagement phase is much like the Education stage. The mediator establishes rapport with the parties and encourages them to tell their stories.

In the Deconstructing phase the mediator:

- deconstructs and externalises the stories.
- shows a party that there is another way of looking at things and that his view is not necessarily more correct, authentic or valid than the other party's point of view.
- challenges a party's stated reasons for having a particular point of view.
- does not attack a party when he is explaining his story but encourages him to imagine that the conflict is someone else's and to look at it through the eyes of an outsider or third-party.

In the Constructing phase the mediator, having helped the parties to externalise the conflict, works with the parties to co-author a new narrative. This is a narrative in which the parties work together against a common problem.

At this point there can be an overlap between the narrative technique and the problem-solving approach. It has been said by Prof Toran Hansen that:

> 'Narrative mediation is thus interested in resolutions that go beyond simple settlement to consider the effects of the mediation on society at large and, like transformative mediation, considers mediation as a means for conflict parties to achieve a higher moral self.'

Both therapeutic and narrative are more ambitious than the standard evaluative and facilitative models. Both draw heavily on the techniques of psychotherapy which as Professor G Neil Martin says is 'usually called the 'talking cure' (although it rarely cures).'

In practice

- Many civil and commercial mediators doubt the value of unrestricted and undirected talk, which tends to be repetitive and self-serving.
- Mediators and their clients are sceptical about its relevance to what they do.
- Its application to conflicts involving parties with ongoing or close relationships is more obvious. But whether it is more effective is a different matter.

See also

COUNSELLING/THREE-STAGE PROCESS/RAPPORT/ THERAPEUTIC/TRANSFORMATIVE

Follow up

Prof Toran Hansen: www.mediate.com>articles>hansenT

Professor G Neil Martin: Psychology 2008

Nash Equilibrium

A central concept in Game Theory.

Arises where each player's strategy is optimal for them given the other player's strategies.

There is no reason for any one player to adopt a different strategy as long as all the other players remain the same. The difficulty is that when there is a Nash Equilibrium no player has any reason to change or move because they will be worse off.

An example is the Prisoner's Dilemma. Go to the entry for **Prisoner's Dilemma**, then come back.

Both prisoners know that:
- a 10 year sentence is better than 20 year one.
- 0 years is better than 2 years.

Needs

So of the three strategies which is the dominant one?

Go to p 537 for the answer.

A player's dominant strategy is the one that leads to the optimal outcome no matter what the other players do.

See also
PRISONERS' DILEMMA/TRUST

Follow up
A Beautiful Mind – film about John Nash.

National Mediation Helpline (NMH)

Set up by HM Court Service with the Civil Mediation Council (CMC).

Provides civil court users in England and Wales with information and advice relating to mediation.

Can put court users in contact with accredited mediation providers who can provide low-cost mediations.

Replaced by the Online Civil Mediation Directory Service.

See also
MOJ/Online Civil Mediation Directory Service

Needs

One of the fundamental concepts of mediation along with 'positions' and 'interests'.

Mediators are trained through open question and active listening to work through parties' positions to their interests,

Needs

and finally to their needs. Sustainable settlements can only be reached, so the theory goes, if a person's needs are met.

Positions, interests and needs overlaps but are rarely identical. Mediators pay tribute in a rather unsophisticated way to Maslow's hierarchy of needs.

In fact what mediators want to discuss with parties are:

- What is really important to them.
- Whether these requirements can be achieved at trial and if so at what cost.
- Whether there is any benefit to achieving some or even all of them earlier through settlement.

More often than not some needs cannot be met at trial even if a party is spectacularly successful.

Mediators are often surprised to see how little thought has been given by the parties and their advisers to needs – as opposed to positions or interests – before the mediation. Why are parties reluctant to think about what they really need? It's hard work, requiring:

- Close analysis.
- Lateral thinking.
- The ability to prioritise.
- Giving up long held ambitions or opinions.

But those who do this before the mediation have a better chance of achieving a favourable outcome in a less stressful environment.

In practice

- Parties with encouragement can work out their needs. They have often not confided these to their advisers.
- Many find the process of recognising reality disturbing but when they do it their anxiety levels drop.

Negotiation

See also

FACILITATIVE/HARVARD – HNP/LIM/INTERESTS/ MASLOW'S HIERARCHY/POSITIONS

Negotiation

The best technique for resolving disputes. Used since the beginning of time.

This simple traditional process has developed into a science and industry of negotiation. In the mediation context there are three key points:

- Not every negotiation is a mediation but every mediation is a negotiation.
- Every negotiation involves the recognition of reality: your own and the other side's.
- Deals are not made by arguing about points but by discussing proposals.

In practice
- We all negotiate all the time.
- Mediation is assisted negotiation.
- The principles and techniques of negotiation don't change much but the context does.

See also
CIALDINI'S BIG SIX

Follow up

Walker *Mediation Advocacy: Representing Clients in Mediation* Ch 16 Negotiation Fast Track Tactics

CEDR *How to Master Negotiation*

Net

Cialdini *Influence*

Churchman *Negotiation: Process, Tactics, Theory* (2nd edn)

Net

The 'net' is what mediation clients want to know.

- The paying party wants to know the ultimate cost to him after deduction of tax allowances, fees etc.
- The receiving party wants to know how much cash he will have in his pocket after everything else has been paid including tax, legal fees, insurance premiums and so on.

Receiving parties are often shocked by how much is deducted from their gross recovery to give their net financial position. Mediators encourage both the paying party and the receiving party to consider their net financial position if they do not settle by comparing three potential outcomes at court:

- A good day in court.
- A bad day in court.
- A middling day in court where you do not lose 100% or win 100%.

In practice

- Net positions are rarely calculated before the mediation. When this is done at the mediation perspectives can shift quite radically.
- Calculate your net position before the mediation.

See also
GROSS/PMA

Follow up

For worked examples see Walker *Mediation Advocacy: Representing Clients in Mediation* para 7.2.

Neutrality

Mediation theorists agonise over whether impartiality and neutrality are the same thing.

Neutrality means that the mediator does not have:

- A stake in the outcome of mediation.
- A pre-existing relationship with one of parties, which could predispose him towards favouring them over the other.
- Any sort of conflict of interest.

Neutrality also means that during the mediation the mediator will not act in a way which favours one party over another.

Whether an evaluative mediator can be truly neutral in this sense remains an open question. Parties who do not like the view expressed by the mediator may regard him as biased against them. This is why many mediators still refuse to be evaluative and retain the facilitative model.

Some mediation theorists argue that:

- Neutrality is outmoded.
- It is never attainable in any event.
- It is not necessarily desirable because it can be disempowering.
- It should be abandoned in favour of mediator engagement in the parties' dispute.

In practice
- Despite the theorists' anxieties most practitioners and their clients are able to work with the idea of neutrality.

See also
IMPARTIALITY

Follow up

Bernard Meyer *Beyond Neutrality*

See for example the works of Bernard Meyer and Greg Rooney.

NLP (Neuro-Linguistic Programming)

NLP is another concept imported into mediation. Opinion is divided.

From its origins in California in the 1970s NLP has become a global business. Many people including successful and respected mediators swear by it. Others dismiss it as discredited pseudoscience.

Its core techniques are:

- Establishing a rapport between the practitioner and the client through pacing and leading both verbal and non-verbal behaviour by reframing, matching and mirroring.
- Gathering information about the client's present state and their desired future state.
- Encouraging clients to consider implications of their desired outcomes.
- Helping clients to feel differently towards challenges and situations.
- Rehearsing the changed feelings.

Examples of NLP techniques used at mediations include:

- Replacing the word 'but' with 'and'.
- Having parties change seats so that they change mental as well as physical perspectives.

Whether you support NLP or not you have to relish the irony that its two creators, Richard Bandler and John Grinder, litigated against each other for 20 years over the intellectual property rights in NLP. None of the NLP models and techniques helped resolve their disputes through communication and behaviour change.

In practice

- NLP is more popular with the therapy wing of mediators than with the problem solvers.
- Mediators cannibalise NLP and use the techniques that they find helpful.

See also

ACTIVE LISTENING/BODY LANGUAGE/PERSPECTIVE/ RAPPORT/REFRAMING

Non-Adjudicative

A non-adjudicative process is one where no decision is made and imposed upon the parties to a dispute.

Negotiation and mediation are non-adjudicative. Litigation, arbitration and adjudication are adjudicative.

Being non-adjudicative is advertised as one of mediation's positive advantages compared to other forms of dispute resolution. But some see it as a weakness.

In practice

- Most mediators, even the most evaluative, remain non-adjudicative.
- Adjudicative models are being developed.

See also

ADJUDICATIVE/ARBITRATION/ABR-MED/EVALUATIVE/ MED-ARB

Non-Binding

A non-binding process or agreement means that the parties are not under any legal obligation to do what they may agree to do. There may be moral or commercial consequences for non-performance but there are no legal ones.

Most mediation agreements require a signed document before settlements reached at mediation become binding. Outside mediation oral agreements can be legally binding but some agreements have to be in writing, eg contracts for the sale of land.

In practice

- Parties who are stuck sometimes ask the mediator to make a recommendation or proposal. Usually this is a non-binding recommendation/proposal.
- Sometimes mediators are asked to make a binding recommendation. If they do they act as an expert or arbitrator making a determination and turning mediation, a non-adjudicative process, into an adjudicative one.
- Be absolutely clear whether a Heads of Agreement or mediator's recommendation is meant to be binding or not.

See also
HOTs/MEDIATOR'S PROPOSAL/RECOMMENDATIONS

Non-Negotiable

Much used phrase at mediations. Mediators do not like to hear it. They prefer parties to be open-minded, capable of lateral thinking, flexible and realistic.

Many people believe that everything has a price. Circumstances can change so that something that once was valuable and important later loses its value or importance and vice versa.

What are the consequences of saying that something is non-negotiable early on in the mediation day?

The advantages are:

- Focusing discussions.
- Avoiding going down blind alleys and wasting time, money and energy.
- Demonstrating seriousness, firmness and coherence.

The disadvantages are:

- Closing down potential lines of discussion which might be outside what people expected to discuss.
- Being perceived as aggressive and unreasonable.
- Inciting the other side to challenge your fixity of purpose. People who are presented with a non-negotiable position often like to test it to see if they can call your bluff.

In practice

Experienced mediators although disappointed to hear that something is non-negotiable are rarely dismayed. They know that:

- Hardly anyone ever makes their final offer or truthfully states their bottom line.
- Many positions that were cast in stone are turned into the fine sand of settlement by the warm waters of discussion.

See also
BOTTOM LINES/DEADLINES/RED LINES/ULTIMATUMS

Non-Verbals

At least 66% of communication is said to be non-verbal. Some say it is even higher.

Non-Verbals

Non-verbal communication is about visual cues. But it is not body language, which everyone has heard about and which fascinates most people. There are many more examples:

Voice	Paralanguage
Clothing	Artifactics
Eye contact	Oculesics
Touch	Haptics
Distance	Proxemics
Body language	Kinesics
Use of time	Chronemics

Remember:

- Different people have different behavioural norms. Maintaining eye contact can be disrespectful and rude in some cultures and evasive and shifty in others.

- Sometimes when someone coughs they just have a sore throat and have not just told an untruth.

In practice

When preparing for mediation:

- Think hard about what you wear. Decide what message you want to send the other side and how they will receive it.

- Reflect on what behaviour or non-verbal cues influence you in a positive way. Smiling is one of them. Visualise yourself adopting them.

- Do the same for negative influencers and visualise yourself not adopting them. This is harder than you might think.

At the mediation:

- When shown to your room think about who sits where. In particular consider where the mediator will sit.

Non-Zero Sum

- During the Joint Opening Session watch and note (without writing anything down) people's gestures and expressions.
- Keep your own hands on the table and express interest in what is being said by leaning forward. Do not express boredom, indifference or contempt.

During mediation:

- If things become tense – lean back.
- To encourage – lean forward.
- Maintain eye contact for as long as you feel comfortable.
- Smile as often as you can without appearing to be a grinning imbecile.

See also

BODY LANGUAGE/CROSS-CULTURE/MESSAGES/ SIGNALS

Non-Zero Sum

The opposite of zero sum. A term derived from game theory where one decision-maker's gain or loss does not necessarily result in the other decision-maker's loss or gain.

Game theory tells us that the two are fundamentally different because in a zero sum game:

- An optimal solution can always be found.
- The players are completely competitive.

But in reality life does not have optimal solutions in this way.

In a non-zero sum game there is:

- No universally accepted solution.
- No single optimum strategy that is preferable to others.

Norm Mediation

- No absolutely predictable outcome.
- Scope for players to be both competitive and cooperative.

In non-zero sum games players have some complementary interests and some opposed interests. That is what happens in real-life mediations.

An example is the Prisoner's Dilemma.

In practice

- People treat non-zero sum games as zero sum games.
- Collaboration and mutualising are harder to achieve than many imagine.

See also

GAME THEORY/MUTUALISING/PRISONER'S DILEMMA/ZERO SUM

Norm Mediation

An attempt by academics, mainly American, to categorise mediation.

The usual three categories of mediation models are:

Norm-advocating mediation. Where the scope of any mediation agreement is to some extent defined by statute or institutional rules or regulations.

Norm-educating mediation. The rationale is that people who are well-informed make better decisions. With the help of the mediator all relevant information is collected. The mediator may contribute his own information. This is in addition to the parties using their own values and standards (norms).

Norm-generating mediation. Where the parties develop their own norms. The model concentrates on the interpersonal issues. Linked with transformative and therapeutic mediation in emphasising the parties' future relationships, changing ways of communication, greater awareness of their own and others' issues.

In practice
- Never referred to in UK civil and commercial mediations: much discussed in academic journals and blogs.

See also
EVALUATIVE/FACILITATIVE/HARVARD/NARRIATIVE/ STYLES OF MEDIATION/TRANSFORMATIVE

Notes

Mediators in their training are exhorted not to take notes when talking to the parties. Taking notes distracts them from paying attention to active listening and non-verbal cues.

In reality lawyers are not fazed by seeing mediators take notes. They know from their court experience that when the judge stops writing he has stopped listening and paying attention to their points.

Some mediators take copious notes during any Joint Opening Sessions and caucuses. They appear to be taking a verbatim minute. Others take very few notes and concentrate on engaging in conversation. They will usually make a note of:
- Any figures.
- Any offers or proposals.
- Shopping lists of points to be discussed during the day.
- Specific requests for information from the other side.
- Specific information to be provided to the other side.

- Any specific wording such as a confidentiality clause.

Most mediators make private notes in the intervals between caucuses when they are on their own.

Mediators must take care:

- Not to leave their notebooks in the wrong room. On the rare occasions when this has happened there have been suspicions that the notebooks have been read.
- To start each caucus with a blank sheet of paper so that those in the room cannot see what has been written. Openly trying to read a mediator's notebook upside down now appears to be acceptable practice especially amongst the younger generation of mediation advocates.

Most mediation agreements prohibit tape-recording conversations and discussions. This is because most mediation agreements contain confidentiality provisions that say that everything that is discussed at mediation is confidential and that a mediator cannot be compelled to produces notes or to give evidence.

Some mediators go further and undertake that at the conclusion of the mediation, whether there has been a settlement or not, they will destroy their notes. This practice is dying out as professional indemnity insurers now routinely provide cover and like to see attendance notes.

But there's a trend for note takers to be present at mediations. Their sole function is to take a full note usually on their laptop. What are these notes for apart from providing a defence in any negligence action brought against them by their client?

In practice

- Parties and mediators take whatever notes they want.
- Surreptitious digital recording is on the increase.

See also
CONFIDENTIALITY

Nothing Is Agreed

Parties and mediators often say that 'nothing is agreed until everything is agreed'. This is for three reasons:

1. Mediation agreements usually stipulate that any settlements reached at mediation are not legally binding until they has been incorporated into a document signed by both parties.
2. Parties like to consider the proposals as a package so that they can see how one element impacts on another and whether overall it represents a fair and reasonable alternative to what could be obtained at court.
3. Although parties and mediators like to work through a list of issues and tick them off as they are discussed no one likes to feel that they are being hemmed in and held to something that was discussed four hours earlier in a slightly different context. During the day new information becomes available. Different perspectives are exchanged and adopted. People change their stance.

In practice

- Parties do like to think that issues are agreed as they go along.
- A sense of cumulative progression generates settlement momentum.
- Going back on a previously agreed point always causes friction. Therefore make clear as you go along that any agreement on a particular issue is provisional and will be reviewed at the end.

NVC (Non Violent Communication)

See also
**NON-BINDING/MEDIATION AGREEMENT/
NON-BINDING/SUBJECT TO CONTRACT**

NVC (Non Violent Communication)

NVC is not just a way of speaking that avoids aggressive or hostile language. It is:

- A communication process devised by Marshall Rosenberg in the 1960s.
- Based on the premise that most conflicts between individual groups arrive from miscommunication about their human needs caused by using coercive or manipulative language intended to induce feelings of fear, guilt or shame.

Certain types of communication alienate people from the experience of compassion towards each other such as:

- Moral judgements.
- Demands.
- Denial of responsibility.
- Comparing people with each other.

Instead NVC users concentrate on:

- Observation – look at what you see. Take note but do not evaluate or judge.
- Feelings – these are not the same as thoughts or judgements.
- Needs – there are universal needs and NVC assumes everything we do is in order to satisfy our needs.
- Request – a request is distinguished from a demand. If you make a request and receive a negative reply you do not act in a coercive way. Instead try to understand through questioning why your request has been rejected.

NVC (Non Violent Communication)

In practice

- Many mediators from the therapy wing are advocates of NVC.
- Surprisingly few lawyers and their clients have heard of it, let alone practise it.

Follow up

Marshall Rosenberg *Non-Violent Communication: A Language of Life*

O

Objections

Despite mediation's obvious benefits and judicial encouragement people in disputes still raise objections to it. Here are common ones with responses.

1 'There is no guaranteed outcome. We might go to mediation and not settle. All that time and money will be wasted.'

Response

- There will be no outcome, ie settlement, unless all parties agree. But if there is a settlement it will be one that is acceptable to you all. The guaranteed outcome that arbitration or litigation provides will not be acceptable to at least one side and possibly to both.

- Preparing for and attending a mediation does not mean that the time, money and effort spent is wasted. Even when there is no settlement the parties often say that there has been progress because they understand both their own case and the other side's case much better. They are often better placed to make a successful Part 36 Offer.

2 'It's too late. We are ready for trial. Counsel has been briefed. We might as well go to trial.'

Response

In saying this you are:

- Committing the sunk cost fallacy. We've already spent so much money we might as well spend more even though it might be a case of throwing good money after bad.

Objections

- Saying that you are going to trial. The alternative is a settlement at the door of the court or halfway through the trial. Do you think it will be easier or harder to settle in those circumstances?
- Giving up hope. It is never too late to settle. Parties settle halfway through the trial before judgment has been given. Sometimes they settle after the judgment has been given. The Court of Appeal operates a mediation scheme. This is where one party already has a court judgment in their favour.

3 'It's too early. We don't know their case yet.'

Response

- It's never too early to settle a dispute. Most disputes never go anywhere near a court or mediation. They are settled by the parties themselves without the involvement of lawyers.
- Be careful not to fall foul of the curse of information. This is a belief that the true answer will emerge if more information is obtained. Not so. People usually feel overwhelmed with information.
- Most parties to a dispute know what their commercial, psychological and personal needs are. They may not have clearly formulated them to themselves or confided them to their lawyers yet.

4 'I am going to win. I don't need to settle.'

- This may be true. But bear in mind that most people fall foul of optimism bias.
- Mediators act as agents of reality for both sides. The other side may realise that they're going to lose and are looking for some help in funding a dignified exit.

Remember at all times, when not accepting an invitation to mediation, the *Halsey* factors and the unpleasant costs consequences of falling foul of them.

Objective

In practice

- Advancing credible objections to mediation is becoming harder.
- Some people prefer, for commercial or psychological reasons, to have an uncertain present and future. It postpones the day of reckoning. But they day will come.

See also

CAMS – COURT OF APPEAL MEDIATION SCHEME/ COGNITIVE BIAS/DOOR OF THE COURT/HALSEY/ NEEDS/PART 36 OFFER

Follow up

CPR, Part 36

Objective

Three different meanings apply at mediations:

1. The goal that a party wishes to achieve. Surprisingly parties are often hazy about this. As part of effective mediation preparation devote more time to structuring your settlement scenarios than preparing your case.

2. Distance. Mediators encourage the parties to stand back from the fray and the inevitable emotional investment in a dispute and consider it more dispassionately and in particular:
   - What is the business case for carrying on with the dispute/litigation?
   - How likely is it that they will achieve what they want to without settlement?

3. The mediator is himself objective. He keeps his feelings and emotions restrained and to a minimum. He acts in an unbiased, fair and even-handed manner.

See also
BIAS/IMPARTIALITY/INTERESTS/NEEDS/NEUTRALITY

ODR (Online Dispute Resolution)

ODR is billed as the next big thing in mediation. Not the same thing as online mediation.

Some mediators see ODR as a threat. It will put them out of work. Others see it as an opportunity to enhance their service.

There are four levels of ODR:

1 Information management. Parties input their details online. This is the simplest.
2 TFN (Technology Facilitated Negotiation) techniques such as double blind bidding and visual blind bidding are used. Most applicable where liability is not in dispute and the parties are trying to agree the numbers.
3 TFN provides specific advice to the parties. Not just by providing a process but by a decision tree or risk analysis.
4 Decisions taken by the system. There is no human intervention.

Is it a threat?

Fully automated computerised systems of dispute resolution are already available. Algorithms based upon the collection of big data about disputes of a particular type are used. They are used for low value claims with a simple factual matrix. As they become more sophisticated and users become more familiar with them they can be used for more complex and higher-value claims.

Some of them provide that at a certain stage in the algorithmic process if an agreement is not reached a human intervenes and makes a decision.

Widely predicted to be transformative of some parts of the mediation market over the next 5 to 10 years. See the pilot project for doing divorce mediation online with Resolve and MODRIA and the recent Susskind report.

Others are less certain, for example Jay Welsh of JAMS considers that ODR's impact on the type of mediations that they administer will be limited.

In practice
- ODR is here. It will grow.
- There is no point in mediators, clients or lawyers resisting it. Better to embrace and influence it.

See also

BLIND BIDDING/DECISIONTREES/ONLINEMEDIATION/ TECHNOLOGY FACILITATED NEGOTIATION.

Follow up

Susskind Report www.judiciary.gov.uk>2015/02

Ethan Katsh www.mediate.com>pdf>katsh

Graham Ross www.civilmediation.org>downloads-get

MODRIA – www.modria.com

JAMS – www.jamsadr.com

Wolf Michael J nyujlp.org

Off-the-record

'Off-the-record' is not the same as 'without prejudice'. If you want your conversation to be without prejudice you must expressly say so.

Offers

All conversations at mediation are with without prejudice because it says so in the mediation agreement. They are also usually confidential.

The phrase 'off-the-record' is used by parties when they tell the mediator information in a caucus that they do not want him to pass it on to the other side. The classic example is when they say that they are considering amending their pleadings to bring in an allegation of fraud or reporting the other side to the police.

Why do this? To convert the mediator to your side? Do you hope to influence the mediator so that in some subliminal way he will try to persuade the other side of the error of their ways?

Be prepared to answer the question which the mediator will inevitably ask: 'Why are you telling me this? What you do want to do with this information?'

In practice

People do it:

- To inform the mediator of factors influencing their thinking and decision-making.
- To subtly influence the mediator so that he subliminally transmits it to the other side.

See also

COGNITIVE BIASES/CONFIDENTIALITY/MESSAGES/ SIGNALS/WITHOUT PREJUDICE

Offers

There are three important offers at mediation: the first, the final and the pivot.

Offers

1 First offer

In most mediations the parties are reluctant to make a first offer. They say that:

- They do not want to bid against themselves.
- They want to see what the other side want.
- They really need a message from the other side that they are going to be realistic during the day.
- They don't want to show their hand.

Usually after the first offer has been made people are discouraged and irritated with each other. Research supports anchoring, ie going first and setting the mood, and making low/high offers to start with is effective.

2 The final offer

This really is the last offer on the day before settlement is either achieved or the parties leave. If you're making it be sure that it is your last word on the subject. If you are receiving it be clear how much worse it is than what you calculate you need.

3 Pivot

This is the offer that changes the mood. Most significant when the parties start the mediation with a claim and counterclaim. Both expect to be net receivers of money. That makes it more challenging to settle. Most cases still settle.

At some stage there is a psychological breakthrough and one party decides that it will not insist on being a net receiver of money.

Even in mediations where it is clear who is the paying party there is an offer which changes the mood. A different message is sent and received. People start to collaborate to try and achieve a workable solution for all sides.

Offers

Tactics

Different negotiators have different views about the pacing, framing and timing of offers.

- Some like to delay making an offer until mid-afternoon. Insurers are particularly prone to this. They see mediation as playing poker not problem-solving.
- Others like to salami-slice by moving in small steps until eventually somewhere in the middle (as they see it) a figure is reached.
- Some like to exchange offers. Others prefer to make offers sequentially.
- Mediators are trained to guard against the danger of premature offers or proposals before interests and needs have been fully explored. In fact the dangers of offers which are too early are much less than the dangers of offers which are too late.

Usually offers have been made and rejected before the mediation takes place. Where this happens the parties attend mediation expecting the offers to be improved. The paying party expects the receiving party to lower their demands. The receiving party expects the paying party to increase their offer.

Some hardball advocates like to start off by saying that previous offers are no longer available. They make their first offer at a lower level than the one that was previously rejected. Several hours are wasted to bring them back to the same level, which then becomes the starting point for settlement discussions.

Sometimes new information makes a previous offer redundant. For example the blighted property sold for more than expected or the patient makes a more complete recovery. This is rare.

In practice
- Work out offers in advance.
- Try and guess what offers the other side will make.
- Going back on previous offers never works and wastes time, energy and goodwill.
- Offers usually fall into one of four categories: insult, extreme, credible and reasonable. Be clear about which category you want your offer to fall into.
- Reactive devaluation means that offers never appear as good to the receiving party as they do to either the offering party or to the mediator.

See also
ANCHORING/COGNITIVE BIAS/EXCHANGING OFFERS/FINAL OFFER/HEALTH WARNINGS/ SALAMI SLICE/ZOPA

Office Holders

Occupy a position by reason of statute. A common example at mediation is Insolvency Practitioners who act as liquidators or trustees in bankruptcy.

They often need to amend the standard confidentiality provisions in the mediation agreement to allow them to fulfil their reporting duties. They will be reluctant to agree not to be able to use information which they learn at mediations.

Parties who feel sensitive about this must be especially careful about what they disclose to the other side if there are officeholders present or involved.

In practice
- Being released from the usual confidentiality provisions is more of a problem with regulators, especially HMRC,

Ombudsman

than with Insolvency Practitioners. But you still need to be aware.
- If you need a relaxation of the standard provisions ask for it before the mediation. Most office holders do not do this and leave it until the day.

See also
CONFIDENTIALITY/LIQUIDATORS

Ombudsman

Originally set up as an independent representative of the public to investigate complaints against Government departments.

Key features
- A form of ADR where the Ombudsman deals with complaints against various entities, both governmental and commercial.
- The Ombudsman is usually a single person but there can be a panel or board.
- Ombudsmen try to resolve complaints through conciliation, and sometimes mediation.
- In the end the Ombudsman issues a decision. It can be either binding or non-binding. Or binding on one party but not the other- usually the complainant.
- Usually Ombudsmen do not hold a hearing but come to a decision on the basis of written evidence and submissions.

Pros
- It is comparatively easy for the complainant to access the procedure.
- It is not confrontational.

- It is often free.
- In many schemes the Ombudsman's ruling is not binding on the complainant but it is binding on the party about whom the complaint is made.

Cons
- It can take an unexpectedly long time for the Ombudsman to investigate. Many services are under resourced and overloaded with cases eg the Financial Ombudsman Service.
- You are dependant on a case handler with whom there is little direct contact.
- You have to be able to present information in written form in an intelligible way. Not everyone can. Many complainants seek some help with their written advocacy.

In practice
- Ombudsmen are likely to be the main challenge to mediators for market share in the conflict resolution market.

Omni-Partiality

A concept particularly used in workplace mediation. The mediator is a friend to everybody.

Transferable to civil and commercial mediation. Mediators are friendly to everybody. All parties want to think that they are the mediator's best friend and that he becomes their advocate in the other room. But being a friend and being friendly are not the same thing.

In practice
- Experienced mediators resist attempts to recruit them as a party's advocate but they do try and appear equally friendly to everybody.

Onions

- When mediators start to reality test parties can wonder why they have stopped being friendly towards them. They think that the mediator has been turned by the other side. They haven't.
- Like Mrs Thatcher, mediators are not for turning.

Onions

Peeling onions is a metaphor to describe how mediators uncover layers. Devised by Marga Schreuder and Ali Hanekoot of the Centre for Conflict Management and the Amsterdam ADR Institute.

A variation of the idea of PIN, ie through questioning getting through to a party's underlying interests.

The basic idea is that behind a position is a belief or general standard. Jacques De Waart gives the following examples:

Position – That illegally built house next door must go.

Standard – Everyone has to obey the law – including my neighbour.

Behind a belief or general standard is a general interest.

Possible general interests: equal treatment/knowing where you stand/preventing precedents being set.

Behind a general interest lies a personal interest.

Possible personal interest: need to be considered/having a degree of control over my life.

Behind a personal interest lies a more personal interest.

Possible more personal interest: have an interrupted view from my window/to be able to rely on my neighbour/to be respected in the street.

See also
INTERESTS/NEEDS/POSITIONS/PIN

Follow up

Association for International Arbitration ed *A Guide to European Mediation* p 163–166

Online Civil Mediation Directory Service

Replaced National Mediation Helpline in 2011.

See also
NATIONAL MEDIATION HELPLINE/MOJ

Follow up

civilmediation.justice.gov.uk

Online Mediation

Where a mediation is conducted by a live mediator who is not physically present with the parties.

Online mediation can be conducted by telephone, Skype, email, or by any of the new technologies such as Zoom.

Particular issues are:

- *Quality of the experience.* Do people behave in the same way when they are face-to-face as when they are online?
- *Security.* This is:
  - The security of the technology.
  - The Process can you be sure that other people are not present who have not signed up to the confidentiality

- provisions in the mediation agreement. You won't necessarily be able to see them.
- *Commitment.* When online, people are often in their usual environment, ie their home or office. No special effort is required to attend a mediation venue. They will be subject to the usual distractions of their normal environment. People find it psychologically easier to log off than to walk out of a live mediation.
- *Quality of the technology.* Despite the claims of their promoters many systems are still clunky and unreliable. If the system doesn't work efficiently people lose faith in the process.

Specialist training is now available for online mediation to equip mediators to cope with the different considerations.

But there are advantages:
- People may not have to spend so much time in the mediation process if they do not have to travel.
- People may spend less money.

In practice
- Its use will grow.
- Embrace it.
- Train in it.
- Use it.

See also
ODR/TELEPHONE MEDIATION/WALK OUT

Follow up

ADRg www.adrgroup.co.uk

VIRTUAL LAB www.virtualmediationlab.com

Opening Statement

An oral statement delivered by a party or its representative when there is a Joint Opening Session.

Traditionally seen by advocates as an opportunity to:
- Demonstrate the strength of their position.
- Set out the main points of their case.
- Overwhelm the opposing party and deflate their expectations.

Doing this gets the mediation off to a bad start. When people feel under attack their defences go up and they stop thinking about settlement.

The purpose of being at mediation is to make peace not war. Therefore when making an opening statement:

- Adopt a slightly formal but conversational tone, not a hectoring, dismissive courtroom one.
- Address your remarks primarily to decision-makers on the other side.
- Present an overall assessment of the current situation rather than a partisan re-statement of your legal case. Situations change as time passes and litigation develops. What was important at the beginning may no longer be important now or be important in the near future.
- Identify the issues, which the parties will have to grapple with in order to achieve a settlement. Only deal with live issues. Abandon dead ones.
- Highlight your good points but acknowledge the other side's good points.
- Keep it under 10 minutes.

Opening Statement

In practice

- You want the decision-maker on the other side to think that you are a competent, well-prepared and reasonable person. If you are a lawyer you want to be someone that on another occasion he might consider instructing.

- The purpose of the Joint Opening Session is to set the mood for the mediation day. Do not raise the temperature, aggravate ill-will or inflame emotions. If you do the mediator will have to spend the next two hours in remedial work before any sensible discussions about the business of the day can start.

See also

JOINT OPENING SESSIONS

Follow up

Walker *Mediation Advocacy: Representing Clients in Mediation* paras 10.10–10.15

P

Panels

In essence lists of mediators with contact details.

4 types

Registers of mediators

They give details of the mediators, eg The Civil Mediation Council. Most have some qualifying criteria.

By invitation

Run by mediation providers who provides administration and marketing services such as Panel of Independent Mediators or In Place of Strife. They usually charge their mediators a percentage of their fee. Varies from 40% to 25%.

Some are often also providers of mediation training, eg CEDR or JAMS.

By application

Also run by mediation providers who provide administration and marketing services. Some charge joining or registration fees such as ADR Group; others, such as Clerksroom, do not.

Some make an administration charge to the clients. Others deduct a percentage from their mediators' fees.

DIY

Group of mediators who band together for marketing purposes. They charge each other a fee and/or percentage. Often based on the traditional barristers' chambers model.

Panels

Some have formal corporate structures with shareholders. Others are much more informal.

Vary greatly in size. But the minimum number of panel mediators to enable the panel to be registered as a mediation provider with the CMC is six.

Pros

From client's point of view:

- A degree of Quality Assurance – particularly if CMC registered.
- Help with logistics – rooms, times, etc.
- Streamlines selection of mediators.
- Knows that the mediator will have PI insurance.

From mediator's point of view:

- Eases administration.
- Promotes marketing.
- CPD events.
- Contact with other mediators.
- Provides PI insurance.

Cons

- From both points of view there can be an extra layer of cost. Sometimes, but not always, cheaper to go to the mediator direct.
- The Panel's administrators can steer mediations in particular directions – particularly to their own trainers if they are also a training organisation.
- Some Panels demand exclusivity.
- Very variable levels of administrative efficiency.

In practice

- Panels proliferate. But are dominated by seven major providers.
- Although most civil and commercial mediators are appointed directly, 45% of appointments are through panels.
- Novice mediators derive greater benefit from panel membership than established mediators with their own reputation and following.

See also

REGULATION/MEDIATION PROVIDERS

Follow up

CEDR Audit 2016 www.cedr.com

Walker *Setting up in Business as a Mediator* pp146–151

Part 36 Offers

A legitimate litigation pressure tactic. They are offers to settle made by a claimant or defendant in proceedings or anticipated proceedings. They can be made:

- before proceedings have started;
- at any time during proceedings;
- during a trial; or
- even at an appeal.

The aim is to put pressure on the other side by exposing them to a costs sanction if the matter proceeds to trial and judgment.

If a Part 36 offer is accepted, that brings an end to the claim. The accepting party is entitled to his costs up to the time of acceptance.

Part 36 Offers

If a Part 36 offer is not accepted and a party at trial does not succeed in beating the offer he can suffer adverse costs consequences. These are having to pay:

- an additional sum not exceeding £75,000, calculated as 10% of amount awarded up to £500,000 and 5% of amount over £500,000 (with a cap of £75,000).
- interest on the damages at a rate not exceeding 10% above the base rate.
- costs on an indemnity basis.
- interest on the costs also at a rate not exceeding 10% above the base rate.

Note that you have to follow the procedure and requirements set out in Part 36 CPR. Deviations can be fatal.

In practice

- Some parties attend mediations in order to discuss the case and gauge the range of settlement figures from the other side to help them formulate an effective Part 36 Offer.
- Where there has been no settlement parties often make Part 36 Offers shortly after the mediation.
- Where mediations take place after a Part 36 Offer has been made then like all pre-mediation offers that have not been accepted it forms part of the parties' mental furniture. The receiving party will expect the paying party to increase the offer.
- The trend among sophisticated users of mediation is to try and settle the matter before mediation. If that is not possible they delay making a Part 36 Offer until after the mediation.

See also
COSTS/EXCHANGING OFFERS/OFFERS/RISK ANALYSIS/SIGNALS

Partnership

Follow-up

Part 36 Civil Procedure Rules

Partnership

The classic definition is an activity carried on by two or more people with a view to profit.

Partnership disputes are a staple of the mediator's diet. They are commercial divorces. They have the same interplay of resentment, emotion, psychological need and money. Often the partners represent themselves, particularly if they are lawyers. This never makes matters easier. There is a lack of objectivity.

Particular features include:

- Difficulties in agreeing figures in particular the dissolution or final account and work in progress (WIP).
- Problems in being able to afford to buy out the departing partner.
- Use of intellectual property rights in precedents, client connections, databases, etc.
- Reputation. Both continuing and departing partners usually want to carry on business or at least preserve their good name and professional standing. A public airing of the dispute in court never enhances anyone's reputation. This is why partnership disputes are particularly suitable for mediation.

In practice

- Disputing partners act in ways that they would never advise their clients to act.
- There is usually less cash available to fund settlement than the partnership accounts suggest.
- WIP is not money.

Patience

See also
COGNITIVE BIASES/OBJECTIVE/REPRESENTATION.

Party Control

A selling point of mediation. See the **TOP TEN**.

See also
AUTONOMY

Patience

Defined as the capacity to accept or tolerate delay, problems, or suffering without becoming annoyed or anxious.

A synonym for:
> forbearance, tolerance, restraint, self-restraint, resignation, stoicism, fortitude, sufferance, endurance, tolerance, indulgence, leniency, kindness, serenity, understanding, composure.

Also defined as a card game played by parties on their iPads during the lull in mediation. Best avoided. Stay engaged.

Anyone who attends mediation in any capacity must be patient.

In practice
- Being passive is not the same as being patient.
- Patience does not mean allowing matters to drag on without any progress and with endless repetition of the same points.

- Setting reasonable and realistic milestones and sticking to them is process management not impatience.
- Sometimes no matter how patient you are you have to call it a day.
- Always remember deals do not get done by walking out.

See also
ENGAGEMENT/GOOD MANNERS

PATNA

Probable Alternative To a Negotiated Agreement.

In practice

- The same thing as RATNA – Realistic Alternative To a Negotiating Agreement.
- Work this out before you go to the mediation. Don't do it on the hoof when you are there.

See also
BATNA/MLATNA/RATNA/WATNA

Peace

Mediators tell parties at mediation that we are here to make peace not war today. Peace making requires a different mind-set and skill set.

People usually nod in agreement when they hear this. But not always.

This anodyne statement produces three non-affirmative reactions:

1 'We're not here to make peace at any price.' The response is 'Does that mean war at any cost?'
2 'We're not here to make peace. We're here to make the best peace.' This is a more aggressive formulation of 1 above and is often delivered by lawyers, especially American ones.
3 'Any settlement must reflect the merits of the case. The other side will have to recognise the weakness of their position.' No-one has a monopoly of good points.

Wanting peace is not some idealistic, wimpish fantasy. As a famous Capo di Tutti Capi said at a meeting of the New York Mafia families: 'Peace is profit.'

And this from someone in whose world disputes are settled by bombs and bullets not by briefs and motions.

In practice

- Peace is not always possible. The best that you can hope for is a ceasefire.
- Some disputes can only be managed so that the conflict is less destructive for all concerned.
- If you're going to mediation put your dealmaker's hat on and remember the Godfather's words.

See also:
MERITS BASED SETTLEMENT/PEACE PREMIUM

Peace Premium

The amount that you save by not going to court. Made up of:

- Legal costs.
- Lost time.

- Opportunity cost of the legal costs and the lost time. What else would you be doing with that money or time?

Peace is worth paying for. This is the premium and is the amount that could be put into the settlement pot.

The longer the time before you attempt settlement the more of the peace premium you spend.

In practice

- Settling disputes earlier is cheaper.
- Spend the peace premium either on settlement or your business not on litigation.

Peer Mediation

This is problem-solving by youth with youth.

Young people, particularly ones in schools or colleges, who are in dispute can meet to solve their issues and problems with the help of a trained youth/student mediator. Schools find it particularly helpful in reducing bullying.

The facilitative joint session model is usually followed.

In practice

- Has been used in the USA for many years. Growing in popularity in the UK.

See also
FACILITATIVE/YOUTH MEDIATION

Follow up

Richbell *How to Master Commercial Mediation* pp 282–288

PEN (Planned Early Negotiation)

Acronym invented in 2011 by John Lande, an American academic and practising mediator.

An attempt to formalise early negotiation as the primary way of resolving disputes rather than by starting legal proceedings. A variation of Collaborative Law pioneered by Family Lawyers.

Aims to reduce the transaction cost of resolving disputes. Most legal cases settle anyway. Recognise that and do it sooner rather than later. Early settlements are cheaper than late ones. Don't spend the peace premium.

Good idea but sounds like putting old wine into new bottles. PEN repackages old techniques such as:

- Identifying successful commercial outcomes for you and the other side.
- Risk analysis.
- Legal analysis.
- Cost benefit analysis.
- Outline litigation plan.
- Review and monitoring mechanism.
- Starting negotiations. Breaking out of the prison of fear.

But if the new packaging attracts customers what's wrong with that?

In practice

- PEN as a formal system has not taken off in UK but is used to a limited extent in USA.
- Many lawyers both in-house and external do something similar but in a less systematic way.

- Both lawyers and clients find it hard to escape the prison of fear.

See also

COLLABORATIVE LAW/PEACE PREMIUM/PMA/ PRISON OF FEAR/RISK ANALYSIS

Pendulum Decision

Where a mediator/arbitrator makes a choice between the parties' final offers that will become legally binding on the parties.

In practice

- Not much used in the UK but likely to become more popular.

See also

MEDALOA

Percentages

Loved by mediators and hated by lawyers, particularly barristers. Mediators use them when encouraging the parties to carry out a risk analysis.

Lawyers tend to prefer verbal rather than numerical expressions of risk or uncertainty. 'We have a very strong case' they say, rather than: 'We have a 70% chance of winning.' Unless you can apply percentage chances calculating risk/reward ratio is impossible.

Third-party litigation funders require chances of success to be expressed in percentages when considering submissions for funding.

Perception

In practice

- You cannot avoid percentages at mediations.
- If your lawyer is reluctant to use percentages – choose a more numerically-orientated one.

See also

DECISION TREES/RISK ANALYSIS/SUMMING THE DIFFERENCE

Follow up

Richbell *How to Master Commercial Mediation* pp 313–323

Walker *Mediation Advocacy: Representing Clients in Mediation* Ch 7

Perception

Mediators repeatedly hear the cliché that 'perception is reality'.

In other words it does not matter what the facts or the position might be objectively, they are what people subjectively think that they are. Everyone has and is entitled to their own reality. There is no truth; just people's own truths.

Such post-modern insights might enliven university seminars but are of limited use in mediations. Of course everybody has their own version of events. Judges face this every day. So do mediators who, even though not acting as judges, often reality test.

Mediators concentrate on:

- Discussing a party's stated interests and needs to see whether they are internally coherent and consistent.
- Identify where a party is expressing conflicting goals/interests/needs.

- Acknowledging a party's perception while pointing out that the other party has a different perception. They encourage perspective shifting.
- Working out how much common ground there is between the different interests/needs of the parties given their different perceptions.

In practice

- At mediation it is often less a question of being right than doing right.
- People see what they want to see. Mediators help them see what they need to see.
- Most people are governed by self-interest. Mediators convert self-interest into shared interest.

See also
PERSPECTIVE/REALITY TESTING

Personality

Mediators are told that it's not the legalities that are important at mediation it's the personalities. As a leading mediation trainer puts it: 'We tell our students, the dispute is not in the facts but in the people.'

If this were true:

- Most mediators who are appointed in civil and commercial disputes would not be lawyers, which they are, they would be psychotherapists or psychologists, which they are not.
- Clients and their solicitors would not appoint sector specialists who know all about the subject matter of the dispute. They would appoint psychotherapists or psychologists who know about personality. But they don't.

Personality

- Most successful mediators, but by no means all, have obvious people skills. They usually have 20 years or more of professional experience dealing with people. Some will have learned more than others from their experience. But all have some idea of what their own personality is like even if they have not taken a Myers Briggs test.
- Some of us are more perceptive than others. It is probably all down to Emotional Intelligence.
- But how do you know whether a mediator has a high Emotional Intelligence Quotient (EIQ)? You don't unless you've used them in the past?
- Nobody ever advertises their EIQ. They may advertise their settlement rate or their class of degree but never their EIQ.

When you appoint a mediator try:

- Asking others for their views.
- Telephoning the mediator.
- Reading their website and blogs.
- Considering what their testimonials say about them.

Most mediators are familiar with the Big Five personality traits:

1 Extroversion.

2 Neuroticism.

3 Conscientiousness.

4 Agreeableness.

5 Openness.

What they won't know is the personalities of the parties and their advisers. More often than not they have never met any of them before and they probably haven't even spoken to the clients.

In practice

- We all form instant views of people.
- We may modify them as during the day we spend time and interact.
- Behaviour is temporary: personality is permanent.

See also

BODY LANGUAGE/COGNITIVE BIASES/RAPPORT

Follow up

Walker *Setting Up in Business as a Mediator* Ch 4

Walker *Mediation Advocacy: Representing Clients in Mediation* Ch 3

Perspective

Experienced mediators do not ask the parties and their lawyers to change their opinions or their minds. But they do ask them do shift their perspective. They encourage them to look at the situation from a different angle.

Mediators will ask you to say:

- What you would do if you were in the other side's position.
- What you think the other side want/need.
- What, if you had been instructed to advise the other side as a lawyer, you would be saying to them.

The more you have done this as part of your pre-mediation preparation the easier you will find it. Practise it before you get there.

In practice

- No lawyer or client will ever publicly admit that they have changed their mind.
- They rarely admit it to the mediator in private.
- New information can change people's minds. Early disclosure of new information is better than late.

Persuasion

Everybody practises persuasion at mediations.

- Advocates try and persuade the other side that they are right and will win at trial.
- Clients try to persuade the other side and the mediator of their willingness and ability to fight all the way to trial and to absorb loss in the unlikely event that they lose.
- Mediators try to persuade the parties to consider not just the cost of settlement but the benefits as well.

In practice

Recognise that:

- Nobody makes a deal for your reasons. They do it for their own.
- No lawyer has ever admitted to being persuaded by the other side's arguments at mediation.
- Time spent trying to persuade the other side that you are right is time wasted. Better to spend the time explaining how a proposal meets their interests as well as your own.

Therefore as a party:

- Spend time both before and at the mediation asking the other side what they need and why.
- Ask yourself: what are the reasons, if any, that I cannot give it to them? Once you have decided that you can, you are in the business of deal-making.

- You can start to ask them: 'If I am able to do that will you be able to do this?'

See also
ADVOCACY/MEDIATION ADVOCACY

Phases – In Mediation

There are two different three-stage phases in mediation: the practical and the philosophical.

Practical

The three stages of most mediations are: Advocacy, Problem-solving and Negotiation.

Advocacy

The parties and their representatives tell the mediator all the points that they are going to make before the judge, if the case does not settle. They try to overwhelm the other side and deflate their expectations.

Problem-solving

The parties look to see if they have the building blocks to construct a platform for settlement if they want to. This is partly analysis and partly exchange with some tentative negotiation. Initial proposals are discussed.

Negotiation

Having decided that they do have the building blocks, they move onto discussing more developed proposals and to agreeing the final wording and final figures.

Philosophical

The classic three stages of mediation are: Education, Exchange and Exploration.

PI (Professional Indemnity) Insurance

In practice
- The phases overlap. The process is not linear.
- Parties will move from one place to another out of order. Most parties return to the Advocacy stage at some stage during the day. This is their comfort zone.
- Progressing through the phases is the most important thing.

See also
EDUCATE/HARVARD/THREE STAGE PROCESS

PI (Personal Injury)

The personal injury sector has not embraced mediation with the same enthusiasm as other legal sectors. They prefer to rely upon the Round Table or Three-Room Settlement discussion process.

In practice
- There is no reason why personal injury claims cannot be successfully mediated in the same way as other disputes.

See also
RTMs – Round Table Meetings

PI (Professional Indemnity) Insurance

This appears in mediations in two different contexts:

1 The mediator's own PI insurance.

   This is not obligatory. Many mediators do not have it. Most successful and experienced mediators do.

PI (Professional Indemnity) Insurance

The Civil Mediation Council requires its members and its registered mediation providers to either have PI insurance or to make sure that their panel members have it.

Panel appointed mediators will normally have the benefit of the panel's policy.

PI insurance is cheap. Insurers do not think that there is much risk of claims being made against mediators.

2 The parties' PI insurance.

Claims against professionals are usually covered by insurance. Often in professional negligence actions there is more than one defendant, which can mean that more than one insurer is involved. This leads to disputes and secondary mediations between insurers.

Claimants want to know whether or not defendants are insured. This has become particularly acute as many professional firms have ceased to trade or become insolvent as a result of the economic depression since 2008.

Professional Indemnity insurance policies are on a claims-made not on a losses-occurring basis. The insurance policy which responds to the claim is the one in force in the year in which the claim is notified to insurers. The negligent act or omission may have occurred some years before when different insurers were involved.

In practice

Most policies have:

- An excess or uninsured element.
- A limit of indemnity.
- Exclusions and warranties.
- All these have to be considered. This means that sometimes a sub-mediation is going on over coverage issues.

See also
INSURERS/MEDIATORS 'LIABILITY

PI (Professional Indemnity) Insurers

Professional indemnity insurers say that they are more enthusiastic about mediation than other insurers. They generally:

- Take a more proactive approach than legal expenses insurers or physical damage insurers.
- Send someone along to mediation.
- Are sophisticated users of litigation and mediation.
- Are initially difficult and try and dominate the process on the day but in the end are realistic and reasonable.

In practice

- Insurers do not attend mediations in person on a surprising number of occasions.
- Insurers do not review reserves just on the basis of telephone calls from their lawyers at the mediation. They need to think about them. This causes delay.

See also
INSURERS

PIN (Positions, Interests and Needs)

The troika that mediators work with is moving the parties from expressing their positions to considering their interests to meeting their needs.

See also
INTERESTS/NEEDS/POSITIONS

Plenary Session

Another word for Joint Session. Where the mediator and the parties all sit together usually at the start of the mediation.

See also
JOINT OPENING SESSION/JOINT SESSIONS

PMA (Pre-Mediation Analysis)

Carrying out a Pre-Mediation Analysis is an essential part of preparation for mediation. Many people do not do it. All they do is prepare a presentation of their best legal points.

Clients and their lawyers need to carry out a PMA together. In a structured way it examines:

- Risk/reward ratio of litigation.
- Cost/benefit ratio of settlement.
- Impact of winning or losing at trial.
- Impact of settling/not settling.
- Client's current and foreseeable needs (tangible/intangible) and resources.
- Client's risk profile.
- How a settlement can be structured to suit clients' needs and the other side's needs.

In practice

- This is rarely done in a considered way. Often rushed though in a meeting on the afternoon before the mediation or in the middle of the mediation.
- When a PMA is completed it often transforms the client's view of the dispute and litigation.

See also

IMPACT/RISK PROFILE/STRUCTURING SETTLEMENT

Follow up

Walker *Mediation Advocacy* para 7.02 for worked example

Point Scoring

An irresistible temptation for parties and advocates, particularly barristers, at mediation.

Always gets in the way of settlement unless carried out in a good-natured spirit of comradely badinage.

In practice

- Try and limit yourself no more than five points a day.

See also

ADVERSARIAL/MEDIATION ADVOCACY/ REPRESENTATION

Positions

The stated expression of:
- What you want.
- Why you are entitled to it.
- What you will do to the other side if they do not give it to you.

Mediators encourage parties to move away from their positions to considering their interests and needs.

Position Papers

In practice

Positions are:

- Often expressed in legal terms and assertions of legal rights.
- Points of departure.

See also

DISCLOSURE/INTERESTS/NEEDS/LIM/PIN

Positional Negotiating

Aka distributive negotiation, haggling. Whatever phrase is used it is the opposite of principled negotiation.

In practice

- There is always some value to be claimed. That is where distributive or positional negotiation comes in.

See also

BARGAINING/DISTRIBUTIVE/HAGGLING/HARVARD/ HORSE TRADING/ZERO SUM

Position Papers

Aka mediation statements. Parties usually send them to the mediator in advance of the mediation.

Often interpreted to mean making a concise but forceful presentation of the strength of your case.

When drafting a position paper be clear:

- Who your audience is.
- What message you want to send.

Position Papers

Audience

- Is it the mediator? Is he a lawyer? What will he want to know? What can he find in other documents? How much time does he have to read everything that is being sent?
- Is it the lawyer on the other side? Are you just locking horns or trying to embarrass him in front of his client and the mediator?
- Is it the decision-maker on the other side? Is he a lawyer? How much has he been involved in the dispute to date? Often the decision-maker has been sent to clear up the problem and has had limited involvement in it prior to mediation.
- Is it your own client? Does he want you to stick it to the other side? Is the position paper a comfort blanket?

Message

Many position papers read like declarations of war or submissions or case statements for an court application.

Barristers admit that they prepare them for the mediator in the same way they prepare a case summary for the judge. They include footnotes and case citations. Some append photocopies of cases.

What the mediator wants is:

- An up-to-date assessment of the current position.
- A clear formulation of the issues that the parties think need to be tackled with his help during the mediation in order to achieve a settlement.
- A guide to the most relevant parts of the documents and mediation bundle that he has been sent.

The key headings:

- Statement of the parties.
- Short description of the nature of the dispute.

Position Papers

- Short descriptions of previous activity – if proceedings have started what stage of the litigation has been reached. What is the next step if settlement is not reached?
- If there have been previous attempts to settle what were they and why did they fail?
- Description of live issues which the mediator will have to tackle in order to achieve a settlement. Brief descriptions of why there is a disagreement between the parties on each of them.
- Identify dead or resolved issues.
- Presentation of financial information, eg schedule of values of properties, summary of balance sheets.
- Summary of costs incurred to date and expected to be incurred to trial.
- Any exceptional or unusual features, eg one of the witnesses is in prison. Or a winding-up petition has been presented.
- Expert evidence/specialist reports. If there are reports. Summarise any conclusions and differences
- Outline of possible settlement frameworks, eg all the properties can be sold and the proceeds divided in proportions to be agreed. Or the properties are not sold but the ownership is rearranged between the parties.

In practice

- Mediators receive their bundle days before they receive position papers.
- Prepare position papers at the same time as the bundle. This concentrates the draughtsman's mind on what documents really are needed for the mediation
- Too many position papers read like declarations of war.

See also
ADVERSARIAL/ADVOCACY/BUNDLES

Follow up

Walker *Mediation Advocacy: Representing Clients in Mediation* pp 208–216

Post Mortem

Takes place on two occasions:

1 At the mediation while the settlement agreement is being prepared for signature. A dangerous time of the day. The parties have made their agreement but not yet signed it. Until they do it is not legally binding. People start to have second thoughts.

2 After the mediation. The agreement has been signed. The parties feel Settler's Remorse. They start asking themselves 'What If?' A waste of time, money and energy.

In practice

- Avoid them if you can.
- Make sure that you record the reasons for settling.

See also
MEDIATION DAY/SETTLER'S REMORSE

Pound Conference

The Roscoe Pound conference of April 1976 held in Minneapolis, Minnesota is celebrated as the birthplace of modern ADR. It was when Prof Frank Sander gave his seminal paper at 'The Pound Conference: Perspectives on Justice in the Future' entitled *The Varieties of Dispute Processing*.

The Conference was called to give legal scholars and jurists the opportunity to discuss:

- Ways of addressing popular dissatisfaction with the American legal system.

- Reforms of the administration and delivery of justice.

To mark its 40th anniversary the IMI is organising the 2016 Global Pound Conference Series. An enormously ambitious project to gather the views of those involved in mediation with meetings proposed in 36 different cities in 26 countries around the world.

Follow up

globalpoundconferences.org

Power

In negotiation this is the ability to control outcomes.

There is objective and subjective power. A large multinational insurance company is more objectively powerful than an individual near-bankrupt policyholder. But if a policyholder has nothing to lose, he has subjective power.

Churchman lists 10 sources of power:

1. Authority
2. Charisma
3. Image
4. Knowledge
5. Legitimacy
6. Options
7. Ruthlessness
8. Time
9. Trustworthiness
10. Understanding

The only one that is sometimes difficult to exercise at mediations is no 7. At least by mediators. Note that many of them are subjective rather than objective.

In fact recent research suggests that there is no difference in negotiation between being powerful and feeling powerful.

In practice
- Be realistic. Sometimes you are in bed with a two-ton gorilla.
- Act as though the force is with you.
- Most parties overestimate their power in public and underestimate it in private.

See also
BALANCE OF POWER/IMBALANCE OF POWER

Follow up
David Churchman *Negotiation* 1995

Pre-Mediation Meetings

Rarely used in England and Wales in civil and commercial mediations. More common in Scotland.

Useful in complex multi-party disputes for example in construction mediations. Particularly where there are several different agendas that have to be considered in parallel along with a mass of technical detail and expert's reports.

Usually concerned more with designing the process for the mediation rather than with the issues or possible settlement options.

In practice
- Often an unnecessary expense of time and money.

Pre-Mediation Telephone Calls

Essential for a successful mediation. Mediators who go in cold to mediation never having spoken to any of the parties or their representatives make life more difficult for everyone.

Parties feel neglected and complain if mediators do not make contact before the mediation.

Mediators should:

- Always telephone the party's representatives (if they are represented) or the parties themselves if they are not.
- Not telephone the parties direct if they are represented. If you do that you are likely to upset the representative and your actions will be seen as a breach of professional etiquette.
- Always say that the conversation is confidential.

The purpose of the phone call is to:

- Introduce yourself.
- Find out who is attending the mediation and what their mediation experience and expectations are.
- Explain how you normally conduct mediations to see if this matches the parties' expectations.
- Give an opportunity to the representative to raise any particular points at this stage before the mediation has begun.

If you have received and read the papers before you make a telephone call you can raise any points that occur to you. Be careful not to get drawn into telephonic cross-examination.

For the representatives/parties these calls allow you to:

- Get to know the mediator a little if you've never spoken to him before.
- Set the mood and the agenda from your point of view.

Pre-Mediation Telephone Calls

- Raise any confidential or sensitive matters with the mediator which you would not want to put in writing.
- Raise any concerns that you have about:
  - The process – for example your client may be nervous about a Joint Opening Session.
  - The other side – for example parties often tell mediators that they are not sure that their opposite number has authority to settle or is approaching the mediation in good faith.

With unrepresented parties mediators can expect to spend time explaining what mediation is, what the process entails, how to prepare for it and what to say or even wear on the day.

Some mediators like to ask the representative for permission to speak to their clients direct. They think this helps establish rapport. Others do not. They want to avoid crossed wires and mixed messages.

Occasionally a solicitor asks the mediator to speak to his own client directly. This is usually because the client has started to express doubts about attending the mediation at all. Reading a hostile or tendentious position paper can trigger this reaction. Do this if asked but always report back to the solicitor.

In practice

- Most parties and/or their lawyers welcome a pre-mediation chat with the mediator.
- Mediators should not leave making the call until the day before the mediation.

See also

AGENDA/ASSESSMENT/POSITION PAPER/RAPPORT

Follow up
Walker *Mediation Advocacy* paras 11.06–07

Precedent H

Much unloved by solicitors in England and Wales. The form for setting out budgets of anticipated costs in legal proceedings.

Introduced as part of the Jackson reforms in April 2013. Designed to enable courts to manage legal costs in litigation. Many were becoming disproportionate.

A side-effect of Precedent H is that more detailed consideration has to be given by the parties and their lawyers to exactly how much litigation is going to cost at a much earlier stage.

Even now many lawyers are still coy about discussing their client's potential liability to legal costs. Complling Precedent H helps avoid this. A realistic appreciation of legal cost is significant for mediations.

Many mediators emphasise the risk of incurring significant legal costs if the case doesn't settle. Sometimes this is of no significance:

- The amount in dispute and what parties could potentially gain if they win at court far outweighs any costs that they may incur.
- For large corporations or extremely rich individuals legal costs are immaterial.

In many other cases the ratio of costs to the amount claimed or recoverable is significant. Saving legal costs is one factor in favour of settlement at any mediation. But it is only one and not always the most important.

Some parties become irritated if they see mediators over-emphasising legal costs. They think that the mediator

Preparation

doubts their ability to pay or their commitment to their cause and is trying to scare them.

In practice
- Round figure calculations of costs, past and future, are all that is required at mediation.
- Most clients have not fully understood the full impact of legal costs on their case.
- If your solicitor has not sent you a copy of the Precedent H ask for one.

See also

COSTS/NET

Follow up

CPR PD 3E

www.justice.gov.uk/courts/procedure-rules/civil/pdf/update/new-precedent-h-guidance.pdf

Cook on Costs 2016

Laura Slater (ed) *Costs: A Practical Guide* (2016)

Preparation

Preparation for mediation needs rebalancing. Currently most parties and their lawyers spend 80% of their time preparing their case and their submissions and less than 20% on structuring possible settlements.

Since the purpose of mediation is to make peace not war the proportions need to change. Preparation is both mental and physical. The essential stages in preparation are:

- Pre-mediation contact with mediator.
- PMA.

- Position paper.
- Bundle.
- Opening statement.

See also

PMA

Follow up

Walker *Mediation Advocacy: Representing Clients in Mediation* Chs 5 and 10

Price

As Warren Buffett says 'Price is what you pay. Value is what you get.'

Do not confuse them.

Most parties concentrate on the cost of settlement, ie the price they pay either by handing over money or reducing their demands. They overlook the benefits of settlement.

Benefits are both tangible and non-tangible. Non-tangible benefits can still be identified and quantified although this is not always easy.

Do this before the mediation. It is much more difficult to do in the middle of a mediation.

Common benefits of settlement are:
- Not having to spend any more money on legal costs.
- Getting rid of the risk and uncertainty.
- Not having to spend time and effort on the dispute.

Principle

- Releasing time, money and energy for the business of their business which is never litigation. That is the business of the lawyers.
- Less stress.
- Reducing distraction.
- Containment of reputational risk.
- Confidentiality.

Remember be realistic in assigning values to non-tangible benefits. Don't just put notional values to them.

In practice

- Before the mediation day parties tend to concentrate on the cost or price of settlement.
- During the mediation day, as they discuss and reflect, they think more about the value of settlement.

See also
COSTS/VALUE

Principle

A word used at every mediation at some stage.

There are two senses:

1 Someone always says: 'It's a matter of principle' or 'It's becoming a matter of principle.'

   Sometimes fortified by supplemental phrases such as:
   - 'I'd rather pay the money to my lawyers and lose than…'
   - 'I just don't want them to get away with it…'
   - 'I don't want this to happen to anybody else…'

If something really is a matter of principle for you, ask yourself what apart from the payment of money can satisfy you. If this is seeing the other side being punished or suffering pain – commercial or personal – be prepared to go all the way to trial. But also be prepared to be disappointed.

In practice

- Most matters that are expressed to be ones of principle can be met by the receipt of money. Sometimes a written apology is also necessary. Rarely is it sufficient on its own.
- Most matters of principle, ie fundamental values which go to the sense of identity, are more accurately described as deeply held grievances, objections, requirements, demands or needs.
- Principles such as fairness or equity are often subjectively interpreted.
- The word has been so overused in negotiations, that it has lost meaning and impact.

2 In principle

The parties have made progress. But they cannot sign a concluded binding settlement agreement. They can however make an agreement in principle.

This can be a staging post along the road to settlement or it can be a dead end. Much depends on post-mediation activity. You have to keep the momentum going if you want to reach a concluded settlement. Sometimes that is helped if the mediator continues in his role. Sometimes it is better if the parties negotiate directly with each other.

Be clear whether any agreements in principle/heads of agreement are intended to be legally binding or not.

In practice

- Try to avoid agreements in principle – they are not settlements.
- Sometimes they cannot be avoided but they are too often used as displacement activity.

Principled Negotiation

The opposite of positional negotiating which is a zero-sum game, ie 'What I gain you lose'. Instead based on 'win-win.'

Allegedly introduced to the world by Fisher and Ury through the Harvard Negotiation Project.

In practice

- Used less than idealists want and more than the realists say.

See also

HARVARD/WIN-WIN/ZERO SUM

Follow up

Fisher Ury *Getting to Yes*

Priorities

Clients hate mediators asking them what their priorities are. They have to analyse, evaluate and choose. This puts responsibility on them.

Clients who have undertaken a PMA find this easier. Parties who haven't can find the mediator's questions stressful. Often they give a list of contradictory or mutually incompatible priorities.

Be ready to be asked about priorities. Much better to have an idea in advance and not to make them up as you go along on the mediation day.

In practice

- Priorities change over time.
- Different members of the negotiating team can have different priorities.

See also
LIM/PIN/PMA

Prison of Fear

Phrase coined by John Lande to describe the typical lawyer's mindset when advising clients on a dispute.

Invitations to negotiation/mediation/settlement are seen by other side's lawyers and clients as a sign of weakness. Your own clients might interpret any willingness as lack of commitment to their cause.

Reluctance to initiate negotiations leads to expensive and protracted litigation. Disputes which start off as commercial ones become more legal even though the chances are that they will end in a commercial settlement. Money goes down the litigation silo rather than into the settlement pot.

So plan your prison break.

In practice

- Fight first: talk later is the mindset of many lawyers and clients.
- In UK it's changing along with the courts' encouragement of mediation.
- Mediation is no longer seen as a sign of weakness.
- Paradoxically the stronger your case the earlier you should try to settle it and collect your money. Mediators do act as agents of reality.

Prisoner's Dilemma

- Remember : 'Jaw Jaw is better than War War' (Winston Churchill).

See also

COMPULSION/DIRECTIONS QUESTIONNAIRE/ HALSEY/MEDIATORS/PEN

Follow up

John Lande *Lawyering With Early Planned Negotiation* American Bar Association

Prisoner's Dilemma

The classic demonstration of the benefits and difficulties of cooperative – as opposed to competitive – behaviour.

Two prisoners are arrested.

1. They are suspected of having committed both a major crime and a minor offence. They are kept in separate rooms and cannot communicate.
2. The prosecution do not have enough evidence to convict them of the major crime. They offer each prisoner the same deal:
   - If you confess to the major offence, but your partner in crime does not, you give evidence against him and go free and he gets 20 years.
   - If you both confess you each get 10 years.
   - If neither of you confesses you each get two years for the minor offence.
3. What do you do? Whatever you do your outcome depends upon what the other side does.

Go to page 539 for the answer.

Privilege

There is no such thing in England and Wales as mediation privilege. The courts have declined to find that it exists over and above the ordinary rules of confidentiality (whether implied or express in a contract) and the without prejudice rule.

This means that;

1 There is no special immunity from suit for mediators or anybody else taking part in the mediation. Hence the exclusion clauses in mediation agreements.

2 Documents which are produced solely for the purpose of the mediation remain confidential and cannot be referred to later. But documents which would be disclosable under the ordinary rules remain disclosable.

3 Officeholders who have statutory duties often require a carve-out or exemption from the blanket confidentiality of mediation proceedings.

See also
DISCLOSURE/MEDIATOR'S LIABLITY/OFFICE HOLDERS/WITHOUT PREJUDICE

Follow up

Brown v Rice [2007] EWHC 625 (Ch)

Problem solving

The key skill at mediation. Mediators encourage the parties to identify the problem, agree the scope and work out how it can be tackled. The problem is the enemy not the other side.

It is the middle phase of the Three Phase procedure.

The more that you have carried out a PMA the better prepared you will be for problem-solving on the day and the less stressful you will find it.

Profession

Procedure

See THREE STAGE

Process

See THREE STAGE

Profession

Is mediation a profession? Many mediators say that it is. This is debatable.

The fact that many mediators have professional qualifications in other sectors such as law, medicine, accountancy, surveying does not make mediation itself a profession. Mediation lacks several of the key characteristics:

- It is not a full-time occupation for most mediators.
- There is no licensing. Anybody can practise as a mediator.
- Mediators do not need to have received any training.
- There is no regulation.
- There is no nationally approved syllabus of specialised training.
- There is no mandatory code of professional ethics.

Various initiatives are under way to supply some of these elements, for example:

- The IMI certification process.
- The EU code of conduct for mediators.
- The CMC register of members.

They are all voluntary. Attempts at regulation are resisted by many mediators.

In practice

- Mediation in England and Wales is more like a cottage industry than a profession.

- This is not necessarily a bad thing. But it impedes development of a mediation voice.

See also
CMC/EU CODE OF CONDUCT/IMI/REGULATION

Proposals

The currency of mediation. Without proposals there is no mediation, let alone settlement.

Mediations that turn into an exchange of arguments and point-scoring do not lead to settlements. Deals are achieved by discussing proposals.

Do not be afraid of making a proposal. Set the agenda. Give the mediator something to work with.

Make it as detailed a proposal as you can. The mediator can then ask the other side what has to be changed in your proposal to make it work for them.

Be prepared to explain the reasoning behind your proposal. In particular how you have calculated the figures.

When you receive the other side's proposal be prepared to discuss and amend it constructively. Be aware of cognitive biases. Much easier to do this if you have carried out a PMA.

In practice
- When a proposal becomes a travelling draft you know you are on the road to settlement.
- The sooner the parties are discussing proposals rather than exchanging information and scoring points the better.

Psychology

See also
ANCHORING/EXCHANGING OFFERS/HEALTH WARNINGS/OFFERS/PMA

Proxemics

See also
SEATING

Psychology

The study of mind and behaviour. Much loved by all participants in the mediation world, especially trainers and commentators:

- Parties think that they are pretty good at reading other people.
- Advocates think that they know how to persuade others.
- Non-lawyer mediators emphasise the primacy of psychological over legal factors in mediation.

The trouble is that psychologists are as good as lawyers at disagreeing with each other and as good as nutritionists at coming up with new theories and fashions.

To gain an accurate psychological understanding of a person takes:

- Much more time and effort than is available at mediation.
- Much more skill, training and practice than most mediators, clients or lawyers have.

Ignore psychology at your peril. Embrace it at your peril.

In practice

Accept that:

- People do deals for their own reasons not yours.
- People do not always know what their own needs or motivations are.
- People are capable of being self-contradictory and acting against their own best interests.

See also

CIALDINI'S BIG SIX/COGNTIVE BIASES/EMOTIONS/ PERSONALITY

Follow up

Walker *Mediation Advocacy* Ch 18 Mind Traps Alert

Walker *Setting Up in Business as a Mediator* Ch 4 Know Yourself

Public Statements

Parties often make a joint announcement as part of the settlement. The wording, timing and method of the release are agreed.

Even where there is no joint announcement a statement is issued. Remember that:

- What happens at mediation is subject to the confidentiality provisions in the mediation agreement.
- Some clauses are tougher than others and say that the fact of mediation and not just the contents of the discussions at mediation are confidential. Most do not.
- Whether the terms of any settlement are confidential is to be negotiated and agreed as part of the settlement.

Public Statements

The basic rules

If there is no settlement:

- The without prejudice rule as well as the confidentiality provisions of the mediation agreement will remain in full force.
- The fact that mediation has taken place and failed is not covered by confidentiality and can be referred to. Unless specifically prohibited in the mediation agreement.
- What was discussed at the mediation cannot be disclosed or referred to.

If there is a settlement:

- The confidentiality provisions remain but the without prejudice rule is modified if there is a dispute about the terms of settlement.
- The fact that the mediation has taken place and succeeded is not covered by confidentiality and can be referred to, unless specifically prohibited in the mediation agreement or the settlement agreement.
- What was discussed at mediation cannot be disclosed or referred to.

NB 1 If the mediation agreement contains an express clause stipulating that the fact of mediation cannot be disclosed that remains in force whether or not there has been a settlement.

2 If the settlement agreement stipulates that its terms are confidential that contractual confidentiality remains in force.

See also
CONFIDENTIALITY

Follow up

Walker *Mediation Advocacy: Representing Clients in Mediation* paras 12.1–12.09 & 13.20

Q

Quality Assurance

The lack of compulsory regulation of mediators means limited quality assurance for customers.

The main ways customers can be assured about the quality of mediators are by finding out:

- How and when was the mediator accredited? Was he accredited by a CMC accredited mediation trainer?
- Is he on any professional panels such as in In Place of Strife, ADR group, CEDR etc?
- Whether his panels insist on proper accreditation, CPD and professional indemnity insurance.
- Has he obtained IMI accreditation?
- What do the testimonials on his website or panel entry say?
- Is he ranked in a Directory such as *Chambers* or *Legal 500* and what do the entries say?
- What your colleagues and network think.

See also

ADR GROUP/CEDR/CHOOSING A MEDIATOR/CMC/IMI/ IN PLACE OF STRIFE/PROFESSION/REGULATION

Follow up

Walker *Mediation Advocacy: Representing Clients in Mediation* Ch 3

Questions – Open/Closed

CMC – www.civilmediation.org/

IMI – imimediation.org/

CEDR – www.cedr.com/

In Place of Strife – www.mediate.co.uk/

ADR Group – www.adrgroup.co.uk/

Questions – Open/Closed

The mediator's main tool. Be prepared both to answer and ask them.

Closed questions are:
- Those which can be answered with a short answer, usually yes or no.
- Used in court during cross-examination to close down discussions, thoughts or lines of enquiry. Not to open them up.
- Used at mediation to confirm or clarify something for example 'Would you accept £50,000?'

Open questions are designed to open up lines of discussion or thought.

The six usual ones are:
- Who?
- What?
- How? The most useful.
- Why? The most dangerous.
- When? The most under used.
- Where?

Questions – Open/Closed

Experienced mediators ask questions for a reason. Think about why they are asking the question at all. You can ask them why they are doing it. They may not, for reasons of confidentiality, be able to tell you.

Not answering questions from the mediator or giving evasive answers usually sends out a negative message. Doubts arise:

- Are you in good faith trying to settle?
- Are you just engaged in a tactical exercise?
- Do you know what you want?
- Are you trying to game the mediator?
- Have you prepared properly?

Some advocates are over-protective of their clients.

- They do not allow them to answer the mediator's questions.
- They do all the answering and most of the talking.
- They insist on discussing most responses with their clients in private without the mediator being present.
- They answer the question without even consulting their clients.
- Their worst sin is when the mediator brings in a proposal from the other side and the lawyer rejects it out of hand without even looking at, let alone speaking to, his client. Doing this sends out multiple negative messages.
- Mediators really don't like lawyers acting in this way. Clients are not always keen either.

In practice

- The most useful question for mediators is 'How'.
- Use 'Why' sparingly. It can appear over-Socratic and hostile. Instead of asking 'Why is this important to you?' Try 'How is this important to you'?

Questions – Open/Closed

See also
KIPLING

Follow up
Walker *Setting up in Business as a Mediator* paras 11.20–22

R

THE SEVEN Rs of Mediation

Parties and advocates at mediation should be

1 Reasonable
2 Ready
3 Realistic
4 Reciprocal
5 Relaxed
6 Responsive
7 Robust

Follow up

Walker *Mediation Advocacy: Representing Clients in mediation*

Ranging Offers

The opposite of a points offer where a single figure is suggested. For example instead of saying £100 you offer £90–£110.

Traditionally thought to be a bad technique because the listener would only hear the figure that suited him best. Recent research suggests that a 'bolstering range offer' is the best.

If you want to achieve the figure of £100 offer a range of £100–£120 rather than a bracketing range offer of £90–£110 or a backdown range offer of £80–£100.

In practice

- Mediators often refer to ranges and brackets when trying to free up the parties' thinking about figures and proposals.
- Parties and their advisers are often reluctant at first to think in terms of ranges. It becomes easier with practice.

See also
ANCHORING/BRACKETING/OFFERS

Rapport

What mediators must have with parties and their advocates.

This means establishing an atmosphere of trust and confidence. Then parties and their lawyers will feel that they can disclose information, ideas, fears and needs which are not immediately apparent from what has been said publicly either in joint sessions or in correspondence/pleadings.

Different mediators have different ways of building rapport. They:

- Chat about football, the weather or holidays.
- Try to discover things in common with the parties or advocates such as places visited or shared acquaintances.
- Encourage the client to tell them their story as often and for as long as they want to.
- Tell jokes.
- Insist on breakfast or lunch together.

Some mediators have the knack of quickly establishing working relationships. Others don't.

As a client or advocate you may never have met the mediator before or even spoken to them. You will naturally be on your guard and a bit suspicious. 'Why should I unburden myself to this stranger?'

In practice
- Establishing rapport is a two-way process. Join in.
- Like it or not mediation is a team effort. Everybody has to play their part to achieve a settlement which is a fair and reasonable alternative to going to trial for all concerned.
- If you lose trust in the mediator stop the mediation.

RATNA (Realistic/Reasonable Alternative to a Negotiated Agreement)

In reality the same thing as PATNA/MLATNA.

See also
PATNA (Probable Alternative to a Negotiated Agreement)/MLATNA (Most Likely Alternative to a Negotiated Agreement)

Realism

Negotiation is a process of the mutual recognition of reality. That is: your own reality and the other party's reality.

By all means start high and hope for the best. But recognise what you are likely to achieve and plan for the worst.

In practice
- Mediation is a process of reality recognition.
- ADR can stand for Alarming Dose of Reality. Be prepared for it.

See also
REALITY TESTING

Reality Testing

Aka reality therapy, bashing and trashing, and destabilising. A technique much loved by mediation trainers and mediators of a certain cast of mind.

The idea is to shake the parties' confidence in their stated positions. The line between robust reality testing and evaluative mediation can be hazy.

- If the mediator challenges your assertions using the arguments and information provided by the other side that is reality testing.
- If the challenges are based on his own opinions about the outcome of the case at trial that is evaluative.

Some mediators feel entitled to tell the parties and their lawyers that their case is rubbish. They tend to be either Americans or QCs who have sat as judges.

More usually reality testing consists of asking a series of questions along the lines of:

- What do you say about their point that…?
- How will you get over the evidential difficulty of…?
- You say this and they say the opposite – why do you think that the judge will prefer your view?
- What evidence do you have to prove that…?
- What happens if your witness does not attend?
- What about the recent case of…?
- I know that your expert says this but their expert says the opposite. What's new? Is this simply a clash of the experts?

The mediation becomes a sort of proxy debate between the parties conducted through the mediator rather than face-to-face. In some ways not very different from a mini-trial

Reality Testing

Or you can be asked point-blank: 'What percentage chance do you give yourself of winning at trial?' This is where reality testing shades into risk analysis.

Clients' expectations can also be reality tested.

- Why do you expect your brother to surrender his half share in one family property in exchange for a quarter share in another one?
- How likely is it that the company can afford to pay £500,000 in one go rather than by instalments over a year?
- What would you do if you were them?

This is where reality testing can shade into perspective shifting. Clients can find it uncomfortable if they have not been prepared.

Settlement proposals can be reality tested:

- Do you think that the other side will accept it?
- Would you accept it if you were them?
- What message are you sending out with this proposal?
- How likely is it that they will accept instalments over three years without security?
- How confident are you that you can meet the instalment dates?

Thinking about these sorts of questions in advance will:

- Make the mediation go much more smoothly.
- Lead to better outcomes.
- Lead to less stress for clients.
- Help you devise credible and robust settlement proposals.

Reading Papers

In practice
- All mediators engage in reality testing.
- Recognising your own reality will make it less testing.
- Reality testing cases is not the same as reality testing proposals. Be clear which is happening.

See also
BASHING AND TRASHING/MINI-TRIAL/PERSPECTIVE/ PMA (Pre-Mediation Analysis)/RISK ANALYSIS

Reading Papers

Do not assume your mediator will have read all the papers that you send. Some do. Some don't.

Lawyer mediators tend to read all the papers. That's what they do in their day job.

Some mediators do not even want any papers. For them the detail of the case is irrelevant. The details may be important to the parties but not to the mediator. They prefer to learn from the clients in their own words about the facts and issues.

If you send papers, check whether the mediator charges for reading them. Some include all preparation in their standard fee. Some include three or four hours – or all reasonable preparation – and charge extra for anything over that. Some mediators seem to be very slow readers.

Mediators who do not carefully read the papers risk alienating the parties. Building trust and confidence takes longer if you cannot show that you have studied the bundle that the clients have spent money on having prepared and sent.

Some sophisticated users of mediation complain that some of the most in-demand commercial mediators do not always appear to be properly prepared.

In practice

- Civil and commercial mediators should read the papers. Their clients – both lawyers and the parties – expect it.
- If you want the mediator to read all the papers send them early – not two days before the mediation.
- If you think that the mediator has not read the papers tell him on the day, not a week later.

See also

BUNDLES/PREPARATION

Reasonable

Has two meanings at mediation.

1 As a rallying cry:

Everyone at mediation believes that they are reasonable. 'Let's be reasonable' they say. Like fairness it's a subjective but powerful concept.

Recognise this. As a reasonableness check ask yourself what you would do if you were the other party.

2 As a euphemism:

'We have a reasonable chance of winning'. Translates as 'We expect to lose'.

In practice

- Take the mediator's guidance about what 'reasonable' means in your particular mediation.
- Most mediators indicate when they think that a party is not being as reasonable as they could be.

See also

COGNITIVE BIAS/DIGNIFIED EXIT

Recommendations

Taboo for traditional facilitative mediators. It is for the parties to find their own solution not for the mediator to suggest one.

In reality:

- Parties expect guidance from mediators on closing a deal.
- Some go further and ask the mediator to make a recommendation. Usually these are non-binding.
- Sometimes they ask mediators to make binding recommendations. Mediators who do this are in fact acting as arbitrators.

If you ask a mediator to make a recommendation, binding or not, be prepared to hear news that is unwelcome or unexpected. Do not forget that the mediator has heard confidential information in both rooms. That may well influence his recommendation but he will not be able to disclose it.

Many mediators make a recommendation without giving any reasons and refuse to enter into any discussion about the recommendation. Certainly they will not discuss their reasoning.

In practice

- All mediators are asked informally what they think about the merits of the case or settlement. Some tell you. Most decline.
- The use of recommendations seems to be growing.

See also
MEDIATOR'S PROPOSAL

Recoverablity

Always raised at mediations. Not always an issue. But it often is.

You have a cast iron claim. But the other party simply cannot pay you. What then?

You have to weigh up the reality. Why spend £50,000 in legal costs chasing a debt of £250,000 to find that having obtained judgment your defendant is insolvent. This is throwing good money after bad.

As lawyers say: 'Obtaining judgment is the easy part. Collecting the money is the hard part.'

Paying parties who claim that they are impecunious have to show the receiving party that that they cannot pay. Don't just tell them. They won't believe you. Be prepared to:

- Produce evidence of assets and liabilities.
- Swear an Affidavit of Means.
- Give a warranty in the settlement agreement.

The chances of collecting on a judgment is a key risk factor to be included in any risk analysis.

The receiving party often takes the view that:

- If the other side cannot pay that is their problem. This is not true. If you want someone to pay you money it is your problem as well. As part of negotiating a settlement, make it easy for them to pay you.
- If the other side does not pay, you will proceed to enforce, for example by bringing insolvency proceedings. Easily said. But it costs more money and takes time. Will you be in a better net cash position at the end of it all after the liquidation has been completed and the insolvency practitioners have had their fees?

Reciprocity

In practice
- Considering recoverability is part of being realistic.
- There is nothing as attractive as cash on the table.
- If you can't pay prove it.

Reciprocity

One of Cialdini's Big Six.

A universal rule. Research shows that every human society follows the rule of reciprocating and the sense of obligation that it engenders.

It is well established that:
- If you do someone a favour they are more likely to do what you want when you ask them later. Fundraisers, for example, include small gifts such as a pen or a small enamel badge with their letters seeking donations.
- Trading is at the heart of any negotiation. Effective negotiators do not make concessions, they trade them.

Giving the other side something first – a pen, a cup of tea or even just a compliment – can pay dividends.

In practice
- There is always some reciprocity in mediations.
- But beware of the fallacy of thinking: 'If I am nice to them they will be nice to me'.

See also
CIALDINI'S BIG SIX

Reframing

Red Line

Aka line in the sand, point of no return or granite cliff edge.

A boundary that cannot be crossed. If an issue is a red line it is non-negotiable.

Originated when Gulbenkian drew red lines on a map for British, American and French oil companies who were working out which parts of the Ottoman Empire they could explore for oil. Look at the problems that have emerged since.

In practice

- Very little is actually non-negotiable.
- Many red and bottom lines vanish or are redrawn.

See also

BOTTOM LINES/DEADLINES

Reframing

A basic mediators' technique. Mediators play back to the speaker what they have just heard but in less toxic language.

For example:

> 'I think my boss is a lying deceitful toad. I wouldn't trust him as far as I could throw him.'

> RF: 'So what I'm hearing is that you have confidence issues with your boss.'

Much practised by inexperienced mediators and those from the therapeutic arm. When used by unskilled practitioners reframing sounds patronising to those whose words are reframed and infuriates them.

Regulation

If your words are reframed and you do not like what you hear say so. Tell the mediator that he is missing the point or overlooking the emphasis. But remember that your original statement may have been exaggerated or tendentious.

In practice
- Practitioners reframe much less often than theorists advise but summarise more.

See also
NVC/SUMMARISING

Regulation

There is no regulation of mediators in England and Wales. Mediation is an unregulated activity.

Many eminent practitioners think that this is a good thing. For example Clive Lewis one of the UK's leading workplace mediation trainers says:

> 'like coaching, mediation is an unregulated industry and is likely to stay unregulated for the foreseeable future. This is a good thing...'

The nearest thing to a regulator in England and Wales is the Civil Mediation Council. This sets minimum standards for those trainers and mediation providers who wish to be members.

In 2015 they introduced a system of individual registration. Again it sets minimum requirements. They include having CPD and PI insurance. These can be found on the CMC's website.

The inherent difficulty is that there is no licensing.
- Anybody can use the description 'mediator.'

- Anybody who has passed any sort of training can call themselves an 'accredited mediator'. Even if they have never attended a mediation, let alone conducted one.
- There is no requirement to keep up with continuous professional development (CPD) or to have any sort of complaints procedure or professional indemnity insurance.

See also

ACCREDITATION/CMC/PROFESSION/QUALITY CONTROL

Follow up

CMC – www.civilmediation.org/

IMI – imimediation.org/

Relationships

As a concept in the mediation context important in three ways:

1 Rebuilding or preserving relationships is one of the advertised advantages of mediation over arbitration or litigation.

 The scope for resetting relationships exists in mediation in a way that it cannot in a court room. Every mediator has seen examples of relationships being restored. Every mediator has also seen examples of relationships not being restored.

2 Broken relationships are said to be behind every dispute. The mediator's job therefore, is to reconnect the parties and, for the purpose of settlement, re-establish the relationship.

Relationships

The idea that behind every dispute lies a broken relationship is promulgated by David Richbell. As he says:

> 'I believe that behind every dispute lies a damaged relationship. Even in the most dispassionate insurer/insurer case, relationships still exist, and it's just not just party to party, but lawyer to lawyer, expert to expert and a mix-up of all of them. It is (or should be) all about relationships.'

This view influences the way in which mediation is practised in the UK.

But this premise is not universally accepted. Not every interaction between parties that leads to a dispute is a relationship. Some are simply transactions or encounters. For example:

- There is no relationship in any meaningful sense between someone who buys a pair of trainers in a discount store on holiday in Spain and then complains when the soles have fallen off back in London. There may have been a degree of interaction but no relationship was formed.

- Making a claim against the driver of the car that drove into the back of you does not arise out of a relationship because the two of you were on the same stretch of road in different cars at the same time. Nor does the collision create one.

Describing something as a relationship imbues it with a sense of personal investment, emotional connection, permanence or continuity. This can be dangerous and lead settlement discussions down blind alleys.

- For example buying insurance through your broker once is not a relationship. If you did it every year some degree of personal connection which could be called a relationship is formed.

- If you buy it online there is no relationship at all no matter how many times you do it. But your legal rights and entitlements and commercial needs may be just the same.

Hence mediators spend time talking to the parties about how they interacted with each other in the past and what has gone wrong.

3   How the participants at the mediation act towards each other. For example if there is a team on one side the mediator has to be alert to the relationships between the various members. Who is the decision-maker? Who has been brought in to clean up the mess? Who caused the mess? Are different departments blaming each other for what has happened?

The relationship between lawyers and their clients is often one that intrigues mediators. Are the lawyers nervous about their client's ability to pay their fees? Are they defending their own position, ie advice that they had previously given?

But mediators usually emphasise that they are not relationship counsellors or psychotherapists. Although some are multi-qualified and on occasions seem to confuse their roles.

In reality small consumer disputes are increasingly sorted out by automated, online systems such as the ones used by PayPal and eBay. There are no relationships with algorithms.

In practice

Parties can be surprisingly reluctant to recognise that:

- Any relationship ever existed.
- Even if it did, that there is any desire or possibility to re-establish it.
- Time and effort spent on exploring relationships can be better spent finding out what the parties need in order to move on to the next stage of their business or personal life.

Representation

See also
EMOTIONS/ODR/TEAMS/VENTING

Follow up

Richbell *How to Master Commercial Mediation* pp129–144

Representation

Representation at mediation is not essential. Most mediation agreements expressly say that parties do not have to be represented at all, let alone be legally represented. They have the right to be represented but not the obligation.

Some mediators:

- Think that parties are better off without any representation, particularly legal.
- Spend their time talking with the parties and not to the representatives even when they are present.

In England and Wales there are usually no representatives at family, community and workplace mediations. The parties:

- Have the right to seek advice – legal or otherwise.
- Do not have to make any sort of settlement until they have taken advice.

But the parties themselves, not their representatives, undertake the actual negotiations at the mediation.

For smaller claims, which are dealt with by a telephone mediation, representatives are not usually present.

In practice
- In most civil and commercial cases parties take representatives and these are usually lawyers.

See also
LAWYERS' ROLES/REPRESENTATIVES

Follow up

Walker *Mediation Advocacy: Representing Clients in Mediation* pp 91–100

Representatives

Whoever represents a client at mediation should:

- Know about the dispute/case/claim.
- Have been through a PMA with the client and know its outcome.
- Have – or be able to quickly win – the client's confidence.
- Have the authority to sign settlement documents on behalf of his firm or the client.
- Have the authority to negotiate legal costs on behalf of the lawyers and insurers.

At mediation the representative must:

- *Appear to be in control* – Be able to answer questions from the other side or the mediator promptly, deal with the unexpected, be proactive and advise clients.
- *Act in a professional and competent way* – Not become flustered, aggressive or lose his temper or patience either with the mediator, clients or the other side.
- *Be restrained* – Avoid extreme language and do not be aggressive towards the other side. Aggression does not assist settlement. It just causes the other side to be defensive.
- *Keep up energy levels and good humour under stress* – Mediation is stressful for clients. They need to be calm and reassured. As the day wears on people grow tired

and frustrated. Representatives must remain optimistic and never become downhearted.

- *Always be able to talk to the mediator and the other side's representative* – Many disputes end up at mediation because of a breakdown in communication. This is understandable between the parties. It is unforgivable between the representatives. They must never become an obstacle to settlement. Channels of communication with the mediator and the other side must be constantly kept open.

In practice

- Very few parties turn up by themselves at a mediation. They usually have either a representative or a supporter.
- Too many *legal* representatives, especially barristers, do not realise that they are there to do a deal.
- Very few representatives have had any specific training in presentation, negotiation or mediation advocacy.

See also

ADVOCACY/GOOD MANNERS/MEDIATION ADVOCACY/ PMA (Pre-Mediation Analysis)/REPRESENTATION

Follow up

Walker *Mediation Advocacy: Representing Clients in Mediation* Ch 6

Representatives' Liability

Mediation advocates owe a duty of care to their clients. This can arise even if they are attending on an unpaid voluntary basis.

Representatives' Liability

Where are the potential areas of liability?

- Advising the client to under-settle. The case or claim was worth more than the client received.
- Advising the client not to settle when they should have, given how matters eventually turned out at trial.
- Letting the client settle under extreme conditions, for example late at night when everybody is tired and hungry and the client has become bamboozled by the flood of new information and comment.
- Failing to explain to the client exactly how much they would receive under a settlement proposal after deduction of third party expenses including lawyers' fees.
- Failing to ensure that the settlement agreement was legally enforceable and provided the client with exactly the remedies that he was agreeing to.

Wise representatives make sure that they:

- are prepared;
- record their pre-mediation advice;
- take a note of the advice given during the mediation;
- ensure their clients understood their advice at the time; and
- confirm it in writing after the mediation.

In practice

Representatives' liability is limited because:

- The decision whether or not to settle is always the clients'. Clients always have the choice whether or not to accept the proposal or to continue with the dispute.
- Provided that, as a representative, you do not take the decision for the client, your liability is the same as when giving advice on the conduct of a claim outside of mediation.

- The English courts have decided that it is not the duty of a solicitor at mediation to ensure that a settlement does take place. He only has to make sure that his client understands whether a legally binding settlement has been made. And if it has, what it means.

See also

REPRESENTATIVES

Follow-up

Frost v Wake Smith and Tofields Solicitors [2013] EWCA Civ 772

Reputation

Businesses worry about reputational risk. Individuals may also have reputations, for example amongst their community, that they wish to uphold.

Mediation offers an effective way of doing this in two ways:

1. Disputes can be settled in private and in confidence. The complaints and details do not have to be aired in court.
2. The terms of settlement can be kept confidential even after court proceedings have been started for example by a Tomlin order.

   This means:
   - potentially embarrassing information private is kept private
   - admissions can be made
   - apologies offered
   - compromises made

without the outside world seeing them as evidence of wrongdoing or admissions of liability.

In practice

- Take care when referring to the benefits of avoiding reputational risks by the use of confidentiality. There is a risk of this being seen as veiled threats or lightly disguised blackmail.
- Confidentiality is an intangible benefit to be factored into the risk/reward calculation. Sometimes it has a real value and you can put a figure on it.
- The damage to reputation is rarely as great or as long-lasting as people think.

See also

BLACKMAIL/COGNITIVE BIAS-LIMELIGHT BIAS/ TOMLIN ORDER

Resistance Figure/Point

Aka bottom line or walk away point. If you reach this, you leave the negotiation and the deal is off.

It is the opposite of your target figure, which is your best outcome or goal.

In most negotiations and mediations target points do not overlap. But resistance points do, which is why most mediations achieve a settlement.

For example the highest price that the buyer is willing to pay is more than the lowest price the seller is willing to accept. The gap between the seller's resistance point and the buyer's resistance point is the Bargaining or Deal Zone or ZOPA ('Zone of Potential Agreement').

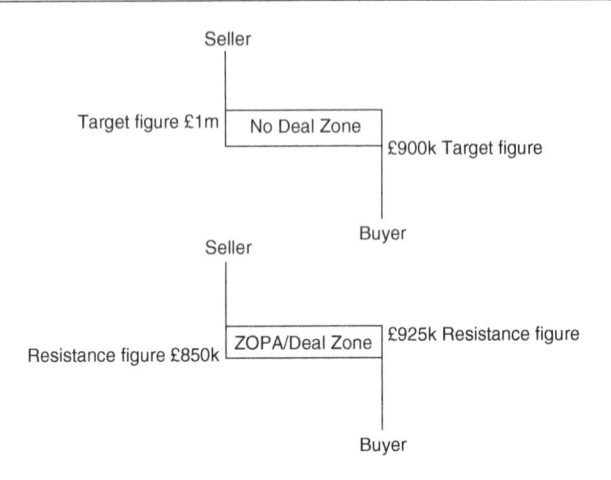

Resolution

```
                           Seller
                             |
       Target figure £1m ┌─────────┐
                         │No Deal Zone│ £900k Target figure
                         └─────────┘
                             |
                           Buyer

                           Seller
                             |
                         ┌─────────┐
   Resistance figure £850k│ZOPA/Deal Zone│ £925k Resistance figure
                         └─────────┘
                             |
                           Buyer
```

In practice
- Know what your resistance point is.
- Stick by it unless there has been a fundamental change in information/circumstances.
- Do not bluff about it.
- Do not lie about it. If you do, deals do not get done but damage is done to your reputation.

See also

BOTTOM LINE/BATNA/WALK AWAY FIGURE/WATNA/ ZOPA

Resolution

Has two meanings in the English mediation context:

1 It is the current name for the Solicitors Family Law Association (SFLA). This is an organisation of 6,500 family lawyers and other professionals in England and Wales. They believe in a constructive, non-confrontational approach to family law matters.

The cornerstone of membership of Resolution is adherence to its Code of Practice.

2 For some commentators this is the essence of what all mediation is. Solving problems is not enough. Resolving conflicts is what is required.

Transformative mediators believe this. They criticise problem-centred mediators who look for solutions, as only doing half the job. Solving the problem is simply applying a sticking plaster.

Unless the reasons for the underlying conflict are identified and dealt with, further disputes will occur. This requires the painstaking uncovering of people's deepest drivers, needs, interest, fears and expectations. Once these are out in the open they can be explored and the parties be educated to prevent future conflicts. This is known as empowering the participants.

In practice

Civil and commercial mediation clients:

- Do not want to be transformed into better people.
- Are suspicious of touchy-feely approaches.
- Want their dispute sorted out in days not weeks.

Follow up

Resolution – resolution.org.uk

Restorative Justice – RJ

RJ developed out of victim-offender mediation and conferencing. Offenders and victims met with a facilitator present and talked to each other.

The idea was to meet the victim's need for an explanation and to make the offender aware of the impact and damage to them. At the same time the offender would be confronted with the consequences of their actions and realise what they had done.

There are similarities with mediation.

- A belief in the value of people talking to each other.
- Creating a safe space in which difficult conversations can be held.
- Disputants who are in an adversarial position.
- The facilitator is non-judgemental, much like a facilitative mediator.
- The skills required overlap – such as active listening, open questioning, rapport building, empathy and making sure that people are heard.
- There is an outcome in the sense that an outcome agreement is drawn up at the end of an RJ session much in the same way as a settlement agreement is drawn up at the end of a successful mediation.

But there are differences.

In RJ:

- The offender must admit guilt. Liability is usually never admitted in mediations.
- No civil, as opposed to criminal, proceedings have been started. Often – but by no means always – legal proceedings have been started in mediation.
- Criminal proceedings are often begun. Hardly ever in mediation.
- The main focus is on emotional damage and physical harm. In mediation it's mainly on financial consequences.
- The structure is clearer and more settled. Mediation is more flexible.

- Joint sessions are the norm with very few breakout sessions. In civil and commercial mediation caucuses are more usual.
- Outcomes are not legally binding. Settlement agreements signed at mediation are.
- The aim is to repair harm. Mediation is to resolve disputes/solve problems.

The Restorative Justice Council is headquartered at Beacon House, 113 Kingsway, London, WC2B 6PP. In November 2015 the Independent Complaints and Appeals Examiner (ICAE) was established. It hears appeals against RJC decisions and complaints against RJC registered trainers and practitioners.

RJC promotes RJ in areas such as early intervention community in housing disputes to avoid them escalating into crimes.

Follow up

The Restorative Justice Council – www.rjc.org.uk

Independent Complaints and Appeals Examiner (ICAE) – www.restorativejustice.org.uk/independent-complaints-and-appeals-examiner

Restrictive Covenants

Restrictive covenants, ie prohibitions against doing something, feature in mediations. They usually involve the:
- Use of land, eg not to use the land as a factory.
- Contracts of employment, eg not to set up a competing business.

The arguments are about the extent and enforceability of the covenants.

Review

Restrictive covenants are often included in settlement agreements. Make sure that they are enforceable. Specialist legal expertise is often required. For example:

- There are specific requirements about positive and negative covenants in relation to land and whether the burden and/or the benefit passes with the land.
- Employment covenants must not be unreasonable in scope or nature. They must not last too long or be too wide. The presumption is that they are in restraint of trade and have to be shown to be reasonable for the protection of the legitimate business interests of the employer.

In practice

- Existing covenants are often modified as part of a settlement.
- Bring your proposed wordings for the covenant with you. Drafting one at the end of a long day, or in the middle of tense negotiations, is difficult.

Review

A stage in the mediation day. Mediators call review meetings with the parties either jointly or separately if they think that momentum is stalling or not enough progress is being made.

The purpose is to discuss:

- What progress has been made.
- Why progress appears to have stalled.
- The obstacles to settlement.
- Whether or not the parties wish to remain committed to the process and to see if they can reach a settlement.

In practice

- Review meetings usually prompt a fresh surge of settlement effort.
- If the mediator suggests a review, go along with it.

See also

DECISION TREE/IMPACT/MEDIATION CLOCK/ MEDIATION DAY/SUMMING THE DIFFERENCES

Follow up

Walker *Mediation Advocacy: Representing Clients at Mediation* pp 170–179

RICS (The Royal Institution of Chartered Surveyors)

RICS was founded in 1868 and has its headquarters in London. It is a professional body that accredits professionals in the land, property and construction sectors worldwide.

Important to mediation in three ways:

1 It operates ACRE Mediation. ACRE stands for Analytical, Commercial, Restorative and Expert.

   Described as RICS's robust, bespoke built environment-focused mediation service.

   It provides:

   - Highly experienced and sector-expert mediators.
   - A process to move the parties either to a pragmatic commercial settlement or a narrowing of the issues – reducing court or arbitration costs.
   - A flexible environment that courts or arbitration cannot provide as it encompasses wide commercial as well as narrow legal realities.

Risk Analysis

2 The RICS Dispute Resolution Service maintains a register of RICS accredited mediators.

3 It provides mediation training.

Follow-up

RICS – www.rics.org/uk/

RICS Dispute Resolution Service – www.rics.org/uk/join/member-accreditations-list/dispute-resolution-service/

Risk Analysis

Risk is the evil twin of uncertainty. Risk and uncertainty are often confused. They are not the same thing.

- Risk can be measured.
- Uncertainty cannot be measured.
- Risk is the estimated likelihood of a known event happening.
- Uncertainty is not knowing what will happen.

Clients want to manage risk. It helps if you can measure it. How do you do that?

Putting present value on future outcomes is one way.

- Using decision trees. They are a diagrammatic structured way of assessing the impact of litigation risk discounts on a claim.

    For example:

    You have a claim for £1m and a 75% chance of winning on liability and a 60% chance of winning on quantum. The value of your claim is £1m × .75 × .6 = £450,000

- Summing the differences:

    This shows the present value of a claim.

For example:

- you have a 70% chance of winning £100,000 (and therefore a 30% chance of losing)
- your costs are £30,000 with irrecoverable costs of £10,000
- and the other side's recoverable costs are £20,000
- then 0.7 × £100,000 + 1 × –£10,000 = £60,000

  +
- 0.3 × –£30,000 + 0.3 × –£20,000 = –£15,000

Present value = £45,000.

In addition you have to assess:

- the credit risk ie the risk of not recovering your judgment.
- the impact of either winning or losing.

In practice

- Clients and their advisers are often reluctant to assess risk in this way. They prefer to rely upon oral statements such as 'We have a very strong case' or 'Better than Evens.'
- Third-Party Funders require a quantitative analysis not just a qualitative one.
- An obstacle to accurate risk analysis is our susceptibility to cognitive biases such as Optimism Bias.

See also

COGNITIVE BIASES/RECOVERABILITY

Follow up

Richbell *How to Master Commercial Mediation* pp 313–323

Walker *Mediation Advocacy: Representing Clients in Mediation* Chs 7 Risk/Benefit Assessment and 18 Mind Traps Alert

Riskin's Grid

Risk Profile

People's appetite for risk varies. To measure their appetite for risk ask them:

Q1 You have £1,000. I offer you a guaranteed additional £500 or a 50/50 chance of an additional £1,000. Which would you take?

Q2 You have £2,000. I offer you a guaranteed loss of £500 or a 50/50 chance of loss of £1,000. Which would you take?

Most people:

- In Q1 choose the guaranteed £500 gain.
- In Q2 choose the 50/50 chance.

This is inconsistent. Those with a high appetite for risk will take the 50/50 chance in both Q1 and Q2. Those with a low appetite for risk will take the guaranteed sum in both.

The fact that most people make inconsistent decisions demonstrates the cognitive bias of the endowment effect.

In practice

- People are more prepared to cap their upside exposure than their downside exposure.
- Hence receiving parties are more conservative than paying parties.

See also

COGNITIVE BIAS

Riskin's Grid

The diagram that caused so much confusion and argument amongst mediators and spawned a thousand articles. The Old Grid.

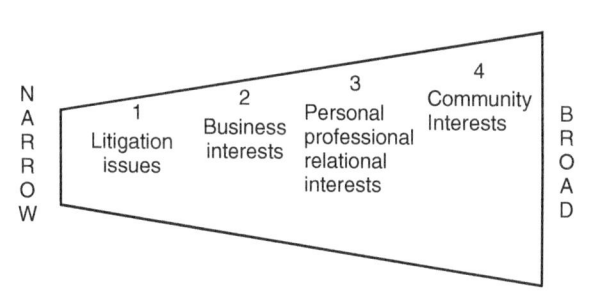

Riskin's Grid

Wonderful illustration of:

- The law of unintended consequences. Professor Riskin was trying to bring clarity but created confusion.
- The rule that once you have published an idea it no longer belongs to you and you may never in future recognise your progeny.

Tries to grapple with the different approaches that mediators take to mediation generally and the particular mediations in which they find themselves. Introduced concepts of facilitative and evaluative mediations.

He recognised the confusion that had been caused and reissued his grid with additional commentary and guidance. Replaced facilitative and evaluative with directive and elicitative. The New Old Grid.

He also tried to move away from mediator orientation grids to decision-making grids. The New New Grid. This has not had the same impact.

The Old Grid still influences much of the mediation training provided in the UK and other jurisdictions.

In practice

- Of interest to mediation trainers and theorists.
- Of relevance to novice mediators newly emerged from their training.
- Of little practical application to practitioners.

Problem definition continuum

NARROW	1 Litigation issues	2 Business interests	3 Personal professional relational interests	4 Community Interests	BROAD

Riskin's Grid

Old Grid

```
                    Role of mediator
                       Evaluative

                 |  Evaluative  |  Evaluative  |
                 |    narrow    |    broad     |
   Problem       |--------------|--------------|    Problem
  definition                                       definition
    narrow       |  Facilitative|  Facilitative|     broad
                 |    narrow    |    broad     |

                       Facilitative
                    Role of mediator
```

New Old Grid

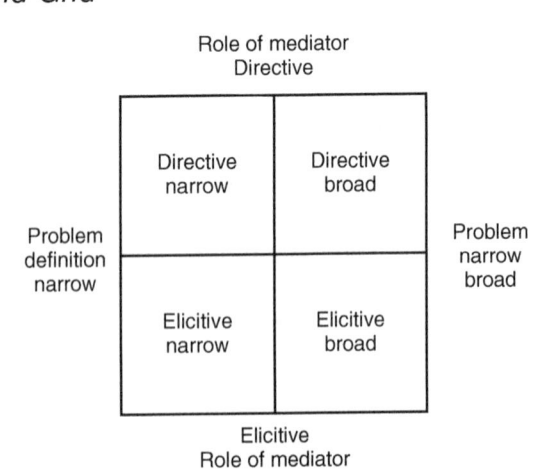

```
                    Role of mediator
                       Directive

                 |   Directive  |   Directive  |
                 |    narrow    |    broad     |
   Problem       |--------------|--------------|    Problem
  definition                                        narrow
    narrow       |   Elicitive  |   Elicitive  |    broad
                 |    narrow    |    broad     |

                       Elicitive
                    Role of mediator
```

See also
DIRECTIVE/ELICITIVE/EVALUATIVE/FACILITATIVE

Follow up

Leonard L Riskin 'Decision-making in Mediation: The New Old Grid and the New New Grid System' Notre Dame Law Review vol 79 issue 1 12-01-2003

Robust

There is no point becoming upset at mediations. You just have to accept that people will try and irritate you, be unreasonable and waste your time.

If you become upset, annoyed or irritated this will affect your ability to take rational decisions and to see the opportunities for making peace rather than engaging in skirmishing.

In practice
- Most mediations are conducted in a good spirit.
- People do lose their temper with each other but not often and not for long.

See also
GOOD MANNERS/MEDIATION DAY/WALL

Rolling Mediations

The conventional model in England and Wales is for civil and commercial mediations to be concluded in a single day's session. Occasionally they go over to a second day. The intention is to conclude a settlement at the end of the session.

Round Table Meetings (RTMs)

By contrast rolling mediations envisage from the outset a series of mediation sessions. These can be:
- Any length but usually between one and two hours.
- Spread over several weeks or months.

In other jurisdictions, for example in Israel, civil and commercial mediations are usually conducted on the rolling session basis and mediations can last several months or even years.

In Family mediations there are usually five or six 90-minute mediations sessions spread over two or three months. They are meant to be cumulative. Progress is made at each session and extended as the parties move towards a Memorandum of Understanding.

Community and workplace mediations tend to follow this pattern although usually with fewer sessions and over a shorter timescale.

In practice
- Rolling sessions are not used much in civil and commercial mediations in the UK

See also
MEDIATION DAY

Round Table Meetings (RTMs)

Aka Joint Settlement Meetings or Three Room Meetings.

Often seen as a cheaper and easier option to a formal mediation.

In practice

- Usually take more time, cost more money and are less effective than mediations.
- Still favoured by personal injury lawyers.

See also

JOINT SETTLEMENT MEETINGS/THREE ROOM MEETINGS

S

Salami-Slicing

Aka nickel and diming or nibbling.

Making a series of small steps that in total achieve more than one large step. Sometimes used pejoratively to describe underhand or even illegal activity.

For example in business, it can be 'shaving' where the sums due are rounded up the whole time. No one notices because the amounts are so small.

In negotiation it is dealing with one issue at a time or obtaining small concessions on multiple points. More frequent in procurement negotiations than mediations but still used.

Advantages

- Useful where there is a low level of trust between the parties. Start with issues of low importance to the other side.
- Can give control of the process to the salami slicer.
- If other side is under time pressure and there is a danger that the salami slicer will terminate the mediation.

Disadvantages

- Takes time.
- Can irritate other side if new issues are constantly raised.
- If issues are interconnected, difficult to separate them out into discrete ones.

Counters

- Stipulate as a ground rule that 'nothing is agreed until everything is agreed'.
- Constantly check if there are any other issues. Ask 'Is there anything else?' 'Is that everything?'
- Say that, as they are seeking concessions on separate points, while you do not mind discussing them individually and as discrete items you will look at the overall package.

In practice

- The first and the last few steps in mediation are the smallest. That is when the parties are at their most nervous.
- People say that they do not want to salami slice and then do it anyway.

See also

ANCHORING/EXCHANGING OFFERS/FIRST OFFERS/ OFFERS/RECIPROCITY

Sandwiches

Important in mediations in two ways.

- Blood sugar

    Low blood sugar levels impede settlement. The parties have to be kept fed and watered. Hosts should always ask if there are any specific dietary requirements.

- Milestone

    One mediator's approach is to ask the parties to exchange offers/proposals before the sandwiches arrive, ie before three hours have passed. In a standard eight-hour

SCMA (The Standing Conference of Mediation Advocates)

mediation why wait until more than half the time has elapsed before discussing settlement?

In practice
- Good food helps get better deals.
- No food can mean no deal.
- Hungry people think about food not settlement options.
- Keep everyone fed and watered.

See also
HOSPITALITY/MASLOW'S HIERARCHY

Follow up
www.psychologicalscience.org>wang

Schools

For mediation in schools see **PEER MEDIATION**.

For schools of thought about mediation see **STYLES OF MEDIATION**.

SCMA (The Standing Conference of Mediation Advocates)

The Standing Conference of Mediation Advocates headquartered in Chancery Lane, London describes itself as the home of mediation advocacy. The SCMA:
- Wants to help members develop their practices.
- Describes itself as

SCMA (The Standing Conference of Mediation Advocates)

'A multi-disciplinary cross-professional association of practitioners established to promote and develop best practice professional excellence in mediation advocacy through individual and corporate training and commercial activities.'

- Has adopted the guidelines of the Law Council of Australia. The key points are:
  - Mediation is not an adversarial process, it is a problem-solving exercise.
  - Lawyers and clients should act at all times in good faith to attempt to achieve settlement of the dispute.
  - A lawyer needs to be able to convince the client on the other side not the lawyer or the mediator. A persuasive rather than adversarial or aggressive approach is preferable and more likely to be successful.
  - Acknowledge the other side's strong points and concerns.
  - Do not mislead, exaggerate or make final offers unnecessarily.

The SCMA is an accredited CMC mediation trainer and provider and its website is a useful resource.

See also

ACCREDITATION/BARRISTERS/MEDIATION ADVOCACY/SOLICITORS

Follow up

www.mediationadvocates.org.uk/home

Law Council of Australia Guidelines for Lawyers in Mediation – www.lawcouncil.asn.au/FEDLIT/images/Guidelines_for_laywers_in_mediations.pdf

SCMS (Small Claims Mediation Scheme)

Small Claims Mediation Scheme is a free scheme operated in the county courts in England and Wales for lower value cases, ie under £10,000. The mediations are usually:

- Conducted by telephone with an hour time limit.
- By mediators who are court employees. Within an hour they try to find out the main issues that require settlement. They may not have access to the court file.
- Arranged after the Directions Questionnaire has been sent out by the court and completed by the parties. If you do not hear from the court about mediation after you have returned the forms saying you would like one, telephone them. Give them two weeks and then follow up until you receive your date.

If a settlement is reached the mediator will record the terms and tell the court. He will not take any steps to enforce the agreement. If a settlement is not reached the case carries on.

Discussions with the mediator are private and confidential and cannot be referred to in any court proceedings.

Anecdotal evidence suggests that:

- Users are happy with the experience.
- The mediators are quite evaluative.

See also
ONLINE MEDIATION/TELEPHONE MEDIATION

Sealed Offers

In the mediation context sealed offers are used when the parties are:

1 Reluctant to make an offer to the other side but they want to indicate an offer to the mediator.

Sealed Offers

The usual reason for reluctance is that one party is not sure whether the other is really interested in trying to come to a settlement. They need some encouragement before they self-disclose.

They are worried that either:

- they will annoy the other side by making too low on offer; or
- they will leave themselves at a negotiating disadvantage by making what they think is a proper offer while the other side makes only a low offer.

They therefore want to know what is in each other's minds. By communicating their opening offers to the mediator who can read them in private they are able to receive from the mediator an indication of whether or not they are on completely different planets or not.

2 At an impasse. Mediators can ask for their Last, Best and Final offers. They can read them in private. They tell the parties whether they are very close or still a long way apart without revealing the size of the gap in numerical terms.

If the offers overlap a settlement is concluded at the midway point.

In practice

- A very effective technique used by many mediators.
- Be careful about rejecting the idea of sealed offers if the mediator suggests it.

See also

AUTO SETTLER/BRACKET/SPLITTING THE DIFFERENCE/

Seating

A neglected topic in mediations despite the science of proxemics, which investigates the use of distance in communicating with people.

What happens?

In the private sessions – caucuses

Representatives:

- If you sit at the head of the table you are electing yourself team leader. Barristers habitually do this. Is this the message you want to send?
- You should leave the chairs nearest to the door for the mediator. It is rude, let alone inefficient, to make the mediator squeeze past people in order to find a seat every time he comes in and out of the caucus sessions.
- You should decide whether or not you or your client wants to be facing the mediator. Generally the mediator will want to be able to establish a lot of eye contact with your client.

Mediators:

- You should try to sit so that you can have direct contact with the decision-maker in the group. Being able to establish and maintain eye contact is a key part of establishing rapport and showing that you are listening.

In joint sessions

- Many mediators like to sit at the head of the table if it is a rectangular one. This gives them a dominant position. The disadvantage is that it forces the other attendees to sit facing each other in two opposing teams. With round tables these problems do not arise but most tables are not round.

- Some mediators prefer to sit in the middle of a rectangular table with the attendees spread around them. This alleviates the problems of two opposing teams or sides.
- Some mediators insist that the clients sit nearest to them. Others allow the teams to organise their own seating. Paradoxically mediators who most emphasise the empowering nature of party autonomy in mediation are the most insistent on who sits where.
- Mediators should be careful about setting up extra layers of stress and complexity.
- Mediators trained in NLP (Neuro-Linguistic Programming) often suggest during the course of the day that people shift seats. This is based on the idea that if you physically change someone's perspective you can change their mental and psychological one as well. It freshens things up.

In practice
- In the end it does not really matter where anybody sits, provided that good relations can be established and maintained.
- The shape of the room and the table often restricts any creative choice of seating.

See also
NLP (Neuro-Linguistic Programming)/PROXEMICS

Secret Weapon

The mediator's secret weapon is that only he knows what is happening in the caucuses in the different parties' rooms.

Some mediation theorists think that this disempowers the parties and recommend that all sessions are joint sessions. Some even ban any confidential or private communications with the mediators.

These practices are not followed in civil and commercial mediations in England and Wales.

In practice

- Much of the shuttle diplomacy is secret diplomacy.
- The managed flow of information is a key mediator skill. He is best placed to advise the parties of what, when and how to disclose information so that it is of maximum effect in clearing obstacles to settlement.

See also
AUTONOMY/JOINT SESSIONS/SHUTTLE

Sector Specialism

Refers to a mediator having experience in the subject matter of the dispute. For example:

- If it is a dispute in the hotel industry he knows about hotels. He may have previously advised hotel owners as a lawyer or accountant or have worked in the hotel industry.
- If it is a professional negligence action arising out of the negligent drafting of a will he may have been a probate and wills solicitor himself.

In civil and commercial mediation there is a trend towards mediators who have a subject or sector specialism. In other words clients and their advisers have more confidence in mediators who know the subject rather than one who knows mediation.

Sector specialists

Pros

- They already know the industry or subject matter. They speak the language. Less time is spent bringing them up to speed.

Sector Specialism

- As experts in the area they are harder to bamboozle.
- They may bring their expert knowledge to help generate solutions.

The unspoken thought is that, as they already know the area, they will understand one party's case much more quickly and readily and will be able to convince the other party that they are wrong.

People at mediations believe that the other side don't agree with them simply because they do not understand or know enough about the subject. If they did they would see the error of their ways. This sometimes happens but not often.

Be careful about believing that through knowledge comes truth. And that truth is your version of events.

Cons

- As experts they are more inclined to express their expertise and act more like expert determinators than like mediators.
- They become more attracted to, and engage in, the detail of the dispute rather than in the process of trying to find common ground for settlement.
- They find it more difficult to stay out of the fray and avoid becoming overtly and sometimes forcefully evaluative.

In practice

- Parties and their advisers like to think that mediators know what they are talking about.
- Lawyers either like to think that they can bamboozle the mediator because he doesn't know anything about the subject or that he is part of the club who knows everything about the subject and will tell the other side where they are wrong.

Selling

See also
GENERALISTS/LAWYERS ROLES/REPRESENTATIVES

Selling

If you find it hard to sell you will find it hard to mediate. If you can mediate then you can sell.

Many mediators regard selling as a difficult and slightly distasteful task. In Daniel Pink's words it is seen 'as a white-collar equivalent of cleaning toilets – necessary perhaps, but unpleasant and even unclean.'

In the mediation context it has three meanings:

1 The mediator selling his services.

   He is developing a business. Mediators have to understand that if they do not actively promote themselves and their business they will not build a sustainable living. You can simply act passively, put your name on a website and wait for the world to come to you. Eventually with a bit of luck people will. How long can you wait? But if you want to generate work you have to promote yourself.

2 The mediator selling during the mediation.

   Most mediators negotiate during mediation. There are multiple negotiations. The mediator negotiates with the parties and their representatives both individually and jointly. He is not necessarily selling a particular proposal or idea apart from the idea of making peace.

   Skilled mediators and skilled salesperson use the same transferable skills, so if you can mediate you can sell. These skills include:

   - Asking open questions.
   - Active listening.
   - Reframing.

Settlement Agreement

- Summarising.
- Rapport building.
- Establishing the client's values and needs.

3 Mediation advocates or representatives sell their client's case/proposal.

This is not about being aggressive. It is about being credible. As the advocate you want to establish a mood for settlement. And show the other side why it is in their interests to accept your proposal.

In practice

- In mediations everyone is selling something.

See also

ACTIVE LISTENING/INTERPERSONAL SKILLS/ QUESTIONS/RAPPORT

Follow up

Walker *Setting Up In Business as a Mediator* Ch 12 Selling the Necessary Skill Set

Walker *Mediation Advocacy: Representing Clients in Mediation* paras 6.23–29 Essential Skills

SEND (Special Educational Needs and Disability Tribunal)

See also

SPECIAL NEEDS

Settlement Agreement

The ultimate aim of all mediations.

Settlement Agreement

Drawing up a settlement agreement always takes longer than you think. This is not just lawyers being pernickety. When people come to write something down after a hard day's negotiation it just takes time.

In practice

- Allow enough time to draw up the agreement even if it is a simple four-paragraph document. Allow at least twice as long as you think it will take.

- Do not try and draft in committee. This takes even longer. Choose one person to produce the first draft and let others comment on it.

- Mediators do not normally become involved in drafting the settlement agreement unless both parties are unrepresented.

- Mediators only become involved in the drafting of the agreement if the representatives find themselves disagreeing over the finer detail.

- Always take your template and standard clauses with you on your laptop – everyone finds it difficult after a hard day's negotiation to start drafting from scratch with a blank screen or page in front of them.

- Make sure that the representatives keep their clients occupied and engaged while the agreement is being drafted. For them the hard work has been done and they just want to go home. They can become impatient and frustrated and start to fear the worst and become prone to second thoughts.

See also

MEDIATION DAY/POST-MORTEM/SETTLER'S REMORSE

Follow-up

Walker *Mediation Advocacy: Representing Clients in Mediation* Ch 14 for a commentary on a precedent settlement agreement

Shuttle

Mediators have borrowed the term 'shuttle diplomacy'. First used to describe Henry Kissinger's efforts after the 1973 Yom Kippur war.

It describes what mediators do when using the caucus model of mediation. The mediator spends time with one party and then with the other acting as an intermediary going back and forth transmitting information, messages and proposals.

Often used as a word of opprobrium by those who believe in the transformative joint session model of mediation.

In practice
- Shuttling is what most civil and commercial mediators spend most of their time doing.

See also
CAUCUS/JOINT SESSIONS/THREE STAGE PROCESS

Signals

These are the messages contained, but not spoken, in words, gestures and clothes.

In mediations the parties want to receive signals that the other party is serious about negotiating and is prepared to move from their stated position. For some reason simply hearing the words: 'We are here with an open mind ready to try and achieve a settlement, if possible' does not actually convince listeners. They want some reinforcement.

You have to walk the walk not just talk the talk.

Silence

In practice:

- When making a proposal think about what message or signal you are sending and how it will be received.
- Be careful about sending mixed messages or signals. 'Here is our offer but we have to leave in an hour' which is three hours earlier than scheduled.
- Remember you are there to make peace so why refuse to say 'Good morning' or shake hands?
- Why assure everyone in the Joint Opening Session that you want to put the past behind you and look forward and then spend the first caucus with the mediator going over the past and asking him to get the other side to explain themselves?
- Venting may be cathartic, as its proponents claim, but it can send out confusing signals.

See also

GOOD MANNERS/JOINT OPENING SESSION/ MESSAGES/VENTING

Silence

Much recommended by theorists and trainers; much less used in practice.

Silence can make people feel uncomfortable. If they feel uncomfortable will they feel under attack in some way? Words of course can convey aggression. But silence isn't always a neutral state.

Pauses, even extended ones, between asking questions and receiving information, can be very effective. But the deliberate prolonged silence needs to be deployed with care. It can feel controlling and manipulative.

In practice

- Everyone at mediation tends to talk too much and not listen enough. This includes mediators.

Size

Size matters in three ways at mediation:

1 The size of the dispute

This is conventionally measured by the amount in dispute. The larger the amount the more the mediator charges. Most operate on some sort of scale fee. Not all do. More and more charge a flat rate for a day's work irrespective of how much money is at stake.

Other measures of the size of the dispute are:

- The number of parties involved.
- The amount of documentation.
- The number of issues and points of dispute.

2 The size of the team

Large disputes have sometimes been settled with one person per side and the mediator.

The golden rule is less is more. But in fact in any moderately-sized dispute there are normally two people on each side. One decision-maker and one supporter or technical person or briefer.

With more than four people Groupthink occurs. Factions can develop. If juniors are brought along either to take a note or to observe and learn, the more senior members of the team, particularly barristers and senior management can feel the need to show off.

3 Size of room

Three people in a boardroom for 20 can be as off-putting and inefficient as six people crammed into a small room for four.

Discussion and development of ideas is easier in a larger rather than a smaller space. People are not physically on top of each other. They do not feel hemmed in. In the larger space they can get up and walk around. All very important at mediations.

In practice
- Bigger disputes mean bigger fees.

See also
FEES/GROUPTHINK/TEAMS

Solicitors

Civil and commercial mediations rarely take place without at least one solicitor present. Community, family and workplace mediators rarely have solicitors present. But often they are advising in the background.

Solicitors at mediation are both their client's advocates and their legal advisers. They also appoint the mediator and so are liaison officers with the mediator as well.

The seven most common faults of solicitors

1 Being more like barristers than barristers in concentrating on evidential and legal issues.

2 Over-identifying with their clients. They have a longer and more sustained relationship with their clients than barristers do. Sometimes they become too much of a good friend to their client. The introduction of funding arrangements such as CFAs and DBAs has made this worse.

3 Not doing a PMA or even discussing the figures with their clients in advance of the mediation. In particular not working out the cost/benefit analysis.

Special Needs

4 Not fully explaining costs to clients. It is not sufficient to just give them a copy of the Precedent H. You have to explain how the cost implications will work out in practice and how much the clients will end up with net in their pocket.

5 Not bringing draft documents with them – not even a template for a Tomlin order.

6 Continuing the guerrilla warfare that has developed in correspondence during the litigation with the other side.

7 Losing their nerve and suddenly deciding that they need counsel's advice after all.

See also

ADVOCACY/CFA/DBA/LAWYERS/LAWYERS ROLES/MEDIATION/PMA/REPRESENTATION/ REPRESENTATIVE

Special Needs

If you disagree with the local authority's decision about a child's special educational needs, appeals should be made to the Special Educational Needs and Disability Tribunal ('SEND').

An appeal can only be made to SEND if a mediation adviser has issued a certificate under section 52(4) or (5) of the Children and Families Act 2014. The Act does not make mediation compulsory. It makes *consideration* of mediation compulsory before most types of cases can be brought to SEND.

The procedure is set out in The Special Educational Needs (Mediation) Regulations.

See also

SEND

Follow up

Children and Families Act 2014, s 52(4) and (5)

The Special Educational Needs and Disability Regulations 2014, SI 2014/1530, regs 32–42

Splitting the Difference

A common and deceptively simple closing technique used in many mediations. Both parties compromise and give up an equal amount. What could be simpler and fairer than that?

Splitting the difference is not necessarily fair. Both sides giving up the same amount doesn't make the outcome fair. What makes it fair is the underlying standards or principled basis of negotiation. If for example the objective valuation of a property is £100,000 and a potential purchaser offers £90,000 why is it fair to accept £95,000?

The standard advice is never to offer to split the difference. Get the other side to offer it first. If they do you can then bracket their offer to your advantage.

For example:

- They offer to split the difference. The difference is £100,000–£200,000. Splitting the difference means £150,000.
- You take the offer of £150,000 to your client and come back and tell them that your client wanted to stick at £200,000 but you persuaded him to split the difference between £150,000 and £200,000, ie at £175,000.
- There's a good chance that the other side will then offer to split the difference again between £150,000 £175,000, ie at £162,500.

Statement of Case

When you split the difference you agree to a solution that is halfway between the two positions. This appears to be fair and therefore difficult to refuse. The trick is to manoeuvre so that the midpoint or halfway position is still an acceptable outcome for you.

These difficulties explain why the Auto-Settler is proving to be so popular.

In practice
- Splitting the difference is considered at every mediation.
- And is used at most.

See also
AUTO-SETTLER/BRACKETING

Statement of Case

Has two meanings in mediation.
1 Mediation statement or position paper.
2 The meaning in the CPR, ie court documents.

These include the claim form, particulars of claim, defence, counterclaim, replies to the defence, etc and requests for further information and clarification.

They contain:
- The factual basis on which the party relies in making their claim or defence.
- The facts on which the party will rely to prove their case.

They are supported by a statement of truth.

According to CPR PD 16.8 there are matters that must be specifically pleaded in statements of case. These include:
- Allegations of fraud.

- The fact of any illegality.
- Details of any misrepresentation, breaches of trust, wilful default.
- Undue influence or unsoundness of mind.
- Notice or knowledge of fact.
- Any facts relating to mitigation of loss or damage.

In practice

- Statements of case (CPR meaning) are included in all mediation bundles.
- Most position papers read like statements of case.
- They are of limited help as agendas for deal making.

See also

ASSESSMENT/BUNDLES/CPR/POSITION PAPERS

Follow up

CPR Part 20

CPR PD 16.8

Strategy

Always advised: rarely devised.

When setting out it's sensible to have an idea of where you would like to end up and how you can get there. At many mediations the parties only have a vague idea of destination or route. And still they settle.

As a minimum you need to have discussed:

- What will happen if you don't settle.
- What will happen if you do settle.

Stress

- What you need.
- How they can they give it to you.
- What they need.
- How you can give it to them.

In practice
- Always stay flexible.
- As Mike Tyson said: 'No plan survives the first punch in the mouth.'

See also
PMA/PREPARATION

Stress

Stress does not mean pressure or strain. It is a physiological response to a demand or threat. Hormones are released to arouse the body for emergency action. These include adrenaline and cortisol.

In a mediation people under stress will not be able to think constructively about settlement. Their prefrontal cortex is impaired as a result of over-firing neurons. This means that the fight or flight response is engaged. Calm rational thought and planning go out of the window.

In practice
- Stress is one of the main barriers to settlement.
- It is the job of the mediator and the representatives to bring the decision-maker's stress levels down to operational level.
- The aggressive adversarial tactics of many advocates, particularly barristers, raise stress levels not reduce them.

See also
AMYGDALA/BARRIERS

Strike Out

This does not refer to the behaviour of high conflict individuals. It means an application to the court in English legal proceedings to remove the whole or part of a statement of case.

The court can strike out on its own motion or on an application.

The main grounds for striking out are:

- The statement of case (usually the Particulars of Claim or Defence) does not disclose the cause of action and there are no reasonable grounds for bringing or defending the claim.

- The statement of case does not contain a sufficiently precise statement of the facts upon which the claimant relies.

- Inadequate reasons are given for a denial or defence.

- The proceedings are an abuse of the process of the court.

- A party has failed to comply with the rules of the court or directions given by the court. This is a case management tool for the judge.

If you tell the mediator and the other side how absolutely hopeless their case is and how they are doomed to fail, you will be asked: why not apply to strike out? If you succeed, that is the end of the case. Of course if you do not succeed you may end up paying costs and emboldening the other side.

Structured Mediation

Parties considering a strike out application sometimes go to mediation for tactical reasons. They want:

- To rehearse their best points before the mediator who is an independent third party to see if they can gauge the likely response from the judge.
- To see whether or not in response to their challenge at mediation the other side produce any further arguments or evidence.

This tactical use of mediation is to be deprecated but it does sometimes happen although rather less in practice than most people think.

In practice

- At mediations strike outs are often discussed but rarely pursued if there is no settlement.

See also
TACTICAL/SUMMARY JUDGMENT

Follow up
CPR 3.4 (2) PD 3A

Structured Mediation

Aka early structured mediation or litigation lite.

A process designed to meet the lawyers' paranoia about trying to settle cases too early. They say that the issues have to be clarified, the law identified and the evidence assembled before the clients can take an informed decision on settlement.

As part of the preparation for mediation the parties follow a procedural timetable which mirrors the steps in litigation, eg:

- Involve the mediator in devising and monitoring it.

- Exchange in correspondence statements of issues with arguments and supporting evidence.
- Exchange key documents and information.
- Technical issues can be addressed by experts exchanging their opinions on a without prejudice basis.

For large-scale multiparty disputes there could be benefit in this.

In practice

- For most civil and commercial disputes this degree of investigation and litigation enquiry is not needed.
- What is needed is early negotiation to try and settle before costs escalate and positions become entrenched.

See also

OFFERS

Follow up

Eversheds post on 16 February 2016 'Mediation: Get well sooner?' – www.eversheds.com/global/en/what/articles/index.page?ArticleID=en/Construction_And_Engineering/Mediation_get_well_sooner

Styles of Mediation

In 2012 a literature review identified 25 different models of mediation. Conferences, academic journals and the Internet are full of passionate exchanges about their respective merits.

Subject to Contract

The Big Four have been identified: evaluative, facilitative, narrative, and transformative.

Most clients are not interested in what theory of mediation their mediator espouses. They want their problems sorted out.

In practice

The three basic rules are:

1. There are mediations that are business and those which are personal.
2. Personal mediations tend to be facilitative, narrative or transformative. Business mediations tend to be evaluative and problem-solving.
3. Personal mediations attract more non-lawyer mediators.

See also

EVALUATIVE/FACILITATIVEATIVE/HARVARD – HNP/NARRATIVE/TRANSFORMATIVE

Follow up

Walker *Mediation Advocacy:* Representing Clients in Mediation Ch 4

Subject to Contract

Use this phrase if you do not want any legal consequences to flow from your negotiations.

Often used to make sure that during negotiations, for example agreeing Heads of Terms, no legally binding contract is inadvertently created.

Negotiated terms that are expressed to be subject to contract are not legally binding until a formal document has been prepared incorporating them and usually signed by the parties.

This is reflected in the standard stipulation in mediation agreements about there being no legally binding agreement until the parties have signed.

In practice

- Doubts do arise about whether a legally binding settlement was actually made. Probably more often than they should.
- Some of these doubts are genuine doubts – most are tactical ones.

See also
TERMINATING

Summarising

A core competency for mediators. Similar but different to Reframing. Aka looping.

Mediators use it:

- To show a party that they have understood and heard what they said. This is showing Acknowledgement.
- To make sure that everyone has understood what has been said in the same way. Misunderstandings are both a frequent cause of dispute and a barrier to settlement. Mediators do a lot of clarifying.
- To play back to the speaker what he has just said so he can hear his own words. Speakers reflect on whether what they said is what they really intended to say or what they want repeated to the other side.
- To reinforce a point.
- To chart progress during the day.
- To remind people of what they have previously said or agreed – Looping.

Summary Judgment

In practice
- Mediators use open questions and summarising more than any other techniques.
- Effective mediation advocates do the same.

See also
ACKNOWLEDGMENT/LOOPING/REFRAMING

Summary Judgment

Procedure where the court without a full trial may give judgment against the claimant or defendant on the whole or part of a claim.

At the hearing oral submissions are made. Oral evidence is not usually given and the court relies on written evidence. The court will give summary judgment if it considers that:

- The claimant has no real prospects of succeeding on the claim or issue.
- The defendant has no real prospect of successfully defending the claim or issue and there is no other compelling reason why the case of issue should be disposed of at a trial.

Similar to a strike out. In fact the court can on a strike out application give summary judgment if it thinks that is the way to dispose of the matter.

Why go to mediation if you are sure that you will get summary judgment?

- How sure are you really?
- They cost money to apply for?
- Depending on the sums involved and the recoverability risk you might be in a net worse position after a successful summary judgment application.

- Are you in a better position to do a deal before or after a summary judgment application?
- Is there anything that you want that a court cannot award you?

In practice

- Discussed at mediation in the same way as strike out.

See also
STRIKE OUT

Follow up
CPR PART 24.2

Summing the Differences

A technique to help parties think creatively about figures and review the monetary worth of their dispute.

At its simplest it looks like this:

- If you go to trial on a claim for £100,000 with legal costs of £40,000 and succeed, your net financial position will be that you will be £60,000 in pocket after payment of legal costs. Plus the contributions of costs that the other side makes eg £30,000. Your irrecoverable costs £10,000. Overall net position £90,000.
- If you lose a trial your legal costs will be £40,000 from your own side and a contribution of £30,000 to the other side. In other words you will be £70,000 out of pocket.
- If you have a 75% chance of winning you have a 25% chance of losing.

    + £90,000 × .75 = £67,500

    +

    − £70,000 × .25 = − £17,500

Your claim is worth £50,000.

Surprises

In practice
- Parties and their advisers only do the first line of the calculation.
- Even just doing that is helpful. But it is not sufficient.

See also
RISK ANALYSIS

Follow up
Walker *Mediation Advocacy: Representing Clients in Mediation* p 119

Surprises

Surprises are inevitable: bombshells are not.

Why deliberately deliver surprises at mediation?

To maximise the impact of the disclosure. Usually this is a recent expert's report, up-to-date valuation or new witness statement. The idea is to rock the other side so that they will feel vulnerable and be prepared to pay or concede.

If you have information which you think will influence the other side's decision-making why not tell them in advance? What is there to be gained by holding it back?

Sometimes lawyers want to save something for cross-examination at trial. They fear that if they reveal it now the other side will be able to prepare their counter and therefore neutralise its devastating effect at trial. In other words they still regard mediation as litigation's antechamber.

Much better to identify with the mediator the obstacles to settlement. If they can be removed by the additional information, disclose it. If not, keep it back.

In practice

- If a surprise is a bombshell the recipients have to take time to process the information. The mediation is adjourned.
- If the surprise is not a bombshell it just slows down the process of formulating settlement proposals while the recipients absorb the information and respond. Much of the day is then spent arguing about the new information, its late disclosure and its implications.
- Very few late disclosures are bombshells.
- Most are irritants and occasionally obstacles to settlement.
- Sometimes surprises are the exit route: new information can make it easier for people to change their minds. Face is saved.

See also
DIGNIFIED EXIT/DISCLOSURE/EXCHANGE/FACE

Sympathy

Empathy's evil twin. Mediators are trained that empathy is good and sympathy is bad.

In reality the distinction is not always clear. What is important is that the mediator builds a rapport with the parties and their advocates. In certain circumstances it is absolutely inappropriate not to express sympathy. For example:

- Someone attends the mediation even though they have had a bereavement the previous day.
- Someone is mugged on the way to the mediation.

Sympathy

Of course you express sympathy.

Sympathy is otherwise banned because as a mediator you must not be seen to be siding with one party against the other. You do not want to become personally drawn into the dispute. If you express sympathy to someone you are expressing support and that may be construed as not being impartial. This can happen.

Expressing empathy also brings its own dangers as explained in the entry for **Empathy**.

In practice

- Clients interpret any expression of sympathy or empathy as support for their position.
- They do not distinguish between empathy and sympathy. What they are looking for is approval from the mediator.

See also

ACKNOWLEDGMENT/APOLOGY/EMPATHY/EMOTION/ RAPPORT

T

TACTICAL

Parties occasionally attend mediations for tactical reasons with no intention of settling. Most mediators, but not all, deprecate this.

Tactical mediations are used when a party wants to:

- Avoid the risk of an adverse costs order at trial for not attending mediation. It's quicker and cheaper to turn up for the day than to make submissions on contested costs hearings at the end of trial.
- Find out what the other side is like. How will they stand up as witnesses? Some advocates try to cross-examine the other side. Most experienced mediators will not permit this.
- Probe the other side to see what evidence they have. This can help their own case preparation.
- Run their best points past the other side to see how worried they are by them. In other words to rehearse.
- Test the quality of any expert evidence. Put the experts together and see what happens.
- Meet the client. Some barristers have never met their clients. They use the mediation as an extended conference.
- Sound out the other side's settlement range. This helps frame effective Part 36 Offers.

Mediation agreements contain a warranty that the parties are attending the mediation in good faith to negotiate a settlement. Attending with no intention to settle but simply for tactical reasons is a breach of that clause. Sooner or later someone will be sued for breach of the agreement.

In practice

- Tactical mediations are rare.
- Even parties who attend the mediation with only a half-hearted commitment to the process can become caught up in the day and end up settling. Usually much to their surprised delight.

See also

MEDIATION AGREEMENT/PART 36 OFFERS/STRIKE OUT

Follow up

CPR Part 36

Tax

Tax features in two ways in mediations.

1 The tax tail often wags the settlement dog. Mediators ask parties and their representatives to make sure that tax advice has been taken before they attend mediation. Both the paying party and the receiving party need to be aware before the mediation of the tax implications of any money flows or property transfers.

   Settlement agreements sometimes include a clause that the parties will cooperate in structuring the payments in the most mutually tax-efficient way. This may give comfort on the day but it is not reassuring for future conduct if there is any element of settler's remorse.

2 Tax disputes

   These are usually:

   - With tax advisers over advice. These are professional negligence mediations.
   - With HMRC. This is a more recent development. They have special features.

In practice
- Parties rarely take tax advice in advance.
- Urgent calls to accountants often happen during the mediation. They always impede settlement momentum.
- Mediating with HMRC is a different experience.

See also
HMRC/LSS/PI/PI INSURANCE/SETTLER'S REMORSE

TCC (Technology and Construction Court)

The Technology and Construction Court is a specialist division of the High Court.

Its judges have given many influential judgments in mediation.

They also provide judicial mediation to the Court Settlement Process (CSP).

See also
CSP/JUDICIAL MEDIATION

Team Mediation

This has two meanings.

1 Mediation by a team of mediators.

    A team of two mediators is co-mediation. Complex mediations may require different skills, cultural and linguistic as well as technical, in order to find enough common ground on which to deal with multiple issues.

    For example the United Nations established the Standby Team in 2008. This is a group of full-time mediation experts that can be rapidly deployed to provide technical advice to UN officials and others leading mediation and conflict prevention efforts. They have expertise in a wide range of issues that tend to arise in negotiations including constitution making, gender issues, natural resources, power-sharing, process design and security arrangements

2 Mediation of disputes within a team.

    This is the more common meaning. It is a type of workplace mediation.

    Mediation providers who offer this service describe it as a specialist and advanced area of expertise. The basic skills deployed in workplace mediation are used. But more attention has to be given to facilitation and process design to ensure that all members of the team feel that they have an opportunity to express their views and feelings.

In practice

- Most mediations except community mediations are carried out by a single mediator.

Teams

Who needs to be in the team?

Teams

It depend on the nature and complexity of the dispute. At its simplest you need:

- a decision maker; and
- anyone whose advice he needs in order to take an informed decision.

In reality the decision-maker likes to have:

- A supporter.
- Someone who knows the factual background to the dispute. This may be the person who has caused the problem in the first place.

Successful teams need to have four things:

1 A clearly understood and agreed goal.

2 An agreed strategy.

3 A shared approach, ie the way of doing things.

4 Complementary skills.

In practice

- It may be useful when putting a team together to consider the 9 Belbin Team Types ranging from Completer-Finisher to Plant. But teams often pick themselves.
- There may be very little choice or discretion about who should attend.

See also

DRC/GROUPTHINK

Follow up

9 Belbin Team Types - www.belbin.com/about/belbin-team-roles/

Government Guidance to the DRC – Webarchive. nationalarchives.co.uk/201301281112038

Telephone mediation

Growing in use. Popular as a low cost alternative to face-to-face mediations.

Used by Her Majesty's Courts Service ('HMCS') to provide free one hour mediations for Small Claims in the Country Court.

Also used by private mediation providers who offer short telephone mediations for small consumer disputes. Often strictly time-limited (60 minutes).

In practice

- No time for much report-building or exploring underlying issues.
- Mediators tend to be very directive and even evaluative.

Terminating

Why?

Most mediation agreements provide that either the parties or the mediator can terminate the mediation at any time without giving a reason.

The usual reasons for an early termination are that one of the parties:

- Has received new information, which it needs to consider before taking settlement discussions any further.
- Is walking out as a negotiation tactic.

Or the mediator thinks that:

- One of the parties (or perhaps both) are there for tactical reasons only and are not trying to settle the dispute.

Terminating

- The parties are so entrenched that there is no prospect of a settlement.

Complaints have been made against mediators for premature termination of a mediation. Although most mediation agreements reserve the right to the mediator to terminate at any time without giving reasons, they also stipulate the duration of the mediation. Parties have complained that they have paid for eight hours of the mediator's time and they expect to receive eight hours of his time.

If you think that the mediator is terminating the mediation prematurely say so at the time. If a mediation provider is administering the mediation contact them and ask them to speak to the mediator.

When?

Problems have arisen about deciding when and if the mediation has actually terminated. The best practice is for mediators to ask the parties to sign a mediation report form saying that the mediation started and finished at the times shown and whether or not it has settled.

Doing this confirms:

- The mediator's time sheet has been completed.
- Whether or not the mediation has in fact finished.

But if the matter did not settle and the parties wish to continue to negotiate through the mediator is the mediation still continuing?

You need to know because of the provisions in the mediation agreement for concluding a legally binding settlement.

- Most mediation agreements provide that there is no legally binding settlement until all the parties have signed a document recording the settlement.
- Outside mediation parties can engage in those discussions without the mediator and can conclude

Terminating

a binding settlement by exchange of emails or in a telephone call.

- Mediators and parties both have to be careful to stipulate on what basis settlement discussions continue and what the formalities of concluding a settlement will be.

There have been two recent cases on this point in the English courts: *Bieber* and *Mrs AB*.

In the *Bieber* case the judge considered the standard clause about there being no binding agreement until a document has been signed by the parties. He said:

- That provision only referred to settlements made during the mediation and not long after the mediation.
- An exchange of emails between the solicitors after the mediation may in any case have complied with that provision applied to negotiations.

In *AB v CD* the mediator was called to give evidence.

In practice

- Mediations are rarely terminated early.
- Most mediations overrun not underrun.
- There appears to be a trend for the parties to expect that settlement will not be made on the day of the mediation but shortly afterwards.

See also
BINDING/MEDIATION AGREEMENT/SURPRISES

Follow up

Bieber and others v Teathers Limited (in liquidation) [2014] EWHC 4205

Mrs AB, Mr AB v CD Limited [2013] EWHC 1376 (TCC)

TFN (Technology Facilitated Negotiation)

The big threat to the TPN. RoboMediator has arrived.

The human mediator will be replaced by an automated decision-making process. The technology is the medium of the negotiation.

Already there are systems in place where the parties can do everything online with no human intervention. There are case evaluation systems where parties enter details of their dispute and the system tells them how strong their case is. The software applies the results of Big Data analysis of similar cases and predicts outcomes.

One day perhaps a Robo-Mediator will be able to deal with parking disputes and noisy dogs in community mediations, build rapport with a tearful claimant in a personal injury case, maintain eye contact and provide non-verbal encouragement to warring family members in a contested will case.

The technology to do this is not currently available.

In practice

- Practitioners' confidence in the use of TFN at mediations is limited by the fact that no computer can yet (in 2016) recognise a banana.
- But TFN will develop and be used more.
- Embrace it. You know it makes sense.

See also
BLIND BIDDING/ONLINE MEDIATION

Theories

It may work in practice but does it work in theory? This is the attitude of many mediation commentators.

There are shelf loads of books and articles about mediation theory. The Internet is full of chat rooms and discussion groups.

Universities produce more and more books, theses and learned papers. Some of it is interesting, even stimulating but little is of any practical relevance to practitioners and their clients.

In practice

- Clients could not care less about mediation theories.
- Experienced mediators do not worry about theories.
- Mediation is a craft. Practitioners develop their own way of doing it.

See also

CRAFT/EVALUATIVE/FACILITATIVE/HARVARD/ NARRATIVE/STYLES OF MEDIATION/THERAPEUTIC

Therapy

Most mediators distinguish mediation from therapy, counselling or coaching. While acknowledging that there are overlaps in objectives and techniques they emphasise the differences. The main ones are:

- Mediation is a group activity rather than an individual one.
- Most mediations involve parties who are in conflict with each other rather than with themselves.
- At most mediations parties are concerned with their legal rights and entitlements.

- Most mediations take place within a short period of time and do not have a series of sessions over many weeks, months or even years.
- Mediation is a process for bringing a dispute to an end not a course of treatment.

The therapeutic wing of mediation has a different view of mediation from the problem-solving wing. This fuels many of the theoretical debates and arguments.

In practice
- Mediators do engage in reality testing or reality therapy.
- Civil and commercial mediators tend to seek solutions to problems, not to rebuild people's lives.

See also
COUNSELLING/NARRATIVE/REALITY TESTING/ ROLLING MEDIATIONS/THERAPEUTIC/ TRANSFORMATIVE

Therapeutic

Another name for transformative mediation

See also
TRANSFORMATIVE

Third Party Funders

Aka litigation funding.

See also
ALF/LITIGATION FUNDING

THOMAS-KILMANN

A well-known conflict style inventory.

It identifies five different styles:

Competing	assertive/uncooperative
Avoiding	unassertive/uncooperative
Accommodating	unassertive/cooperative
Collaborating	assertive/cooperative
Compromising	medium assertive/cooperative

- Assertive means the extent to which an individual tries to satisfy his own needs.
- Cooperative means the extent to which an individual tries to satisfy the other person's needs.

Negotiators may find it useful to know which is their own dominant conflict resolution style.

In practice

- Nobody at mediation ever tells anybody what their TKI score is.
- There is never an opportunity to administer the TKI which takes 15 minutes and an hour's interpretation by a trained interpreter.
- Do people act in the way they do because of the situation that they find themselves in or because of their TKI category?

See also
CIALDINI'S BIG SIX/COGNITIVE BIAS/PERSONALITY

Follow up
Walker *Mediation Advocacy: Representing Clients in Mediation* Ch 17 What type of negotiator am I?, Ch 18 Mind Trap Alerts

Thought showers

The new more politically correct description of brainstorming.

See also
BRAINSTORMING

Threats

The negotiator's last resort.

If you make threats in order to bring home to the other side the disadvantages to them of not settling be careful that:

- You do not trespass into blackmail.
- You do not compromise the without prejudice confidentiality.
- You do not open yourself up to a claim of duress, thereby making any agreement voidable, ie liable to be set aside.
- You do not simply annoy the other side so much that their defences go up and their ability to think about settlement closes down.
- They do not call your bluff.

In practice:

- It's much better to frame threats as warnings.
- Most threats have a negative effect.

See also
BLACKMAIL/DURESS

Follow up
Ferster v Ferster [2016] EWCA Civ 717

Three Room Meetings

Another name for joint settlement meetings or roundtable meetings.

In the past these have been particularly favoured by personal injury practitioners.

See also
JOINT SETTLEMENT MEETINGS/PI – PERSONAL INJURY

Three Stages

The classic Mediation model has three stages: Educate, Exchange, Explore.

1 Educate

In this stage mediators want to find out what each side regards as important in the dispute and what it thinks the other side regards as important. They use a combination of open questions and active listening.

They ask three questions:

1 What is important?
2 Why is it important?
3 How do you want to achieve it?

They do this with all the parties to see how much the responses overlap. The greater the overlap, the greater the common ground and the more chance of a settlement.

Clients are often thrown by these questions – usually because they have not prepared properly. Ask yourself these questions as soon as you decide you want to go to mediation.

2 Exchange

Mediators want to:

- Find out what each side needs to know about the other's position.
  - Parties make assumptions and become frustrated at not knowing what the other side really wants or is saying.
- Fill in gaps in each side's information and understanding. If people have different information they are more likely to have different perspectives. The more shared information, the more chance of shared perspectives. In this way mediators try to expand the common ground.

Parties are often reluctant to exchange information. They worry that they may be disclosing something about themselves that can be used against them or that they are giving something away. It is the mediator's job to allay these concerns.

- He reminds parties that the mediation is confidential. What they say to each other during the mediation day cannot be referred to later.

- He respects their confidentiality and only discloses to each party what he has been authorised to disclose to unblock communication and correct misunderstandings.

By the time most parties come to mediation they are not communicating directly with each other. They are usually doing it through lawyers. In any dispute there are misunderstandings because of poor communication. Mediators try and clear them up.

3 Exploring

Mediators work with each party to formulate proposals for settlement.

Time

They tell parties that:

- Settlements are achieved not by the parties arguing points of evidence or law but by discussing proposals. The sooner they put proposals on the table for discussion the more chance they give themselves of a settlement on the day.
- They need to formulate settlement proposals as part of their preparation before they attend the mediation.
- They are free to think laterally and creatively. Mediations are safe places to have dangerous thoughts.

In practice

- Progress though the three stages is not linear or continuous. Discussions zig-zag in and out of them.
- Take guidance from the mediator. Remember his secret weapon.

See also

EDUCATE/EXCHANGE/EXPLORING/SECRET WEAPON

Tick the Box

Some people attend mediation just to comply with the procedural steps in the litigation and avoid an adverse costs order. They want to tick the box. This is a form of tactical mediation.

See also

COMPULSON/HALSEY/TACTICAL

Time

Important in three ways in the mediation context.

- When do we mediate?

Time

- How long do we mediate for?
- How do we spend the time at mediation?

1 When to mediate?

You can mediate whenever you want to. You can do it:

- As soon as you have a dispute that you have not been able to settle by direct negotiation.
- Before you issue proceedings.
- At the first opportunity during the proceedings.
- Late in the litigation life cycle when all the steps are being taken to prepare for trial.
- Just before trial or even during the trial.
- After judgment has been given or even on appeal.

There is a debate about the dangers of mediating too early or too late.

Too early and you will not:

- Fully understand the legal and evidential issues.
- Not be able to take a fully formed decision based upon the alternative of going to trial.
- Be sure that you are not underselling or overpaying.

Too late and:

- The legal costs will have all been spent and become an obstacle to settlement.
- People's positions will have become entrenched.
- The sunk cost fallacy operates.
- The peace premium will have been spent.

In practice

- There is no mythical ideal time to mediate. Once people have worked out what they need to achieve, go to mediation.

Time

- The sooner you make peace the better. The dangers of going to mediation too early are much less than the dangers of going too late.

2 How long to mediate for?

Mediations expand to fill the time available. If you book four hours with an absolute cut-off the chances are you will settle within four hours. If you book two days you will take two days.

Some disputes are more complex and will take longer. There is a danger of pushing ahead too quickly so that people do not feel they have been able to have their day in court. They need to be given time to feel that mediation has become a new comfort zone for them.

But a lot of time is wasted at mediations.

The better the preparation the more time that can be saved. Much time is spent with the lawyers taking instructions from their clients. Too often clients meet their barrister for the first time at the mediation. Taking instructions and giving advice should be done before the mediation.

The standard mediation day for a civil and commercial mediation is eight hours.

In practice

- Most mediations which start at 10am finish between 6 and 7:30pm. It always takes longer than people think to record the settlement or draft the *Tomlin* Order.
- Going beyond 10 hours is usually counter-productive. People become too tired. Professionals may be used to working all night but clients – even hard-boiled commercial ones – are usually not.

3 What to spend time talking about?

Time management is a key mediator skill. Some mediators set milestones at the start of the day in their opening statement.

Take a lead from the mediator. He will ask you to consider certain things, carry out calculations and provide information. Do as he asks. It will save time.

Spend time talking about proposals for the future – not explanations and justifications for the past.

In practice

- It's never too early to mediate.
- Mediations can be successfully conducted in less than the standard eight hours.
- Preparing well before the mediation saves time on the day.
- Talk about the future not the past.

See also

MEDIATION CLOCK/MEDIATION DAY/PEACE PREMIUM/TIME LIMITED MEDIATIONS/TOMLIN ORDER

Time-limited Mediations

Last less than a full day and have an absolute cut-off:

Key features

- The time limit is short. Scheme or court annexed mediations are often limited to two or three hours.
- There is no expectation that the parties or the mediator will stay beyond this time.
- Quite often there are no facilities to enable them to do that. For example in the old Central London County Court

Time-limited Mediations

mediation scheme which lasted from 16.30 to 19.30. Settlement agreements were sometimes signed by the headlights on car bonnets in Park Crescent.

Pros

- They are more streamlined. They have to be.
- Having a time limit concentrates people's minds. A surprising number of mediations settle within the time-limit on terms which the parties can accept and which give them satisfaction.
- They cost less.

Cons

- The significance of the time limit can be exaggerated. Some parties can feel pressured to make a decision.
- Generally mediations expand to fill the time available so this can save time.
- Optimism bias leads people to underestimate the time it takes to complete any task. Parties who are working hard and in good faith to reach a settlement can find that they just run out of time.

In practice

- Time-limited mediations are becoming more popular.
- Clients want to save time and money. Their lawyers are becoming more practised at mediation and do it better.
- It always takes longer than you think to draft the settlement agreement. Leave enough time to do this.

See also

OPTIMISM BIAS/TELEPHONE MEDIATIONS/ SETTLEMENT AGREEMENT/TIME

Tit-for-Tat

Often seen in mediations where one party does something and the other replies with an equivalent action.

Some negotiation theorists have endorsed it as an effective negotiation technique. Support has mainly come from game theory and the work of Robert Axelrod.

Although it may work in the iterated Prisoner's Dilemma experiment in the real world it is not seen as cooperative or principled negotiation. Rather it leads to escalating conflict.

Negotiators who use tit-for-tat are often seen as fair but hard. These qualities are admired in some quarters. And trading like for like is easy to do. Not much creative thought is required. Hence principled negotiators decry it.

Tit-for-tat behaviour does not always lead to an escalation of conflict. Cooperation can develop lead to 'live and let live' behaviour. The classic example being the Christmas truce in the First World War.

In practice
- Very difficult for parties to avoid some tit for tat during a mediation.
- Don't let tit-for-tat become a habit.
- Slows settlement momentum.

See also
CIALDINI'S BIG SIX/EXCHANGING OFFERS/GAME THEORY/PRISONER'S DILEMMA/TOUGHNESS

Follow up
Axelrod *The Evolution of Cooperation* (Revised edn, 2006)

Tomlin Order

A form of consent order used in the English legal system.

Under a Tomlin Order the proceedings are stayed on terms which have been agreed in advance between the parties and which are set out in a schedule attached to the order.

Particularly useful where:
- Terms are agreed without admission of liability.
- Terms go beyond what the court could have ordered by way of remedy at the trial of the action.
- The parties wish some or all of the terms to remain confidential.

There are other advantages:
- It is not necessary to commence fresh proceedings to enforce the order. If a party defaults the innocent party can apply immediately for a judgment and enforce that judgment.
- It does not count as a judgment and therefore does not appear on the register of court judgments. This can be useful if, for example, the party has to raise funds by way of mortgage or loan to pay under the terms of settlement.

But note

As a Tomlin order is not a judgment it does not automatically attract judgment interest. If you want interest to accrue until full payment or in the case of default include a clause saying so in the schedule.

In practice

- The usual way of recording a settlement where legal proceedings are underway.
- Always take a precedent with you. Make sure it is the latest version.

Top Ten

The ten elements in the classic definition of mediation – go to p x.

1 Voluntary
2 Confidential
3 Process
4 Parties
5 Dispute
6 Choose
7 Neutral
8 Third Party
9 Help
10 Own solution

See also

INTRODUCTION/MEDIATION/AUTONOMY/ CONFIDENTIALITY/DIPUTE/FACILITATIVE/ IMPARTIALITY/NEUTRALITY/PROCESS/TPN/ VOLUNTARY

Follow up

Walker *Mediation Advocacy: Representing Clients at Mediation* Ch 2

Toughness

Mediators encourage parties to be tough on:
- The problem – not on the people.
- On positions – but not on values.

- Their own perceptions, reasoning and cognitive biases.

For negotiators being tough does not mean being unyielding and offensive. Although some think that it does. It means being patient, consistent and persevering with the issues and goals that are important to you and trading small concessions in order to achieve them. So be patient.

In practice

- Always follow your interests.
- Avoid unilateral concessions.

See also

COGNITIVE BIAS/GAME THEORY/IF/PATIENCE/ PRINCIPLED NEOGTIATION/TIT-FOR-TAT

Toxic Mediations

This does not mean mediations about oil spillages or environmental pollution. Although they can be. Toxic mediations are ones which are so difficult to sort out that a permanent solution is probably impossible. They are usually about:

- Large-scale disputes involving lots of people and lots of money.
- International or cross-community issues.
- Political as well as economic interests.
- Sacred values.

Often they do not lead to a resolution or a solution but an agreed way of behaving in the future to manage the inherent conflicts and problems. Mediators who practice in this area spend a great deal of time on process design. Often they act as facilitators rather than mediators in the classic sense.

In practice
- A specialised area of mediation practice.
- Not often encountered in civil and commercial mediations.

See also
ENVIRONMENTAL MEDIATIONS

Follow up
Richbell *How to Master Commercial Mediation* pp 296–297

TPN (Third Part Neutral)

The TPN is the Mediator.

See also
IMPARTIALITY/NEUTRALITY

Traction

Word much used at mediation to connote:
- Momentum.
- Support.
- Potential for discussion and development.

Mediators want to gain traction.

See also
MOMENTUM

Tradeables

The heart of negotiation is trading concessions.

An essential part of pre-mediation preparation is to work out what:

- You could trade.
- You think the other side wants.
- You think they have that they could trade with you.

Doing this involves considering how deals can be structured and prioritising and putting values on different elements.

See also

COMPROMISE/IF/PMA – Pre Mediation Analysis/ RECIPROCITY

Training

Many people who want to be mediators think that they do not need any specific training. They are confident that in their professional life they already mediate, negotiate, exercise people skills and solve conflicts. They know what they're doing. They have learned on the job.

People in this category are diplomats, judges, barristers, solicitors, therapists, journalists, etc. They have all dealt with people and been in some way engaged in getting them to change their minds or behaviour.

Others:

- May have been more directly involved in negotiation as a job, eg commercial and contract negotiators.
- Such as psychotherapists or psychologists think that they already understand how people make decisions on what motivates them.

Training

- Have been handling employment issues such as HR professionals.

This may all be true but:

- Most of those who go on a formal training course for any type of mediation realise that the skills they already have will be applied in different contexts. To be effective the right technique has to be applied in the right context. Doing the right thing at the wrong time in the wrong place is no good to anybody.
- Everyone can acquire bad habits and become set in their ways.

Credibility

There is no requirement to undergo training. If you do undertake training you want a worthwhile qualification. There is no mandatory licensing and certification in the UK. But you gain credibility if you have been trained by a CMC-accredited mediation trainer.

The CMC stipulates the requirements that trainers must provide – for example the training must be at least 40 hours contact time, 50% must be in role play and those who assess the trainees must not be the same people who trained them.

A list of accredited trainers can be found on the CMC website.

It is worthwhile contacting several trainers before committing yourself to one.

Questions to ask are:

- Where will the training be held? You may have to include accommodation costs if you are travelling to the venue.
- What pre-reading and work will be required?
- What materials will be issued?
- Who will the trainers be?

Training

- How much training have they done?
- How much mediating have they done/are currently doing?

Conversion courses

Most initial training is for a particular type of mediation for example civil and commercial, family, workplace.

Some mediators want to be able to offer a wide range of services and go on conversion courses. These are usually abbreviated initial training courses taking account of the fact that the attendees have already being trained in basic mediation techniques.

CPD

Continuing professional development is required by most mediation providers and by the CMC.

An important part of CPD is not just learning about new techniques but refreshing the way you carry out mediation by talking to other mediators and hearing about the experiences of practitioners.

In practice

- Many mediators are sceptical about the quality and quantity of training on offer. There seems to be no end to it.
- The sour thought is often expressed that there is more money to be made of training mediators than in mediating.

See also
REGULATION

Follow up

Walker *Mediation Advocacy: Representing Clients in Mediation* Ch 3 How to get the best out of Training

CMC Registered Providers and Mediators – www.civilmediation.org/members-disclaimer

ADR Group - www.adrgroup.co.uk/

CEDR - http://www.cedr.com/

Transactional Analysis (TA)

A theory much loved by mediation trainers.

TA is defined by the International Transactional Analysis Association as: 'a theory of personality and systematic psychotherapy for personal growth and personal change'.

Developed by Eric Berne and popularised in his book *Games People Play*, It analyses social transactions by reference to an ego state.

Berne's three ego states are:

1 Parent
2 Adult
3 Child

Mediation trainers like it because it is also a system or theory of communication. Each of the three ego states has its own system of communication language.

- The Parent state is the language of values. You can be a nurturing parent or a controlling (critical) parent.

- The Adult state is the language of logic and rationality. This is the Grown up State and is for many people what they want as an ideal.

- The Child state is the language of emotions. You can be a Natural Child, Little Professor or Adaptive Child.

Transformative

In communication there is a sender and a receiver. Berne's idea is that effective communication works when the sender and receiver are in the same ego state. This is a complementary transaction. For example adult-adult means you can have a rational conversation.

If you have crossed transactions for example parent-child the communication will be more difficult.

In practice

- Mediators often see childish behaviour at mediations but they tend not to relate them back to Berne's series of ego states.
- Mediators who are also coaches, therapists and followers of the therapeutic/transformative school of mediation pay more attention to this than civil and commercial mediators.
- Parties at mediation do not want to be told that they are in child ego states.

Follow Up

Eric Berne *Games People Play* (1964)

Thomas Harris *I'm OK–You're OK* (1996)

Transformative

Transformative mediation was developed by Robert Baruch Bush and Roger Folger in 1994 as part of the reaction against problem-solving mediations.

It is consistent with the facilitative mediation model in emphasising the parties' freedom to choose. But the big difference is that the transformative mediator is:

- Helping the parties learn from their past experience.

- Helping the parties to develop new skills for use in the future with an improved and better sense of control over their own lives.

- More interested in changing how people see the world and each other than about finding a settlement or solution.

In other words the parties are being encouraged to examine their past, identify problems and work through them for the future. For some, such as the respected commentators Boulle and Nesic, transformative mediation is the same as therapeutic mediation.

Its primary objective is not settlement: it is behaviour change.

In practice

- Not widely used in the UK outside community and workplace mediation.

Follow up

Boulle, Nesic *Mediator Skills and Techniques: Triangle of Influence* pp 13–15

Translators

Mediation is about active listening and open questioning. Language is the medium.

If there are language problems at the mediation, parties can engage their own translator/interpreter. That is up to them.

As mediator, having your own interpreter helps avoid potential problems about confidentiality over what is discussed in any caucuses.

Mediators have to:

- Establish their interpreter's competence.

- Make themselves comfortable with letting go of control.

Traditionally mediators see themselves as managers of the process. The problem belongs to the clients. So does the solution. The process belongs to the mediator.

When as a mediator you are working with an interpreter you are ceding control to a large extent. If you are uncomfortable with this ambiguity don't do mediations with language problems.

As a party/representative, hire your own interpreter. For the same reasons that the mediator should hire his own. In particular it overcomes problems about confidentiality.

In practice

- In the UK most mediations are conducted in English.
- Increasingly non-native English speakers are parties or representatives.
- Taking extra care to make sure that everybody's understanding of what is going on is the same pays dividends.

Trust

Notable by its absence at mediations.

The mediator has:

- To build trust between himself and the parties. This is rapport. If a mediator wants to find out the parties' deepest needs he will have to overcome their natural suspicion of him as a stranger.
- To build trust between the parties. This is credibility. One of the biggest barriers to settlement is the credibility gap. The parties have simply lost trust in each other. Generally at least an operational level is established during the mediation.

Trust

- To make good use of his initial fund of trust and goodwill.

Parties often start with almost no trust towards each other. As the day goes on and they send each other positive signals about settlement, and they can see that both sides are trying to work towards a deal, trust starts to germinate.

In practice

- Trust is difficult to cultivate in a hostile competitive environment. It is much easier in a cooperative one.
- Trustworthy people tend to be more trusting.

But take heart. Here are three quotations to contemplate about trust:

1 For mediators:

'Love all, trust a few, do wrong to none.'

William Shakespeare, *All's Well That Ends Well*.

ie Be friendly but on your guard.

2 For mediators, advocates and clients:

'Trust but verify'.

Ronald Reagan

ie Always double check. Never assume.

3 For advocates and their clients:

'Men trust their ears less than their eyes.'

Herodotus

ie Show them. Don't just tell them.

See also
GOODWILL/RAPPORT

Follow up
CEDR *How to Master Negotiation* Ch 7

U

Ultimatums

Often issued at mediations and just as often ignored.

The law of diminishing returns sets in early on with ultimatums. The more you issue the less effect that they have.

Decide what is the key issue that you need to force. Is it a process point or a substantive one? Before issuing the ultimatum take a sounding from the mediator. And ask yourself what happens if they do not comply? Do you walk out?

In practice

- Pressure does need to be applied at times during mediations.
- Can usually be done with the help of the mediator and without issuing ultimatums.

See also

DEADLINES/WALK OUT

Ultimatum Game

An example of a cognitive bias:
- We believe that we refuse or accept an offer on the basis of logic rather than on status.
- We will refuse an offer if we think it unfair.
- Fairness is determined by our perception of what we receive compared with what the other party receives.

Ultimatum Game

In the Ultimatum Game there is a Proposer and a Responder. The Proposer has access to a fund of £100. He proposes to split it with the Responder.

- The Responder can either accept or reject the proposal.
- If he accepts it both the Proposer and the Responder receive the amount suggested in the proposal.
- If he rejects it neither the Responder nor the Proposer receives anything.

The results show that Responders will reject an offer which they consider unfair. 50/50 splits are considered fair. Proposals where Responders receive less than 30% are usually rejected.

In other words people would rather receive nothing at all than £29 where the Proposer receives £71.

Three reasons have been given for this:

1. Altruistic punishment. Responders would rather suffer receiving nothing at all in order to teach the Proposer a lesson.
2. Lack of self-control. Intoxicated Responders are much more likely to reject offers in order to teach the Proposer a lesson than sober ones.
3. The stakes are too low. If the figure was £100 million and therefore the net receipt to Responder was £29 million they would not reject it.

In practice

Mediators frequently hear:

- One party saying they do not want the other to get away with it in the future or that they do not what happened to them to happen to someone else. This is altruistic punishment.
- Parties describing their refusal as a matter of principle.

- One party rejecting a proposed settlement because they think the other side is doing better, comparatively, to an unfair degree 'It's just not fair. My head says I should accept but my heart says no.'

See also
COGNITIVE BIAS/EMOTION/FAIR

Uncertainty

Risk's evil twin. They are often confused.

- Uncertainty is not knowing what will happen.
- Risk is the probability that a known outcome will happen.

Most of us cope with risk better than we cope with uncertainty. At civil and commercial mediations many people say that they just want the situation finished. They want to know where they are. They want certainty.

People have different capacities for dealing with uncertainty and ambiguity. This appears to be related to the amygdala.

At mediations be aware of the difference between risk and uncertainty.

Here is an example known as the **Ellsberg Paradox**.

There are two bags.

- Bag A contains 100 balls. 50 are black. 50 are red.
- Bag B contains 100 balls. You do not know how many are red or how many are black.

In Round 1 if you pick out a ball without looking and it's a red ball you win £100.

Which bag will you choose?

Uncertainty

Most people choose bag A.

In Round 2 you win £100 if you pick a black ball.

Which bag will you choose?

At mediation unease with uncertainty leads people to:

- Request more and more information. They do this even when the information can have no bearing on their decision-making or even the outcome of the trial. People just want to know. They can fall foul of the curse of knowledge.
- Be influenced by the pseudo-certain effect, ie I know that you have told me that I have only a 50% chance of winning at trial but I would rather take my chances.
- Overlook probabilities and fall foul of the zero risk bias.

Another example is **Zero Risk**

There are two methods of treating poisoned water.

- Method 1 reduces the risk of dying from 5% to 2%.
- Method 2 reduces it from 1% to 0%, completely eliminates the risk.

Which method you choose?

Answers

Zero Risk

Most people choose Method 2. This is illogical. It only reduces the risk by 1%. Method 1 reduces the risk by 3%. So with Method 1 3% fewer people die. Under Method 2, 1% fewer people die. Method 1 is three times as effective.

Using the **Ellsberg Paradox** which would you choose?

Probably A again.

Unconditional Offer

But that is illogical. In Round 1 you assumed that Bag B contained fewer than 50 red balls. Therefore it must have contained more black balls. In Round 2 you should have chosen Bag B.

See also

AMYGDALA/COGNITIVE BIAS/RISK ANALYSIS

Follow up

Kahnemann *Thinking, Fast and Slow*

Walker *Mediation Advocacy: Representing Clients in Mediation* Ch 18 Mind Traps Alert

Unconditional Offer

Avoid making unconditional offers. Trade concessions. Use the word '**if**.'

Making conditional offers has three advantages:

1 It leaves you with wiggle room.
2 It draws out information.
3 It encourages them to trade something with you in return.

In practice

- People forget to trade. They just react and make counter-offers.
- Set the agenda. Keep the initiative. Be clear where you are going.

See also

EXCHANGING OFFERS/IF/RECIPROCITY

Ungley Order

An order of the court requiring parties to litigation to consider ADR. If the party thinks ADR is unsuitable they have to be prepared to justify their opinion at the conclusion of any trial.

See also
JORDAN ORDER

Unicorn Mediator

How will you recognise a unicorn mediator when you meet one?

Here are some tips:

1 Constantin-Adi Gavrile, a successful and respected Romanian mediator, lists 212 qualities that mediators need-starting with 'Active' and finishing with 'Worthy,' and including along the way:

> 'adaptable altruistic, analytical, assertive, balanced, calm, centered, charismatic, cheerful, communicative, creative, dependable, devoted, disciplined, easy-going, and empathic, fair, focused, honest, humble, incorruptible, inspirational, intuitive......'

2 Clive Lewis, one of the UK's leading workplace mediators, lists the contents of the large imaginary toolbox of skills which mediators take with them:

> 'patience, questioning, listening, humour, reframing, summarising, negotiating, reality testing, scribing, ideas, prompter, refreshments checker and stationery checker.'

3 A 2007 US survey into the skills and qualities of successful mediators listed:

> 'rapport building, deep listening skills, trustworthiness, strong ethics, creativity, patience, persistence,

humour, able to win confidence, friendly, likeable, high integrity, well-prepared, knowledgeable of the law, asks reality checking questions, well-prepared.'

In practice

- No mediator is equally good at all these things or has all these qualities.
- The unicorn mediator does not exist.

See also
CHOOSING THE MEDIATOR/INTERPERSONAL SKILLS

Follow up

Constantin-Adi Gavrile Kluwer Mediation Blog 19 February 2012

Lewis *How to Master Workplace and Employment Mediation* p 221

A 2007 US survey Goldberg and Shaw The Secret of Successful (and Unsuccessful) Mediators (2007) 23(4) Negotiation Journal 398

Unreasonable Conduct

Is wider than unreasonable refusals to go to mediation at all but includes it. Other common examples seen by mediators include:

- Rudeness – not even shaking hands with the mediator, let alone the other side.
- Dismissive gestures when the other side is talking.
- Deliberately not listening to the other side or the mediator by staring out the window, texting or talking to somebody else.

Unreasonable Conduct

- Not engaging in negotiation. This is potentially the most significant legally.

At present because of the veil of confidentiality the courts do not often have the opportunity of examining the conduct of a party at mediation. It sometimes happens. For example the parties can agree to waive confidentiality in order to put an issue before the court. This happened in the case of *Malmesbury* where the court made the following comments:

> 'A party who agrees to mediation but then causes the mediation to fail by reason of an unreasonable position in the mediation is in reality in the same position as a party who unreasonably refuses to mediate.'

Mediators are bracing themselves for the first full-frontal assault on party confidentiality based upon non-compliance with the terms in the mediation agreement to negotiate in good faith with authority to settle.

Given Mr Justice Ramsey's formulation of mediation confidentiality in the case of *Farm Assist* it is easy to see how – sooner rather than later – the court will persuade itself that it can look in detail at what happened at a mediation.

In practice

- When unreasonable behaviour occurs at mediation the mediator's job is to absorb it and dilute the impact.
- Take note of hints and guidance from the mediator as to what conduct is being regarded as unreasonable by the other side.
- If the other side think that you are being unreasonable they will find it harder to do a deal with you.

See also
CIALDINI'S BIG SIX/CONFIDENTIALITY/GOOD MANNERS/HALSEY/NEGOTIATION

Follow up

Farm Assist Ltd v Secretary of State for Environment Food & Rural Affairs [2008] EWCH 3079 (TCC)

Earl of Malmesbury v Strutt & Parker [2008] EWHC 434

V

Value

The very thing that mediators want to help the parties create. Often confused with price.

Made up of two things:

- The value created by settlement. Gaining something that you could not gain at court even if you win.
- The value of settlement. Something that you can do if you are not litigating.

Value created by settlement

Aka Growing the pie. Creating value is a core principle of principled negotiation as defined by the Harvard Negotiation Project. This says that:

- Instead of regarding mediation as a zero sum negotiation where the more one side wins the more the other side loses, consider proposals for mutual gain.
- a win-win situation is better than win-lose or lose-lose.

A classic example is a dispute over a boundary.

- All the court could do is decide where the boundary line is.
- Often in boundary disputes it is to the mutual advantage of the parties if the boundary is rearranged.
- Sometimes this means land swaps. An exchange of land is not something that a court could ever order.
- It is frequently the outcome of a mediated boundary dispute. Both sides walk away with something to their benefit, which they could never have achieved in court.

Valuations

Principled negotiation emphasises that parties resolve disputes when they see that there is more value in settling than in continuing to fight.

Value of settlement

Mediators encourage parties to consider the value, ie the benefit of settlement not just the cost. Once they do this and put values on intangibles – such as saving management time, reducing stress or protecting reputation – settlement becomes easier.

The value of settlement changes over time. At the start of litigation the parties see value in winning the litigation. As time passes priorities change. For example one of the parties receives a bid for its business. They now want to settle the litigation and not have to disclose it as part of the due diligence process.

In practice

- Clients and their advisers need to monitor changes in value.
- Mediators encourage parties to think about both the present value and the future value of settlement.

See also

GROWING THE PIE/HARVARD/PRICE/WIN-WIN/ ZERO SUM

Valuations

Feature in mediations in three ways:

1 The dispute is about a valuation. These are usually professional negligence actions against surveyors, financial advisers, estate agents or auctioneers. All parties rely upon expert evidence as to whether or not

Valuations

the valuer was negligent and what the true measure of loss is.

2 Valuation evidence is used in all kinds of dispute, eg shareholder disputes, contested probate where there are several properties, damage to goods, rights of way/ boundaries.

3 In any dispute where as part of the settlement there is payment by instalments secured over property. The receiving party needs to know the value of his security.

Expert valuation evidence is often essential. What astonishes mediators is:

- How often parties attend mediation with no up-to-date valuation evidence. Sometimes there are no valuations at all. Anxious telephone calls to accountants or Internet searches on ZOOPLA fill the afternoon.

- How far apart the expert valuers can be. Mediators often wonder whether the valuers are valuing the same thing.

- Sometimes valuers are apart because they have been given different information. When they pool the information their range usually narrows. More usually they have taken different assumptions. But they always make the assumptions that favour the party that has instructed them. Or they just use different methodologies.

- Despite the duties imposed upon experts by the court and in particular by CPR Part 35, experts still think that their job is to support the party which instructed them.

In practice

- Once valuers have signed off on their reports they find it difficult to change their opinion.

- If valuation experts attend mediation the temptation for them is to become even more entrenched as they engage in a battle of the experts. Whatever mediation is, it is not a battleground for gladiatorial experts.

- In all valuations remember the old Question and Answer routine:

  Q How much is this worth?

  A Are you buying or selling?

See also

EXPERTS/HOT TUBBING/PREPARATION

Follow up

CPR 35, Part 35

VAT

Value Added Tax cannot be avoided at mediations. It crops up:

1 When talking about legal costs. Precedent H figures do not include VAT. Some paying parties are registered for VAT others are not. This can increase the net cost to them on settlement.

2 Some receiving parties are registered for VAT. This means they cannot claim VAT on their legal costs from the paying party.

3 When talking about the cost of remedial works the same VAT considerations apply.

4 Mediators' fees are potentially vatable. Compulsory registration is triggered when their turnover reaches £82,000 a year (2016).

  Mediators can apply to use the flat-rate scheme if their turnover is less than £150,000 a year. This gives them a beneficial rate and a simplified procedure.

See also

COSTS/FEES/GROSS/NET/TAX

Follow up

www.gov.uk>publications>vat

Venting

As a word, losing popularity. As a concept, retaining its popularity amongst mediation commentators and trainers.

The mantra is that 'suppressed emotions sabotage settlements'.

The rationale is that:

- People in disputes find it difficult to concentrate on settlements until they have been able to express their emotions, particularly strong emotions such as anger. Once they have got it out of their system or cleared the air they will feel acknowledged and heard and be able to concentrate on settlement.

- Parties should be passionate and express strong emotions. The other side should be aware of how strongly a party feels. Why should they be shielded? At least they should be aware of the impact on others of what they have done.

The opposite school of thought says 'expressed emotion sabotages settlements'. This is particularly true if a strong, negative emotion such as anger is expressed publicly for example in a Joint Opening Session.

They point out that:

- Research shows that expressing anger does not make people feel better.

- After expressing anger people often feel vulnerable especially if they have done it in public. They have let their self-control slip. That potentially makes them more malleable either in the hands of the mediator or the other side.

Venting

- Anger increases a person's state of arousal. This in turn makes it more difficult for the pre-cortex to be engaged and therefore to be thinking about the future and settlement. Instead it is being flooded by neurotransmitters such as dopamine.

Contradictions

1 Mediators sell mediation as a process, which provides a safe environment for people to discuss matters frankly and openly. Why should someone be exposed to an emotional onslaught from the other side?
2 Mediators are encouraged to detoxify language through reframing. This will make communication easier. Why therefore encourage someone to deliver toxic language directly to the other side?
3 The listeners. What is the impact on them?
    - Do they feel guilty and more inclined to apologise or pay up?
    - Do they feel under attack and therefore defensive?
    - Do they feel encouraged that if the matter does not settle they will be able to needle the other side in court to the point that they self-destruct?

The answers are not always clear and seldom predictable.

Impact statements

Clients can usefully explain to the mediator and decision-maker on the other side the impact that the dispute has had upon them.

See also

ACKNOWLEDGMENT/AMYGDALA/EMOTIONS/IMPACT STATEMENTS

Follow up

Walker *Mediation Advocacy: Representing Clients in Mediation* para 9.09

Venue

Should the venue be neutral?

The advantages are:
- Everybody is equally inconvenienced by having to travel.
- Home ground advantage, if there is any, is neutralised.
- No one feels intimidated by being in somebody else's opulent premises.

Some mediators advise that the venue should be set in woodlands by water. This will create the necessary tranquil atmosphere to promote settlement discussions.

In practice
- Neutral venues cost money. Usually one of the parties offers to host the venue at no charge.
- In fact there is a tactical advantage in having the mediation in the other party's office. It is much easier to walk out of their office than out of your own.
- Venues are often in built-up areas with traffic noise.
- Wooded waterside oases of tranquillity are not usually on offer.

Who gets the best room?

A common mistake made by the host is to put themselves and their clients in the best room. That usually means a boardroom with space and a view. Smarter hosts consider who is likely to be the paying party. Those who will be paying should have the best room.

People pay money:
- Because they have to.
- Because they are buying something that they want.
- Because they like you.

Voluntary

Are people more likely to pay money if they feel uncomfortable and resentful or comfortable and appreciated?

Checklist

A short checklist of points for a mediation venue:

- How much will they charge?
- When will they close?
- Will photocopying and printing facilities be available both during and out of hours?
- Is there Internet/Wi-fi?
- What refreshments will be available and for how long?
- Are the rooms soundproof? Surprisingly often in modern buildings, with glass offices and demountable partitions, they are not.

See also
HOSPTALITY/SANDWICHES/WALK OUT

Follow up

Walker *Mediation Advocacy: Representing Clients in Mediation* Ch 8.29–30

Voluntary

One of the **TOP TEN**. In practice mediation is not really voluntary.

See also
COMPULSION/INTRODUCTION/TOP TEN

W

Walk Away Figure

Aka resistance figure or bottom line. But this is the one where you really do pack your bags and leave if it is not accepted.

Do not give up hope if you reach your walk away figure and walk away. A high proportion of those mediations which do not settle on the day settle within a week or two later.

But of course there are always those which don't and end up in court.

In practice
- Most mediations settle on the day.
- If there is any chance of a settlement, take it. Things don't always get better.

See also
BOTTOM LINE/DEAL ZONE/RESISTANCE FIGURE/ZOPA

Walk out

At mediations someone always talks about walking out. They do this either:
- In the early stages. They say: 'If the other side are still insisting on being paid money by us we will be leaving by lunchtime.' This is expectation management.
- At the late stages. People are making their final offers. There is deadlock. One side puts their coat on. They're reinforcing the message that there is nothing more coming from their side.

In practice

- Most people do not walk out even when they have put their coats on and packed their bags. If they stay and take their coats off a settlement is usually reached.
- If you want to make peace you have to keep on talking and that is better done face-to-face.
- So don't walk out unless you really do have a plane to catch.

See also
OFFERS/TERMINATING/VENUE

Wall

The low point of the mediation day.

Always around 15.30 during the usual afternoon lull anyway. At mediation is aggravated by:

- Parties not exchanging offers, eg insurers like to wait until 1600 before making an offer.
- Everyone being cooped up for six hours with no fresh air or excercise.
- Drinking too much coffee.
- Boredom and impatience.

Be like marathon runners and just go through the wall. The mediator will have seen it all before. He will help you.

In practice

- Every mediation hits the wall.
- Some walls are higher than others.
- Staying engaged. Go with the mediator's suggestions.

See also

MEDIATION CLOCK/MEDIATION DATES/ ENGAGEMENTS/REVIEW

War Stories

A staple of every gathering of mediators.

- Active mediators find mediating a lonely occupation. They like to swap stories and exchange experiences. It is a way of learning.

- Inactive mediators who have not done many mediations like to hear what it's really like at the mediation front. It is a way of learning.

In practice

- Being a mediator is being a performer. Performers like audiences.

- Rarely do war stories put the teller in a bad light.

- You can learn a lot by listening to other mediators telling war stories. You can also be bored to death.

Warranties

In the mediation context warranties appear in three ways:

1 Most mediation agreements contain a warranty that the parties will attend mediation in good faith to negotiate a settlement and have authority to settle. It is only a matter of time before a case comes before the court alleging that a party attended a mediation in breach of warranty. The problem is that the damages that could be claimed will be relatively low, essentially just wasted costs.

2 In settlement agreements warranties are sometimes given to the effect that certain stated information is

Waterfall Clause

correct. For example a paying party may warrant that their net assets do not exceed a certain amount. If it turns out that the warranty is incorrect the agreement can be overturned.

Inserting a warranty in a settlement agreement is a useful way of allowing a settlement to be made even though there may be gaps in the information provided.

3 Warranty claims can be the subject of mediations. They usually arise in disputes over warranties contained:

- In sale and purchase agreements of shares or businesses. Vendors give warranties about the state of the accounts, trading conditions and so on. After completion purchasers often challenge the accuracy of the warranties.
- In insurance policies where insurers rely upon breach of warranty to decline a claim, eg an alarm warranty in a theft claim.

In practice

- Warranties in one of their three meanings are mentioned in most mediations.
- Most parties and their lawyers do not take warranty templates with them.

Follow up

Richbell *How to Master Commercial Mediation* pp 231–235

Waterfall Clause

Provisions in a contract that apply when a dispute arises. There is a cascading or escalating process.

The conventional stages are:

Waterfall Clause

- Within a stipulated time the parties meet in good faith to try and settle.
- If they have not done that within the stipulated timeframe they appoint a mediator.
- If the mediation does not produce a settlement within the stipulated time the parties appoint an arbitrator or are free to issue proceedings by way of litigation.

There may be additional interim steps such as appointing a neutral fact finder before the matter goes to mediation or having discussions within the organisations in dispute at a higher level than the operational level before appointing a third party.

The English courts will enforce agreements to mediate. The test that they apply asks:

1. Is there is an unequivocal commitment to go to mediation?
2. What process is to be implemented and how?
3. What does the process require the parties to do?

In practice

- More and more agreements contain a contractual obligation to mediate.
- Ignore mediation clauses at your peril.

Follow up

SulamericaCIA Nacional de Seguros SA & Ors v Enesa Engenharia SA & Ors [2012] EWCA Civ 638

Emirates Trading Agency LLC v Prime Mineral Exports Private Ltd [2014] EWHC 2104 (Comm)

Walker *Mediation Advocacy: Representing Clients in Mediation* paras 8.02–8.05

WATNA (Worst Alternative to a Negotiated Agreement)

WATNA is the opposite of BATNA (Best Alternative to a Negotiated Agreement).

Harvard – HNP tells you that the stronger your BATNA the stronger your negotiating position. They do not emphasise the corollary: the weaker your WATNA the weaker your negotiating position.

As part of the PMA work it out. Most people are reluctant to do this. It is an unpleasant experience. Clients do not want to contemplate the abyss. Lawyers do not want to scare clients off litigation.

In practice

- The word WATNA is never used at mediations.
- Mediators discuss the alternative outcomes for the parties if they cannot settle. Be prepared for this. It can be disconcerting.

See also

BATNA/HARVARD – HNP/PMA – Pre-Mediation Analysis/RISK ANALYSIS

What If?

'If' is the negotiator's most powerful word. '**What if?**' is the mediator's most powerful question.

Be prepared to hear it many times from mediators. For example they will ask:

- What if this case does not settle?
- What if you go to trial and win?

- What if they can't pay?
- What if you go to trial and lose? What will the impact be?
- What if this case settles, what will life be like?
- What if you offered this…?
- What if they offered that…?
- What if we get together again and review progress?
- What if the lawyers have a word?

Responding with

- 'That is a hypothetical question.'
- 'We are not going to lose.'
- 'We have already had those discussions.'

Is neither helpful nor impressive and suggests that no prior thought has been given to these questions.

In practice

- When preparing for mediation ask: 'What if?'. It frees up thinking as well as getting you ready for the mediator's questions.
- You will be asked this question at mediation. Be prepared for it.

Win-Win

The clarion call of Fisher and Ury and the Harvard Negotiation Project.

Aka growing the pie.

This is the outcome of principled negotiation. Follow the principles and you can engage in cooperative problem-solving, which will create value so that everybody is better off. That is the idea.

Without Prejudice

Not everybody agrees. Win-win in the true sense is where neither side can get a better deal. There is no gold or value left on the table.

In practice:

1. Sometimes there are limited negotiation variables. In money claims there are two:
   - What are you going to pay?
   - When are you going to pay?

   Everything else such as interest rates and security to cover instalments are variations on a theme.
2. People are not always interested in maintaining relationships. The dispute was a one-off transaction. There is no prospect of future business.
3. The playing field is never level. One side is always under more time, financial or logistical pressure than the other.
4. The opposite of win/win is often not win/lose. It's lose/lose. It takes time for parties who have invested money, time and reputation in litigation to come to this realisation.

See also

GROWING THE PIE/HARVARD – HNP/PMA (Pre-Mediation Analysis)/PRINCIPLED NEGOTIATION

Follow up

Fisher and Ury *Getting to Yes* 2012

Harvard Negotiation Project www.pon.harvard.edu>hnp

Without Prejudice

A rule that provides protection for parties who are genuinely trying to settle a dispute. If they are engaged in genuine

Without Prejudice

settlement discussions any statement that they make whether orally or in writing may not be referred to in open (ie not without prejudice) correspondence or in any court proceedings as evidence of an admission.

The purpose of the without prejudice rule is to encourage parties to engage in frank discussions to try and reach settlement of disputes.

Without prejudice communications are also referred to as 'privileged', ie they don't have to be disclosed.

The rule is not absolute. There are exceptions. The court can consider without prejudice communications in the following circumstances:

1 To determine whether or not a binding settlement agreement was reached.
2 To determine whether or not a concluded settlement agreement should be set aside on grounds of misrepresentation, fraud or undue influence.
3 To determine whether an issue of estoppel has arisen.
4 To determine whether or not perjury for blackmail or other impropriety has been committed during the negotiations.
5 Evidence of the fact of without prejudice negotiations may be admitted to explain any delay.
6 Evidence of a negotiation may be admitted in relation to whether not the claimant acted reasonably to mitigate any loss in the context of agreeing a settlement.
7 By agreement the parties may agree that any correspondence is 'without prejudice save as to costs'. This means that the court may refer to proposals and offers made in correspondence when considering who pays costs at the end of the trial.

8 Terms of a settlement agreement may be disclosable even if relevant and commercially sensitive material cannot be redacted in the interests of justice.

9 In certain types of applications to the court, for example for injunctions, the applicant must give full and frank disclosure.

The court may refer to information made available in the course of without prejudice discussions if it is necessary when interpreting an agreement to know what information or facts were common knowledge that have a bearing on the meaning of the settlement agreement.

The without prejudice protection is additional and separate to the protection of the confidentiality clauses expressly or impliedly contained in the mediation agreement.

In practice

- Problems rarely arise.
- But parties often need to be reassured more than once that all discussions are without prejudice and confidential.

See also

BLACKMAIL/CONFIDENTIALITY/THREATS

Follow up

Walker *Mediation Advocacy: Representing Clients in Mediation* para 12.03

Witnesses

Both assets and liabilities. At trial your own witnesses are often your biggest liability and the other side's biggest asset.

Why bring witnesses to mediation? What are they going to add?

Witness Statements

- The mediator is not a judge. Mediators are not there to hear the evidence and make a decision on its probative value.

- There will be no opportunity to cross-examine the witness. What purpose would be gained by the proffering side if this happened? The cross-examiner has much more to gain by undermining the witness's confidence and rehearsing his questions.

In English law there is no property in a witness and if at a mediation one side thinks that the other side's witness could be valuable they can approach them after the mediation and ask for a witness statement.

Sometimes the parties who need to be present at the mediation are also potential witnesses at trial. To avoid exposing yourself to cross-examination or just hostile questioning take a representative.

In practice

- The golden rule is: do not bring witnesses who are not part of the decision-making process. They just make the team larger and their presence encourages the other side to seek information from them.

- Expert witnesses are in a different position. But usually they are not required in person at mediation.

- Mediators are not finders of fact like judges. You do not have to prove anything to them.

See also
CROSS-EXAMINATION/EXPERTS/TEAMS

Witness Statements

Mediations take place at different stages in the dispute cycle. Sometimes before proceedings have even started. Sometimes after exchange of witness statements.

Witness Statements

Why use them at mediation?

1 To give the factual background included

Witness statements are often in the mediation bundles. They are useful background briefing but are not essential. Most mediations take place without any witness statements.

2 To show the strength of their case

Judges rely more on the oral evidence given before them at trial than what is said in witness statements. Many witnesses do not come up to proof, ie give their evidence in a less compelling way than appears in their witness statements. This is a risk factor that the parties have to take into account.

3 To scare the other side with the future

Routinely parties tell each other and the mediator that they can bring evidence from a witness to establish a point in their favour. The mediator wonders why, if the evidence is important, the witness statement has not already been obtained. Lawyers know there is often a gap between what clients tells them the witness is going to say and what the witness actually says in a signed witness statement.

Sometimes a party has witness evidence that they do not want to show to the other side. They are prepared to show it to the mediator who can confirm to the other side that he has seen it. Mediators have to be careful that they do not become part of the evidence.

In practice

- Witness statements are a lot less useful at most mediations than people who make them think that they will be.

See also
ABSENTEES/EXPERTS/SURPRISES/TEAMS

Working Figures

Mediators tell the parties that in order to achieve a settlement there will need to be some working figures for the purpose of the mediation. If the parties work from different figures they will see things differently.

Working figures are ones which are used solely for the purpose of settlement. They cannot be relied upon in any litigation. By co-operating in compiling working figures no one is giving up any point or making any admissions.

Do not resist the mediator's attempts to get the parties to agree some working figures for the purposes of the mediation day.

In practice

- Producing some working figures happens at every mediation. Progress cannot really be made without them.
- Producing working figures often soaks up more time at mediation than it should.
- Prepare figures in advance.

See also
GROWING THE PIE/PMA/VALUATIONS

Workplace Mediation

Used where there is a dispute between parties who work together. This can be between employees or between employee and employer.

The general aim is to try and preserve the relationship.

Workplace Mediation

This contrasts with employment mediation where the employment relationship has terminated or is on the brink of being terminated.

Workplace mediation can morph into employment mediation. Below are the key differences.

Employment mediation is more:

- Commercially focused.
- Like a commercial negotiation.
- Likely to involve lawyers and legal points.
- Concerned with severance terms.
- Likely to lead to a legally binding agreement.

Workplace mediation is more:

- Concerned with the preservation of an ongoing relationship.
- Agreeing processes for future behaviour and conduct which are not legally binding.
- Concerned with people's attitudes and emotions rather than their legal rights or entitlements.
- Likely to take place without lawyers being present.
- Likely to take place over several sessions rather than in one day.
- Likely to be concerned with internal communication and decision-making processes within the employing organisation.

It is an expanding sphere of mediation activity. Generally workplace mediators:

- Get paid less than civil and commercial mediators.
- Are more likely to be non-lawyers.

- Emphasise their listening skills and their bottomless well of patience.
- Would also like to do civil and commercial mediation.

See also

EMPLOYMENT MEDIATION//REPRESENTATION/ ROLLING MEDIATIONS

Follow-up

Clive Lewis *How to Master Workplace and Employment Mediation*

X

X – The Magic Ingredient

Mediation is often described as a magical process. Its supporters wax lyrical about the magic of mediation.

Even High Court judges who tend to speak in prose refer almost poetically to the extraordinary results which can be achieved at mediation. With the help of an experienced mediator even the most embittered and entrenched parties are able to settle their disputes.

Why does it work when direct negotiation does not? There is no universal answer:

1. It is the opportunity for people to truly express their innermost needs feelings and emotions.
2. Mediation is a safe environment compared with the court room.
3. The parties know that they can leave at any time.
4. In theory they can say what they like without fear of redress. It is all without prejudice and confidential.
5. The whole process is empowering.

All these factors come into play. But the biggest single reason why mediation works is that a stranger is present. The very fact that there is a third party in the room changes the climate. People just behave differently towards each other.

What is the ingredient that makes some mediations successful and not others?

X – The Magic Ingredient

It is the ability of the mediator:

- to get the parties to talk to him and possibly to each other.
- to direct the talk towards the obstacles to settlement.

Open-ended ranting about the past does not help.

In practice

- The best mediations are like conversations.
- The magic ingredient X is to have a conversation with the decision-makers on both sides in which they do most of the talking.
- Sounds easy. But some mediators are just better at doing it than others.

See also

ACKNOWLEDGEMENT/ACTIVE LISTENING/GOOD MANNERS/MASLOW'S HIERARCHY/NEGOTIATION

Follow up

Ghaith v Indesit Company UK Ltd [2012] EWCA Civ 642 Ward LJ at 29

Y

Yes but

A variation of **'if'**. Keeps concessions tradeable.

Very useful at mediations when you are approaching or have just entered the Deal Zone/ZOPA (Zone of Potential Agreement). '**Yes** we could accept that figure **but** only if you give us six months to pay....'

See also
DEAL ZONE/IF/TRADEABLES/ZOPA

Youth Mediation

Aka peer mediation. Youth mediation takes place outside schools: peer mediation takes place within schools.

In both the mediators are drawn from the same background as the disputants.

The term is widely used for mediation involving gangs. Although the context in which youth mediations takes place is different from civil and commercial mediations – personal safety and violence being real concerns – the qualities required and the processes followed are similar:

- Mediators have to be able to listen and ask non-threatening opening questions.
- They have to establish rapport, ie trust.
- They have to set the boundaries of confidentiality.
- Shuttle mediation with caucuses and private sessions is more usual than joint sessions.

Key differences

- Agreements are not legally binding. They are protocols or processes for future behaviour.
- Confidentiality will not be absolute.
- Greater use of co-mediation than usual in commercial mediation.
- The 3Rs of gang behaviour are likely to figure: Respect, Revenge, Revenue.
- Criminal activity is likely to feature even more than in some areas of commercial mediations.

See also
PEER MEDIATION

Z

Zero sum

In a zero sum game one person's gain/loss equals the other person's gain/loss.

This is the opposite of the win-win situation. That is a positive sum game. The total of all the gains and losses of the participants is positive.

This is not the same as a lose/lose situation where the total of all the gains and losses of the participants is negative. In the zero sum game the total is constant. It is only the shares that vary.

Positional negotiation is described as zero sum: principled negotiation as positive sum.

- Avoid zero sum negotiations if you can. If you cannot, always know where your exit route is.
- The better alternative is to try and create extra value which everybody can share.

In practice

- Parties at mediation often have a zero sum mindset.
- Mediators try hard to change it.
- Hanging onto your zero sum mindset can blind you to unexpected benefits.

See also

GAME THEORY/NON-ZERO SUM GAME/PRINCIPLED NEGOTIATION/WIN-WIN

Zone Of Uncertainty

Like the corridor of uncertainty in cricket outside the batsman's off stump. The area where tricky decisions have to be taken:

- Whether or not to accept the deal or walk away. It's tempting but can you do better?
- The proposal offered is not quite enough but it is not too little either. What should you do?

Just like the batsman deciding whether to leave or play the ball. Leave it and he could be bowled or be LBW. Play it and maybe take an outside edge and be caught.

This is where the preparation pays off. If you have thought about:

- Your BATNA/WATNA.
- Your net cash position.
- The benefit of settlement particularly intangible benefits.
- Your appetite for risk and uncertainty.

You will find it a lot easier to deal with offers that land in the Zone of Uncertainty.

Asking yourself what you think the other side wants will help you land your proposals in their zone of uncertainty.

See also

BATNA/PMA – Pre-Mediation Agreement/WATNA

Follow up

Walker *Mediation Advocacy: Representing Clients in Mediation* Chs 5 and 7

ZOPA

Zone Of Potential Agreement is the area in which bargaining can take place and be likely to lead to an agreement.

It is defined by each side's reservation price/resistance figure or bottom line. If these overlap there is a ZOPA. If they do not there is not and therefore no prospect of a settlement. See diagram on p 416.

In mediations reservation prices and bottom lines are not absolute and immutable. As the parties process new information about each other and review their own position red lines are drawn in the shifting sands of settlement discussions and bottom lines move.

See also
BATNA/BOTTOM LINE/DEAL ZONE/PREPARATION/ PRICE/RESISTANCE FIGURE/WATNA

Answer to the Prisoner's Dilemma

Take the two prisoners, Bill and Pete.

They know that if they both confess they will each get 10 years in prison.

If one confesses and the other doesn't the one who confesses will go free and the other will spend 20 years in prison.

If neither of them confesses they will both get two years for the minor offence.

Remember: Bill and Pete are in separate locked rooms. They cannot make contact and they have to make their decision at the same time.

The obvious answer is that the best choice for both Bill and Pete is that neither of them confesses. They will both get two years.

Not according to game theory. You look at the dominant strategy. A dominant strategy is a strategy that is the best payoff no matter what the other player chooses.

Take Bill. Assume that Pete is going to confess. What's the best strategy for Bill?

Scenario One

If Pete confesses and Bill does not, Bill will go to prison for 20 years. But if Pete does confess Bill will only go to prison for 10 years.

In this case it is better for Bill to confess.

Answer to the Prisoner's Dilemma

Scenario Two

Let's assume that Pete is not going to confess. If Bill confesses he will go free. If he doesn't confess he'll get 10 years.

Conclusion

Bill's best choice is to confess no matter what Pete does. Since in both cases Bill's best option is to confess then confessing becomes his dominant pure strategy.

Since Pete is in the same position as Bill his best option is the same.

Of course the best outcome for each of would have been a two-year sentence. They could only have achieved this by staying silent and neither of them confessing.

In other words they would have had to have trusted each other not to act in such a way as to try and get the very best individual outcome, ie walking free. Since they probably think the worst of each other – ie demonising behaviour – they are not able to achieve that.

In mediation the parties may be in different rooms, unlocked of course but they can communicate through the mediator. Through him options can be discussed. The win-win outcome is achievable.

Bibliography

Allen, Tony, *Mediation Law and Civil Practice* (Bloomsbury Professional, 2013)

Association for International Arbitration, ed. *European Mediation Training for Practitioners of Justice: A Guide to European Mediation* (Maklu, 2012)

Axelrod, Robert, *The Evoluation of Cooperation* revised ed (Basic Books 2006)

Blake, Susan, Browne, Julie and Sime, Stuart, *The Jackson ADR Handbook* (2nd edn, Oxford University Press, 2016)

Bond, Greg, ed, *Mediation Practice* (ICC 2016)

Boulle, Laurence, and Nesic, Miyana, *Mediator Skills and Techniques: Triangle of Influence* (Bloomsbury Professional, 2010)

Brooker, Penny, *Mediation Law: Journey through Institutionalism to Juridification* (Routledge, 2013)

CEDR, *How to Master Negotiation* (Bloomsbury Professional, 2015)

Churchman, David, *Negotiation: Process, Tactics, Theory*, 2nd ed (University Press of America, 1995)

Cialdini, Robert B., *Influence: Science and Practice* (5th ed, Pearson, 2009)

Fisher, Roger, Ury, William and Paton, Bruce, ed, *Getting to Yes* (Random House, 2012)

Garby, Thierry, *AGREED!: Negotiation/mediation in the 21st Century* (ICC, 2016)

Kahneman, Daniel, *Thinking, Fast and Slow* (Penguin, 2011)

Lewis, Clive, *How to Master Workplace and Employment Mediation* (Bloomsbury Professional, 2015)

Luntz, Frank, *Words That Work* (Hachette, 2007)

Bibliography

Middleton, Simon and Rowley, Jason, *Cook on Costs 2016* (LexisNexis, 2015)

Myerson, Roger B., *Game Theory: Analysis of Conflict* (Harvard University Press, 1997)

Randolph, Paul, *The Psychology of Conflict* (Bloomsbury, 2016)

Richbell, David, *How too Master Commercial Mediation* (Bloomsbury Professional, 2015)

Slater, Laura, ed, *Costs Law: A Practioner's Guide* (ARK, 2016)

Ury, William, *Getting Past No* (Random House, 1991)

Walker, Stephen, *Mediation Advocacy: Representing Clients in Mediation* (Bloomsbury Professional, 2015)

Walker, Stephen, *Setting Up in Business as a Mediator* (Bloomsbury Professional, 2015)

Walker, Stephen and Smith, David, *Advising and Representing Clients at Mediation* (Wildy, Simmonds & Hill Publishing, 2013)